I0823600

WE ARE NATURE DEFENDING ITSELF

AN ANTHOLOGY OF WOMEN ON BODIES, BORDERS & PLACE

Cordelia E. Barrera

Texas A&M University Press
College Station

First edition

♾ This paper meets the requirements of ANSI/NISO Z39.48-1992 (Permanence of Paper).
Binding materials have been chosen for durability.

Library of Congress Control Number: 2025029556
Identifiers: LCCN: 2025029556 | ISBN 9781648433733 (cloth) | ISBN 9781648433740 (ebook)
LC record available at https://lccn.loc.gov/2025029556

Contents

Introduction

I have been practicing yoga for years, and I hold one class dearer than the rest. This is my Ritual Yin class, which I attend on Monday evenings. Ritual Yin, as taught by my instructor Haley, hinges on strength, flexibility, and balance. Muscle memory, grounding, sense of being, support—these are only a few of the "softening and surrendering" activities that shape our routine. In Yin, we induce rootedness, holding long poses for up to ten minutes at a time. The idea is to lean into the ways the body remembers, perceives and desires balance, and holds muscle memory beyond conscious thought. Mantras are essential to anchoring our individual physical, spiritual, or psychological journeys, and Haley modifies these according to the season, substance, or mood of the wider world we inhabit. Yet our final mantra of the evening is always the same, our reminder to be ever watchful, vigilant, and protective of that which sustains and nurtures us as humans: "Remember," she affirms, "we are not defending nature, we are nature defending itself."

This mantra never left my mind as I communicated with the women who contributed to this collection; I believe it shapes the mindset of each author's psyche, whether consciously or not. In the stories, poems, essays, and reflections that follow, closeness to the earth is a way of life in which landscape manifests a kind of soul, a communal process that links human forms to the complex webs of life that sustain us and, in turn, are sustained by us.

At the simplest level, *place* refers to a particular position or point in space. In geographical terms, place is generally thought of as antithetical to space, which is a continuous area or expanse, free, available, unoccupied. Where space is all about openness and freedom, places embed stability and rootedness onto a landscape. Places, writes Lauret Savoy in *Trace: Memory, History, Race, and the American Landscape*, extend beyond memory toward origin, direction, and orientation. Homes, buildings, plots of land, neighborhoods, cities, rivers—sites and locations that are tied to memories, past practices, or even entire cultures—have meaning beyond the present, as they contain experiences where the traffic of the past evokes continuity and process, but only if and when we are mindful of such lifeways.

Places, then, are crowded by the substance of past lives and ways of living and being. They contain experiences that are aural, tactile, felt, inhabited, and generative. Thinking and writing about place gives life and richness to things both mundane and notable—walking, planting, caregiving, washing clothes, doing dishes, and writing in defiance of things often silenced.

This anthology foregrounds issues of rootedness, cooperation, nurturance, and identity to illustrate how women's writing about place moves us *beyond* landscape as capital, or as an open space of infinite exploitable resources. By representing voices from a diversity of women—some likely unknown, some rising stars, and others who are established poets, authors, and professionals in fields touching women's studies, ecocriticism, memoir, poetry, and prose—the works collected here are meant to move readers toward an expanded definition of land/landscape/territory to expose a genealogy of practices that point to *reciprocal* relationships with the landscape. The aim is to broaden a reader's understanding of concrete ways women think, work, and are guided ecologically and holistically about the places that shape our lives and livelihoods. In expanding the ways landscape and the natural world foreground issues of female empowerment, this collection cultivates and adds to concrete ways we might *all* build more meaningful relationships with the landscapes of our lives as we move toward a hopeful, sustainable future.

In part 1, "Bodies," readers are asked to experience and *feel* a history of the body's contact with landscapes and places as repositories of knowledge. Peering into deep folds of time and memory—even those worn by adversity, grief, and devastation—are living and sometimes hard-won practices that epitomize an ecological consciousness. Part 2, "Landscapes," extends beyond particulars of home and private and public life to situate issues of place as sites and locations of radical action. Each essay, poem, or story in this collection speaks to the ways women think critically, ethically, and creatively about place and landscape to epitomize an ecological consciousness that assumes responsibility and implies engagement with ways of knowing that are cooperative, porous, visceral, felt, and lived. In part 3, "Practices," we find ruminations and traditions of remembering. This section highlights reciprocal relationships to the natural world in terms of place-based knowledge that extends outward to the ways "women's work" in and around the home shapes communal processes that reinforce continuity across time and space. Readers will note that some entries in the collection are short enough to be read in a few minutes, while others require a more nuanced reading, maybe even a bit more time to absorb. Some authors submitted two or more pieces that fit with the overall theme, and so where space was adequate, these women have multiple appearances in the collection.

Before building, before planting or harvesting, it's essential to know—to recognize and appreciate—what roots remain alive. The force of determined roots in any place always resonates. This is perhaps the greatest life lesson within this collection.

Cordelia E. Barrera
December 2024

We Are Nature Defending Itself

Part I

Bodies

Land is more than the rocks and trees, the animal and plant life that make up the territory of Aztlán or Navajo Nation or Maya Mesoamerica . . . land is also the factories where we work, the water our children drink, and the housing project where we live. For women, lesbians, and gay men, land is that physical mass called our bodies.

Cherríe Moraga, *The Last Generation*

I change myself, I change the world.

Gloria Anzaldúa, *Borderlands / La Frontera*

A River of Women

A river of women
softened this valley,
hummed through the heart
of night lulling
babies and abuelas
into petals of sleep.

El río de mujeres
gathered the peach light
of dawn for warmth like a shawl,
slid the glow
into the desert's roots,
eased its grayest thirst.

The river of women
penetrates boulders, climbs
crags jagged as hate,
weaves through clawing thorns
to depths parched, shriveled
offers ripples of hope.

Río de mujeres,
soften our valley,
braid through its silence
carving your freedom
to the song you learn
on your winding way.

"A River of Women" by Pat Mora, first published in *Agua Santa / Holy Water*, Beacon, 1995.

River of women,
stream on in this valley,
gather all spirits,
deepen and rise,
sustaining your daughters
who dream in the sun.

I Want to Be a Maguey in My Next Life

Face to the sun all day.
Burst offspring into the air
Like a piñata.

Store water.
Bloom a tasseled flower
Stretching itself to the sky.
Stretching, stretching to the sky,
What luxury.

I want to belong to these lands
That existed before the world
Was round.

Pinch the asses of those who
Come too close to me.
Give aguamiel to the one who dares
Suck my juice.

And die from this communion.
Dissolve like ash.
Return to live on earth.

Violent.
Detonate from a field like Parícutin.
Return return return to be reborn.
Die to eternally be.

"I Want to Be a Maguey in My Next Life" by Sandra Cisneros first appeared in *Woman without Shame: Poems*, Vintage, 2023.

What If We Are Not Broken by Our Histories?

i.

A forest meadow opens; here deep in winter
snowdrifts rise and fall like perfect meringue.
Our scarred land, the scorch beneath—invisible.
How we stand alone at the choosing edge.

What jagged secrets did my uncles swallow
of boarding school eyes locked like walls,
of night roads and distant ditches, of hunger
churning (266 miles of longing, of hiding)?

Come home. Stand in a circle of gravehouses.
Ondaas, wood sinking into our soft clay earth
further each spring—into *Gaa-waabaabiganikaag*.
What shall we offer them better than survival?

ii.

Though braids have fallen on pipestone floors
each cut strand of dirty DNA swept away,
roots renew. As raspberries after fire tribal stories
vine—spread and ripen under White Earth skies.

Each year new hands score and harvest birch bark,
relatives pole & knock knock & pole in wild rice beds,
tiny tots lift fringed rainbow shawls, step and spin,
as carefully together we place heaped spirit plates.

Just so, remember. Our solemn toes sunk deep
buried in fecal terror—a history we call capitalism.
How we make of every waste a fertile soil.
Oh resplendent mushrooms, sit now and feast.

Sugar Babies

Though the southern Colorado soil was normally hard and cakey, it had snowed and then rained an unusual amount that spring. Some of the boys in my eighth-grade class decided it was the perfect ground for playing army. They borrowed shovels and picks from their fathers' sheds, placing the tools on their bicycle handlebars and riding out to the western edge of our town, Saguarita, a place where the land with its silken fibers of swaying grass resembled a sleeping woman with her face pressed firmly to the pillow, a golden blond by day, a raven-haired beauty by night.

The first boy to hit bone was Robbie Martinez. He did so with the blunt edge of a rusted shovel. Out of the recently drenched earth, he lifted a piece of brittle faded whiteness and tossed it downwind like nothing more than a scrap of paper. "Look," he said, kneeling as if he was praying. "Everybody come look."

The other boys gathered around. There in the ground lay broken pieces of bowls with black zigzagging designs. Next to those broken bowls were human teeth, scattered like dried kernels of yellow corn. Above them the sun had begun to fade behind the tallest peak of the Sangre de Cristo Mountains. The sky was pale and bleak, like the bloated belly of a lizard passing above.

"Don't touch it," Robbie said. "None of it. We need to tell somebody."

And tell they did. The entire town. Everyone, it seemed, was a witness.

* * *

Days after their discovery, our final eighth-grade project was announced. We gathered in the gym for an assembly. The teachers brought together the boys from technical education class and the girls from home economics. We sat Indian style in ten rows beneath dangling ropes and resting

"Sugar Babies" by Kali Fajardo-Anstine first appeared in *Sabrina & Corina: Stories*, One World / Penguin Random House, 2019.

basketball hoops. The room smelled like a tennis ball dipped in old socks and the cement walls were padded in purple vinyl—supposedly to minimize dodgeball injuries. I thought it looked like a loony bin.

Mrs. Sharply, a bug-eyed woman with a neck like a giraffe's but a torso like a rhino's, stood before us on a wooden box. "For the remaining two weeks of your junior high career," she said, "you will care for another life." She then reached behind her into a paper grocery bag, revealing a sack of C&H pure cane sugar. "Sugar babies. We will be raising our very own sugar babies."

Older kids had gossiped about notorious school projects. We had heard stories of piglet dissections, the infamous "growing and changing" unit, rocket launches with carbon dioxide canisters, and a cow's lung blackened and doused in cigarette smoke, but no one had warned us about this.

"Sugar babies are a lot of responsibility," Mrs. Sharply said as she stepped down from her box and paced with the sugar sack. She explained we were to be graded on skills like feeding, bonding, budgeting, and more. She then passed around diaper directions.

"We do it all alone?" It was Solana Segura. She was behind me, her perpetual whimper causing every sentence to end like a little howl. "Like single moms and stuff?"

Somewhere, down the rows, a boy croaked, "But the DNA shows I am *not* the father."

We chirped with laughter until Mrs. Sharply held up two fingers, signaling silence. "Of course not. You'll be in committed partnerships. We're drawing names."

A teacher's aide in Payless flats scurried like a magician's assistant toward Mrs. Sharply. She carried two Folgers cans decorated in pink and blue glitter. Mrs. Sharply set down her sugar, taking the cans from the aide and giving each a good shake. From the pink can, the first name she pulled was Mimi Yazzie, who stood and slinked forward, burying her face into her arms as Mrs. Sharply called out her partner, Mike Ramos. This cycle of humiliation lasted for several more rounds before I was partnered with Roberto Martinez, the bone boy.

After school, Robbie and I sat outside on the swings. He was a scrawny kid with frequently chapped lips and a light dusting of freckles across his low nose. He played soccer and always wore a beat-up blue windbreaker and knockoff Adidas sneakers, with four stripes instead of three. The sugar baby was planted snug in his lap, balanced ever so gently between his two stick-arms. His dark eyes were so big and wide they resembled two brown pigeon eggs, and he spoke with a quavering, squeaky voice. "They said we have to name it. Do you want to pick it out, Sierra?"

"No, you name it." I swung up. "And you take it home tonight." I swung down. "I'll watch it tomorrow, but only if I have to."

"That's cool," he said. "What about Miranda? That's my grandma's name."

"Whatever," I sighed, leaning back on the swing. "Name it after your grandmother. Name it after your entire family. I don't care." I pumped until the rusted chain pulled taut. Then I jumped, landing in the mushy gravel with both feet. I took off for home.

***

"Ain't that something," my father said as he and I ate breakfast the next morning. On our small black-and-white TV above the microwave, aerial shots of the dig site were being shown on the news. The land appeared as an enormous shadow box with scraps of ancient people instead of thimbles and porcelain knickknacks.

"Can we go see it?" I asked, spooning my last bit of cornflakes into my mouth.

"I suspect they don't want us to do that," he said, keeping his eyes on the TV. There were deep lines around his eyelids, his hair was purely silver, and his hands were spotted from years of working as a roofer beneath the Colorado sun. People had begun to mistake him for my grandfather.

"Why not? We should be allowed to." I walked to the sink and tossed my dirty dish inside. "It's where we're from. It's our people."

My father scratched his chin. There was a thin turquoise ring on his finger where there had once been a gold wedding band. "Don't leave a dish in the sink," he said. "How many times I got to tell you that, Sierra?"

I turned back and soaped up my bowl. "I mean it. I want to go."

"Things like this have always happened around here. It's nothing special."

I told him it was new to me as I scrubbed my dish with a green and yellow sponge, the milky water gargling loudly down the drain's black rubber lips. As I rinsed the bowl once more, I peered through the window above the sink. The morning was clear, and in the distance the mountains were crystal blue like an enormous wave. As if sailing across those waters, a small white pickup truck with a front-end bra pulled down our street and rumbled over the gravel in our driveway. Long dark hair clouded the truck's windshield, and very red and very long fingernails were coiled around the steering wheel. A silver rosary dangled above the dash.

"Papa," I called over my shoulder, drying my hands on my jeans.

My father rose and stood tall behind me, smelling of leather and dirt. "Looks like she's back again." He grunted some, swishing spit around inside his mouth before shooting a stream of yolky bile into the sink. "Go outside, Sierra. Say hello to your mother."

My mother first left three years earlier. It happened one morning after she cooked breakfast. I watched as she gathered her keys and coat and walked into our wintry yard without any shoes. She left footprints as slight as bird tracks in the snow. When I asked my father later why she had left, he simply said, "Sometimes a person's unhappiness can make them forget they are a part of something bigger, something like a family, a people, even a tribe."

My mother occasionally would come home for a day or two to gather forgotten necklaces or purses, though over time my father moved her things from the bedroom to a box in the crawl space. Her visits were infrequent enough that I learned to live without her. It wasn't easy at first. Sometimes I'd hear a funny story at school or church and my first thought would be, *You have to tell Mama*. But over time that urge to be with her, to tell her things, to be a part of her—it went away. Just like she always did.

* * *

On my mother's first night back, she couldn't find an apron so she made dinner in one of my father's old T-shirts. With the kitchen TV up loud on *Entertainment Tonight*, she cooked pork chops sizzled in their own fat and smothered in green chili. Whenever I'd glance up from my math homework on the coffee table, I'd catch glimpses of her in the kitchen rummaging through junk drawers and cabinets. I wondered what she was searching for and thought to offer my help, but I realized I didn't care if my mother found anything in our home again.

When she finally called my father and me to the big table, I pulled my sugar sack—Miranda Martinez-Cordova—from my backpack. "Dinnertime," I whispered, admiring the face I had given her with a Sharpie.

Her eyes were big and wide with short lines for lashes. Her mouth was a blissfully flat smirk.

"Your favorite," my mother said, handing a plate to my father. He casually spun it above his head and eased into his seat at the table. The two of them were acting as if nothing had happened, as if my mother had always been there cooking in the kitchen. I felt like my father was a liar, someone who could pretend everything was fine when, really, how could he be anything but sad?

"Do you want something to drink, Sierra?" asked my mother. "No," I said, covering Miranda's mouth. "I don't want anything."

"Nonsense," said my mother. "You're becoming a woman. Women need vitamins and nutrients. You'll have some milk."

My mother opened a cupboard, the small one beside the stove where the glasses had once been, but my father corrected her with a flick of his knife. "Left of the sink."

My mother tilted her head and steadied her mouth into a tight smile. After pouring the milk, she placed the glass in front of me and quickly glanced at Miranda. Robbie had dressed her in one of his little sister's old striped pink onesies. "Does your doll want a plate?"

"She's not a doll. And she's way too young for solids."

My mother laughed and took her seat, closing her eyes while my father led us in prayer. Miranda and I kept our eyes open. My mother had taken off the old T-shirt and wore a blue dress with white-embroidered flowers that had many loose threads. Her lips were thinner and her black hair was shorter than I remembered. She used to only wear silver, but she had on a gold necklace, the thin braided chain glowing against her bronze skin.

After we said amen, my parents made the sign of the cross and my mother opened her reddish-brown eyes. Her eye makeup appeared as a buildup of silt. "You know," she said, turning to me, "I thought we were out of salt. I was going to have you run next door to ask Mrs. Kelly if we could borrow some."

"She's dead." I hunched down and rested my chin on Miranda's head.

"What?"

"She's not alive anymore."

My father gently said, "Old Mrs. Kelly passed away last winter, Josie."

My mother mouthed an "Oh" and looked at her plate. She briskly apologized and we continued dinner in silence. Above us the ceiling fan spun in rapid circles, slicing the air, sending waves of coolness over each of us. My mother and father kept glancing at one another—smiling, chewing, smiling, sipping, and smiling some more. After some time, I got sick of their cheeriness and gulped the last of my milk. Then, as loud as possible, I slammed my empty glass on the table.

"So *Josie*," I said, "what brings you down from Denver? Or do you normally drive around cooking pork chops for people?"

"Sierra," my father barked. "Don't you call your mother by her first name." He shook his head and I avoided his strict gaze.

My mother smiled sweetly. "Tell me about all those Indian graves the boys from your school found out west."

My stomach suddenly lurched with the sounds of digestive failure. "I don't know anything about it," I said, stroking Miranda.

"Sure you do," my father interjected. "That Roberto Martinez, the boy who found the bones, he's your partner for that sugar thing. Your school project."

"To think," my mother said. "This whole time those bones were right in Saguarita beneath our feet."

"That's not true," I said. "They weren't beneath *your* feet."

She giggled a bit. "I was here for a long while, Sierra. I think I know a thing or two about Saguarita."

Though I wanted to tell her she didn't know about anything, I turned my face to my lap and went quiet. After dinner, I sat in my room, where I pressed my ear against the cool white door. Muffled and low, I could hear my father in the living room ask my mother about her drive—road conditions, springtime flurries, if the mountain goats hobbled along the pass. He didn't ask why she was back or if she missed us—questions that hurt me to think about. I moved away from the door and tossed Miranda into the corner.

* * *

"She cried all night. I didn't get any sleep," I told Robbie the next morning as I shoved Miranda into his arms. We met outside thirty minutes before school in our usual spot by the swings. It was chilly and the air smelled like pancake breakfast and frost.

"How could she cry?" he asked. "She's only sugar."

The sun was coming up. The light leaked over the land in velvety streaks of pinks and golds. My mother once told me this meant the angels were baking cookies. "Isn't that what babies do? Cry and crap themselves and cry some more?"

"Hey," Robbie said, his chapped mouth bunched to the side. "Where's her outfit?"

"Lost it."

Robbie sighed and bent down to his backpack. He pulled a diaper from the front mesh pocket. "Give her here. We'll lose points if she's wearing the same diaper from last night." He lay Miranda on the loose gravel and frowned at the new sad, sleepy face I had given her that morning. Her eyelashes were tarantula-like and her mouth was downturned. Robbie fumbled with the diaper, applying and reapplying the adhesive sides.

"So," I said, standing above him, "what was it like?"

"What was what like, Sierra?"

"Finding those dead people. Was it scary?"

Robbie got the diaper to stick. He patted Miranda's black marker face and stood up with a bounce. "Not scary," he said. "But it was weird, you know? We've lived here our whole lives and no one knew about all this old stuff in the ground."

"I guess," I said, thinking of the piñon trees where my father had hung a bluish hammock in our yard. Their roots, he said, had undoubtedly grazed the dead bodies of our ancestors, both Spanish and Indian. I used to play in the shade of those piñons, cracking their nuts with two rocks held firmly in my hands. After pulling away the hard shells, I'd toss the spongy insides into my mouth. I didn't swallow them, though. I was afraid of letting any amount of death, from the soil or elsewhere, work its way into me. "Everything is old here. I mean *everything*."

Robbie nodded. He was rocking Miranda back and forth in such a way I'd only seen small girls do with dolls. "I heard your mom's back again. My grandma saw her buying pork chops at Rainbow Market."

I kicked at the gravel, scuffing my Mary Janes. Dust flew between us. "The bitch is back."

Robbie pretended to cover Miranda's ears. "Dude," he said, "don't call your mom a bitch. What if Miranda called you a bitch?"

"Guess it's a good thing babies can't talk," I said. "Especially ones made of sugar."

Robbie was smiling and had lifted Miranda into the air. He briefly held her against the sky before bringing her back down. "Remember when your mom was our group leader for Day on the Prairie?"

"Yeah," I said, lowering my voice.

"And we all got lost looking for that old barn she said was haunted? Then she let us eat three packs of Oreos? And you had to go to the bathroom in the bushes." Robbie laughed, but I frowned and he quickly turned serious. "Why is she back this time?"

The school bell sounded. Class was starting in ten minutes. We reached for our backpacks and walked toward the front doors. I lifted Miranda from Robbie's arms. "Who knows with that woman? Maybe she wants to see the dig site. Or maybe she likes taking vacations to her old life."

* * *

Within a week, my mother blended into our home as well as Miranda did. Which is to say, not very well at all. When it was just my father, he worked late and usually only had time to heat up a frozen pizza or fix a box of macaroni. Our small purple house was often messy, though we each had a chore list that was conquered by Sunday. With my mother back, the home took on a new order, a different rhythm. She cooked unhealthy but comforting foods, the house constantly emitting a pungent odor of bacon grease and red chili powder. Other times she cleaned. She'd twirl around with a broom, swaying her hips to the music on the radio—an oldies station or some honky-tonk crap. Most evenings, after my father came home from work, he'd unlace his boots in the foyer and then move his arm along my mother's slight waist. Together they'd rock back and forth to the music. It was nauseating.

Each day after school, I'd come home to discover that my mother had made my bed and placed my stuffed animals in a dog pile above my pillows. I'd immediately throw them to the floor. With a detergent that reeked of artificial springtime and cottony clouds, she also did my laundry, taking the time to match my socks, a luxury I hadn't experienced in years. One afternoon, as I sat on the couch, my feet covered in those matching socks and kicked up on the armrest, my mother walked by and swiped them down like she was swatting a fly. "What're you doing inside? It's a beautiful day." Her arms were planted firmly at her sides. She wore a brightly colored tunic and black leggings, making her appear like a 1960s glamour model. She was young still, only in her mid-thirties.

"It's hotter than a pig's armpit out there." I craned my neck, looking past her at the television. An Herbal Essences shampoo commercial was on and long-haired women were moaning under waterfalls.

"You have such a foul mouth," my mother said. "And pigs don't have armpits, genius." She began lifting sofa pillows as though searching for something. "Hey, where's that sugar bag you carry around? Your little baby for school."

"She's with her father. He has her until the weekend."

"Oh," my mother said. "Well, get up off this sofa. We're going for a drive."

I couldn't remember the last time I had been alone with my mother in a car. "What? Where to?"

She smiled, the seams of her mouth running with red lipstick.

"You'll see."

We parked on a steep hill overlooking the dig site. Below us, archaeologists in white hats and khaki shorts swarmed the gutted earth like invasive ants. The plot was as long and wide as a shallow public swimming pool and was divvied up into human-size squares. The sky was cloudless and blue, except for the sun's golden orb. At the horizon, there was a crashing display of earth and air. My mother stood before me and held her arms out, flapping them as if they were useless wings. Wind blew her hair, twirling the strands around her face, hiding her eyes behind sections of black. For the first time since she'd come home, I remembered how beautiful I once found her to be. As a little girl, I'd play dress-up in her satin nightdresses and lacy bras, admiring their slight weight and wondering if I'd ever own clothes like that.

"What do you think?" she asked. "Isn't it pretty?"

I shrugged and stood beside her. The wind carried her jasmine scent.

"Ever feel like the land is swallowing you whole, Sierra? That all of this beauty is wrapped around you so tight it's like being in a rattlesnake's mouth?"

"I see this all the time," I said. "And I don't feel like I'm being eaten alive by anything."

My mother gave me a sideways glance. "You will someday. Maybe it'll come later for you than it did for me. Children tend to do that. Marriage. Life. All these things." Moving behind me, she hunched down and slipped her cold hands over my eyes. "Try it. Close your eyes and hold your arms against the wind. You'll feel it."

I allowed my arms to float up and coast. A kaleidoscope of images spun against my closed lids. I saw the day when I was ten years old, right before my mother left for the first time. She took me to the pueblo where her grandmother was born in New Mexico. Holding my hand, my mother walked us through a small adobe church. She touched the pews with the tips of her red nails as we moved closer to the altar. We stepped into a side room where we lit white candles with long, slim sticks. My mother sent prayers for all those she loved into the sky with smoke, but I sent only one. *Please*, I pleaded to the Virgin, *don't let my mother cry anymore*. I was sick of finding her silently weeping, the sobs bobbing in her throat—at the stove, in the bathtub, kneeling in the dead garden beside our house.

When I opened my eyes, my mother was beside me, a strange blank expression on her face. "Did you feel it?" she asked.

"No," I said. "I didn't feel anything." Goose pimples rose on my neck and arms. "It's just windy and cold."

"All right, Sierra. Then let's get home. I'll start dinner."

As she headed for her pickup, I looked over the hill's edge and down into the dig site once more. The archaeologists were huddled in small groups. The rich odor of disrupted earth blew into me. Everything was terrifyingly silent. I thought about how quiet the world could sound and how when I stood there beside my mother, for a moment, I was afraid she had left me on the hillside, stranded forever.

* * *

"Xerophthalmia," Mrs. Sharply said, "is one of many childhood diseases your babies could get." It was the following Monday, the final week of sugar babies. Another assembly was being held in the gym. Two kids in front of me had swaddled their baby in a blanket, while others around us had glued on googly eyes and red yarn mouths. Robbie sat beside me with Miranda. She looked exceptionally fashionable. That morning I had wrapped a quilted pillowcase around her like a muumuu dress.

"Among other things," Mrs. Sharply continued, "xerophthalmia is a vitamin A deficiency that makes it so a person can't produce tears."

I leaned over to Robbie. "I wish you had that disease. Then you'd stop whining about me drawing on Miranda." I had recently drawn crucifixes and anchors across her back. Tattoos, I called them, but Robbie said she looked like a bathroom wall.

"She's a baby," he whispered with closed eyes. "Babies don't need tattoos."

"Sugar," I said. "She is a bag of sugar."

"Now think for a moment," Mrs. Sharply said, waving both arms in the air. "Think of all the times you cry. Sometimes they are happy, and sometimes they are sad. But crying is natural. Take a moment to remember the last time *you* cried."

The gymnasium went silent. Only the hiss of the fluorescent lights above us could be heard. Students hung their heads, as if possessed by their darkest, most sorrowful memories. I waited for the other students to finish reminiscing about their dear old dead grandparents and broken bones.

"Now, parents," said Mrs. Sharply, "you can see that not being able to cry would be an awful condition. For homework, we will each need to research a childhood disease. Tomorrow we will draw diseases from a hat. Some babies will get a disease, but—just like in life—some will not. It's the luck of the draw."

* * *

Later that day, Robbie hurried after me as I walked home. His backpack seemed comically wider than he did. "You have to take Miranda," he said. "I have soccer tonight." From the giant backpack, he scooped Miranda out, slowly handing her over. She was somehow heavier than usual.

"What the heck have you been feeding her?" I asked. Robbie petted her belly. "That was weird, Mrs. Sharply asking about crying."

"She's a real wacko," I said, hoisting Miranda on my hip. The sky was endlessly blue with paper wisps of clouds. I caught myself tilting Miranda up to see. "So when was it, Robbie? The last time you cried?"

"That's sort of personal, Sierra."

"Roberto Martinez, I'm your child's mother. I deserve to know these things."

"All right." Robbie took a deep breath. "After I found the bones, that night I woke up and thought I saw a skeleton woman at the foot of my bed. I didn't know who she was, but later my grandma told me it was Doña Sebastiana, the lady version of the grim reaper. Death."

"You cried from a bad dream?"

"No, Sierra. It was more than that." Robbie scratched his head and his scalp sounded sandy. "What about you? When's the last time you cried?"

I peered down the block at my little purple house. My mother's pickup wasn't in the driveway and I figured she had gone to Rainbow Market for more pork chops, but for a moment something in my chest ached, a gnawing worry that she was gone again, this time for good. I broke into a sprint and ran toward home. "I don't cry," I called over my shoulder. "Only little girls and babies do that."

***

"I have some new tattoo ideas," I said to Miranda, who sat on the kitchen table, stiffly leaning to the left in a column of sunlight. I was sifting through the junk drawer looking for markers. I had opened every window, and for the first time in days, the house didn't smell like pork. It reeked with the richness of the mountains and desert, rain and sage and cedar pulled together as one. When I realized the drawer only had rubber bands and dead batteries, I said, "Don't worry, you little sack of cavities. I have some markers in my room."

I crawled beneath my bed, over the uncrushed carpet, surrounded by gobs of lint and balled hair. I was looking for a shoebox filled with art supplies, but I ended up fishing out my private-property box instead, the place where I kept movie ticket stubs, old diaries, and birthday cards from my mother. She made the cards herself and I imagined her in some sunny apartment in downtown Denver. Houseplants and cacti lined the windows while filtered city light fell upon her at the sofa, licking stamps and writing out her old address.

Sitting on my floor, my legs spread and the birthday cards dumped around me like confetti, I ran my fingers over their sharp edges and smooth ribbons. I came upon one from my eleventh birthday, the first card my mother sent after she left. I held the purple and gold paper in my palm, then opened the card as if it were the warm, beating heart of an animal. My mother had placed three marigolds inside and they nearly crumbled in my hands.

> To my baby, Sierra. Today is your birthday, and when you were born, I knew everything would change, that every day would be your day, that nothing would be the same.

I climbed onto my bed, where I nestled into Miranda. "See this," I said. "This is from *my* mom." I looked at her sad face, and for a split second, I imagined Miranda as a real infant, a baby who breathed and cried. I rolled her to my lips and dryly kissed her forehead. "I don't know if I'm very nice to you," I whispered.

I then caught a glimpse of my mother standing in the doorway. She was leaning into the wall, limp and fragile. Her reddish-brown eyes were without makeup and her hair was stacked in a sloppy pile on top of her head. "You're good with her."

"She isn't real," I said.

My mother stepped toward me, moving gracefully in her skin. She sat on the foot of my bed with very straight posture and stiff arms. She seemed nervous—the way cats stiffen their backs before danger strikes. "It's sort of strange they make you kids do this. You're only thirteen, but I can understand how they think it prepares you, I suppose. Not that having a sack of sugar for two weeks would prepare anyone for a new life."

I pulled Miranda closer and wiggled my thumb over her quilted midsection.

"I'm not sure if anyone is prepared for raising a child. It doesn't seem to be something we can practice before it actually happens."

I shrugged and rolled Miranda onto my belly. "Where did you go today?"

My mother stared straight ahead, her eyes glassy. "For a drive through the canyon. Would you believe it? I saw two hawks. They were playing in the wind."

Hawks were common in Saguarita. We had an entire unit in sixth grade about them. They danced before mating, could dive 150 miles per hour, stayed with one partner all their lives. I was surprised that my mother paid them any attention. "What kinds of birds do you see in the city?" I asked.

"Crows," said my mother. "Just a bunch of crows." She paused, tracing Miranda's eyelashes with her long red nails. "How long do you have her?"

"A few more days," I said, rubbing Miranda's back slowly. "I can't wait to get rid of this thing. She's so annoying."

"Imagine someday when it's a real baby. It will be much harder."

"That's the point," I said. "Miranda isn't real. If she was, I'd be a lot nicer to her, like Robbie is. He's better at taking care of her."

My mother folded her hands neatly in her lap. She kneaded her fingers back and forth and a trickle of sadness moved between us like a static shock. "Can you believe that when you were born, I was only three years older than you are now?" She forced a laugh, dropped her gaze to the carpet. "I had to stop going to school."

"Did you miss it?" I asked.

My mother sighed and considered my question for a long time. "I didn't know I could miss school. I thought I was just sad, but I take classes now. At a community college. You could go there someday."

My mother went quiet. She pulled the rubber band from her head, allowing her hair to unravel around her shoulders and neck. She looked gloriously dark and light at the same time. There was a shining glint in her brown eyes. She looked younger. She looked happy. "I bet you'll be an artist someday, Sierra." My mother pointed to the tattoos across Miranda's back. "That's what I wanted to be." She smiled and we both laughed. "Here," she said. "Let me braid your hair. I can do a tight one that will last for a few days."

I pulled away at first but soon moved back toward my mother. I was ashamed of myself that I still wanted her close to me, even after everything she had done. I eventually rested my head in her chilly hands and tried to forget how bad my mother had hurt me. Her fingers wove through my hair like she was sewing a quilt. I nearly fell asleep in her arms as I held Miranda in my own. Lying there with my mother in the afternoon light of my bedroom, I imagined her far into the future, driving day and night, her little white truck sliding from mountain peak to valley, through snow and heat waves, windstorms and lightning. Her headlights beam bright and warm, shining into town, the place where I'll live when I'm finally a grown-up and my mother's black hair is silver and her face is well lined. In the distance, I see her arriving, joyously waving to me, her last stop.

* * *

When I woke up the next morning, my father was alone at the kitchen table eating oatmeal and reading the newspaper. Part of me wanted to ask where my mother was, but I knew she was already heading north over the pass, back to that sunny apartment of hers in Denver. Even her chair was gone from the table. My father scooted a bowl of cereal toward me. He then smacked the paper with his hand. "I'll be damned," he said. "Those Indians on the ridge, they got some formal petition going. They're closing up the dig site." His eyes met mine over the top of the paper. "Sorry I didn't take you to see it, Sierra. There will be another one someday."

"I did see it," I said. "Mama took me."

My father swallowed hard and shook out the paper. It sounded like rain. "Want some orange juice with your breakfast? I got the kind without pulp that you like."

"No, Papa," I said, "I'm not feeling too good. Would it be OK if I stayed home from school?"

He raised his white eyebrows. They reflected the low sunlight pouring into the kitchen through the sheer curtains above the sink. "If you feel that bad, then of course you can."

I spent most of the day in bed with Miranda cupped in my arms. We listened to the radio perched on my windowsill. The country songs my mother liked filled the small bedroom, and every now and then I'd lean over with Miranda close to my chest and feel like crying. Then, at three o'clock, there was a quick knock on the door.

Robbie stood on my stoop covered in a mist of sweat around his temples and beneath his mouth.

"What're you doing here?" I asked. "And why are you out of breath? Did you skip or something?"

He wagged his head back and forth. "It's awful, Sierra. Just awful."

"I'm sure you're a wonderful skipper. Don't be so hard on yourself."

"No, not that. It's Miranda." He hunched over and took a huge breath. "She's dead."

"Miranda can't die, moron."

Robbie peered at me, a deep sadness in his gaze. "We pulled diseases out of a hat today. Most kids didn't get anything bad. Some got chicken pox. But Miranda, she got SIDS. If you don't know what that is because you didn't do your homework, it means sudden infant death syndrome."

"I know what SIDS is," I said. "What are we supposed to do now? Throw her away?"

"But we can't," Robbie whined. "It's Miranda."

I stared at him for a long while, counting how many times he blinked without tears rolling out of his eyes. Then I said, "I have an idea."

Robbie and I parked our bikes near the edge of the hill overlooking the dig site. I had wrapped Miranda in a black pillowcase. She resembled a baby nun. I pulled her from my handlebar basket and one last time arched her face to the heavens. There was a mass of gray clouds. They spread evenly over the land like a patchwork of fog. "Look," I whispered. "Even the sky is sad for you."

Robbie stood beside me at the border between the hill and the dig site. He reached out with a thin chicken wing of an arm and patted Miranda softly on the head. We stood at the edge of the hill for some time, listening to the grumbling moans of the clouds and the far-off crackling of thunder. I picked out a spot easy to aim for in the middle of the pit. Then, tipping back, I readied myself to launch Miranda above my head with both arms, but Robbie stopped me "You're going to throw Miranda in there?"

"What else can we do?"

With those big sad eyes, he looked into the dig site. Then he looked at me. "I can kick her farther."

"You're going to kick our baby into her grave?" The wind carried my voice away from me as if it wasn't my own to begin with.

"I play soccer, Sierra."

Taking her from my arms, he delicately set Miranda on the edge of the hill, her limp body leaning mostly to the left. He backed up a few steps and then pushed himself forward with huge strides, his arms flying. When his tennis shoe made contact with Miranda, her body lifted from the earth as though she was nothing more than a helium balloon. She twirled in the air as her sugar insides spiraled out of her body from a hole Robbie's foot had torn in the bag. The sugar blew with the wind, sprinkling the dirt with bits of white. How pretty, I thought, and she landed with a thud.

To Make a Child an Ancestor, a Home

Or

The Year of the Murder Hornets

If a hornet buzzes and you're afraid of stings, in the gums, in the top of the cervix, when you're pinched by pants that don't quite fit your soft stomach, you come to fear buzzing. The hornets live in the underbrush of this northern Washington landscape you're visiting, you imagine, but also the dilapidated studio apartment that haunts your property, a part of a century-old compound in the Central New Mexico valley. Their neat little subsidized houses stacked in corners of filth. You do admire the hornets' ability to look past neighborhood and set up something that feels like a womb, one that you can keep coming back to. You don't let people look in the windows of the studio anymore, and you count yourself as people. You keep furniture stored there, but without a proper roof and with rains and with dust and with missing leaded glass panes, you recognize that most things will have been ruined. The hornets, you're sure, are fine.

Later this fall, you'll knock the shack down to build anew, something freshly cornered. Saws will buzz and your debt portfolio will deepen. Hopefully, the building will be done before the baby is done and before your hard stomach unstiffens and returns to its pinched softness. Or maybe, it's better to wait. Forgo the buzzing until the baby is in someone else's arms for seven hundred and fifty dollars a month, and you leave the compound and return to a desk by a window that overlooks a tree that your great-great-great-great-grandmother could have planted, if not separated by time and distance and a binding of hands. Maybe there's fear enough in motherhood to want nothing else but neurons, building. On reflection, you feel like it's important to have the old studio still rotting; it feels like an insurance for bringing up a new acidic life—a baby needs a little death to couch it, lest it become the death couched for some other birth.

This is all to say that you have built fear like a home, which, of course it is. A nest of hornets, a rock of mildewed furniture that some animal, you're sure, has scented with itself, the potential ghost of your baby too familiar now, in the promise that they will be held in some other woman's arms while you work—a home of pressing fears and their comforts. You treat your teeth like a nest, and every two years, you're guilted into letting a hygienist, with latex hands, dry your tonsils as she cleans the hornet hive from the deposit of your gums, the gums that you do not prod regularly and must now be numbed and scraped, healed against subtle contamination. You moan whenever the needle meets nerve, and here is the pinch again.

This is how you talk about your body, your home, your desert, which was not built by your people and was, in fact, stolen out from other hands so that you could sign sixty-five pieces of paper assigning the land as *yours*. You signed the paper and ripped up the carpet and down the paneling and paint, scraped and dug so that it felt like *yours*. Sucked your breath when you looked at the studio, falling soft at the wall seams. The fetus inside you feels *yours* in the same way that the hornets do, in that they are here, and you love them and you fear them and you would not like to look inside the window to see how they are doing, given the chance. Given the chance to see the rot and what's missing. But you do, with the baby, with the bugs, and you are both terrified and relieved to know that everything you expected to be rotting is, and all that you hoped to be living is still buzzing around in there, and what a simple comfort: to fear the most and to find it.

Diana López

The Seven Directions

Bárbara was named after a saint who was locked in a tower but found comfort by looking to the sky with its clouds and sun and moon, who magically healed people with the waters of her bathhouse, who ran into the crevice of a hill that had cracked open when she needed protection, who wore a magic robe that shielded her from the torches of her persecutors. Bárbara's mother would tell her these stories and then point out how the saint interacted with the four elements of nature, "the air of her tower, the water of her bathhouse, the earth of the hill, and the fire of her enemies."

Then Bárbara's father would chime in. "And don't forget to mention that the saint died when her father chopped off her head." He had a good laugh about this.

"Your dad can be a real pain in the ass," her mother, Ashley, said.

Secretly, Bárbara agreed. Secretly, she thought both her parents were a pain in the ass.

It was her mother who insisted on her formal name, with the accent mark and the rolled *r*'s, and her dad, Rudy, who used the short version, Barb. Never mind that a barb wasn't kind, that it was meant to pierce things.

They lived in Corpus Christi, always going to the beach, but when Bárbara turned fifteen, she didn't want to go anymore. She seemed to be always on her period, and she hated how she looked in her bathing suit because she was stretched out and gangly. The waves and sandcastle building and walks along the shore were no longer interesting. She just wanted to stay in her room with its ceiling fan and comforter and internet access, but there was no getting out of these trips to the beach.

So she got in the car, stuck between lawn chairs and a bucket of smelly bait. As soon as they found a place to park, her dad got busy with fishing, while her mother took a deep breath of salty air and started pointing at things. "Look at the pelican. Look at the seagull. Look at the crab." She picked up a shell, and even though it was broken, she said, "Don't you just love nature?"

Bárbara rolled her eyes. "Oh, yeah, I love it," she said. "The oil rigs, the garbage." She lifted a paper plate half buried in the sand. It was smeared with something yellow—mustard, probably. She threw it like a frisbee, and it landed on the ocean, floating for a minute before absorbing the water, getting heavy with it, and sinking. She couldn't help thinking of everything lost at sea—the treasure ships, the explorers, the slaves, the capsized boats filled with immigrants just looking for a better life.

"You need to listen," her mother said. "The wind and the waves, they will speak to you." Ashley closed her eyes, tilted her head.

"And what are they saying?" Bárbara teased. "What's the chisme?"

"No chisme,"[1] her mother answered. "They're whispering words—*wistful, wanderlust*—and some foreign stuff I don't understand. Maybe from the Karankawas."[2]

"Oh, wow, Mom. That's deep. As deep as the sea."

Her mother opened her eyes. "You should give it a try."

Bárbara laughed.

"Or if you can't listen, give the ocean a word. The wind will pick it up and carry it around the world. Who knows? Maybe someday, it'll come back to you."

"That's so dumb," Bárbara said.

"Maybe, but it can't hurt."

"Why don't *you* give it a word?"

"OK. I will." Her mother closed her eyes again and, after a long minute, said, "Embrace." She held the *s* sound of *embrace* for a very long time.

Then she kneeled, took a bobby pin from her hair, and stuck it in the sand.

"It's afternoon," Ashley said, "so the sun is in the west. That means the shadow's facing east." With her finger, she traced the shadow, and then he made a line in the opposite direction. "Perpendicular to this is north and south." She made another line to form a cross. At each tip, she gathered the sand and fashioned mounds about as high as coffee cups. "Whenever

1 Gossip.

2 American Indian cultural group whose ancestral homeland stretches along the Gulf Coast of Texas from Galveston Bay southwest to Corpus Christi Bay.

you feel lost," she explained, "find your center, and touch base with the seven sacred directions."

"You mean *four* directions," Bárbara corrected.

"No, there's seven," her mother said. She dug a hole to bury the bobby pin, and after patting smooth the sand, she placed the broken shell upon it. "East, west, north, south," she said, lightly touching the mounds; "below," she tapped the ground; "above," she lifted her hands to the sky; "and center," she tapped the shell and placed her hand over her heart.

Then she uttered something in Spanish. Bárbara didn't know if it was a poem, or a prayer, or an ancient chant, but she didn't ask. This whole thing was embarrassing and dumb. The tide would rise, and in a few hours, the ocean would wash away this "nature thing" her mother had made.

They sat on their lawn chairs and looked at the sea. Now and then, people walked by, and some stopped to talk.

The whole time, Rudy kept fishing, catching perch or fish too small to keep. "If I don't get something in the next twenty minutes, I'm done." As soon as he announced this, his fishing line went taut. The rod arced from the force of it. Rudy leaned back and anchored the base of the rod against his belly. He kept pulling, only to have the rod lurch forward again. Then something splashed nearby. "That's it! Did you see it?" He struggled, his face a grimace, the muscles of his arms and legs tensed up. It was a battle, but eventually, the line slackened. "I can feel it giving in!" Inch by inch, he turned the handle on the reel, until finally hoisting his catch. A good-sized redfish gaped at the sky.

Rudy grabbed it, threaded a line through its gills, and tethered it to the floating bait bucket. "If we fillet the fish right now," he explained, "it'll rot before we get a chance to cook it at home." Bárbara nodded, but no way was she eating that fish. She understood that meat came from animals, but she didn't want to see them before they died.

The next hour was uneventful. As Bárbara predicted, the tide rose and washed away Ashley's offering to the seven directions.

* * *

The following month, they headed to the Hill Country. Her parents had reserved a cabin near the Frio River and wanted to spend a long weekend there.

As they drove, monarch butterflies kept splatting against the windshield, and Rudy couldn't help asking, "What's the last thing a butterfly sees when it hits the car?"

It was an old joke, and Bárbara knew the answer. "It's ass!"

She and her father laughed at this, but Ashley just shook her head. "You know those monarchs are migrating all the way to Mexico," she said. "Can you imagine? Those little things?"

"It's not one monarch who makes the whole trip," Bárbara said. She liked when she was smarter than her parents. "They lay eggs along the way. It's the children and grandchildren and great-grandchildren and great-great-great-grandchildren of the original butterflies that take over the journey. Think about it. There's no way a single butterfly can do it, not when they only live for a month."

She meant to one-up her mother, but it didn't work. "That's even *more* amazing," Ashley said, "to start a journey you'll never finish."

"It is *not* amazing, Mom. It's stupid. I mean, what's the point?"

"It's like this multigenerational relay, isn't it?" Ashley said.

Bárbara didn't reply. Once her mother got an idea, she stayed with it.

They got to the cabin, and right after they unpacked, Bárbara changed into her bathing suit, adding an oversized T-shirt to hide herself. She slipped on water shoes, and she and Rudy grabbed the inner tubes. The plan was for Ashley to meet them at a boat ramp downstream.

Bárbara had been on the waterslides and the lazy river of Hurricane Alley, Corpus Christi's water park, but it wasn't the same as being on a real river. She and her father settled onto their tubes and let the water carry them. She leaned back, closing her eyes to the sun. Whenever she got too hot, she splashed water on herself. It was called the Frio River because of how cold it was, and she liked the contrast of temperatures. Sometimes, they hit short rapids. Those were fun, and she got good at kicking off the rocks and tucking her arms to avoid scraping them. Twice the water got too shallow, so they had to portage the tubes for a while, but most of the time, the river was deep enough. She spotted a few woodpeckers, hummingbirds, and mockingbirds. Around a curve, a deer lapped at the water. And the butterflies were still around. She watched one fall onto the river, its wings outspread like the sail of a reclining boat. She tried to scoop it out, but the current pulled her in another direction.

Then they got to a point where a narrow island split the river.

"If you paddle hard enough, you can take the faster side," her father said.

"You know it!" she answered.

She thought he'd join her, but he stayed on the slower side. Soon, she couldn't see him at all, but she knew the island wasn't very long and they'd meet up again.

When she reached the white water, the current was faster than she had imagined. She got pinballed from side to side. Her tube tilted a few times, nearly flipping. She was more afraid than excited, but she couldn't get out of this. There was no path but through. The river flowed. It had always flowed, and it didn't care who or what it carried.

Then there was a drop, maybe five or six feet, but she wasn't prepared for it. She went over, and when she hit the bottom, she slipped out of the inner tube and got pushed under. She tried grabbing hold of something, but the rocks were slippery with moss.

She finally surfaced, but only because the river spit her out. "Hey! Hey!" she called, flailing as she tried to swim against the current.

"Barb!" It was her father. They had passed the narrow island, and her father was now on the land.

She was free floating in the rapids now. The river tossed her, spun her, and dunked her. It was like every nauseating ride at the carnival.

"Grab at that tree!" her father called. She caught a glimpse of him. He was behind her, but catching up. "Grab it!"

She saw which tree he meant. She tried to stand but got knocked down each time. She tried to dog-paddle, but she was still getting pushed around. When she got near the tree, she scrambled for it, but before she could take hold, the roots snagged her legs. She was tethered just like that redfish on the beach. She tried wriggling free, but she went under. She was on her back, getting more and more tangled in the roots, getting heavier and heavier. Strands of hair undulated above her face. She couldn't lift her head. She wasn't very deep, but six inches was no different from six feet when you were beneath water. How long could she hold her breath? She'd drown if she didn't do something soon. But what could she do? She could only take things in, the sights and the sounds. She could only listen, and that's when she heard, "Embrace." It was clearly her mother's voice with that extended *s* sound. Bárbara lay in the river, her legs and her arms spread out, and formed a cross, pointing in four directions. Below was the riverbed; above, the water's surface; and in the center, herself.

Suddenly, and just in time, her father reached her and yanked her out. She sucked at the air and coughed a bit.

"Are you OK?" he asked.

She nodded.

"Were you scared? Because I was scared."

"At first," she said.

After she caught her breath, they walked along the bank. The inner tubes were long gone. When they reached the meeting point, Ashley called out to them.

"Where were you? What took so long?"

"Barb almost drowned," Rudy said.

Ashley ran to Bárbara, brushing back her hair, patting her shoulders, counting her fingers.

"I'm OK, Mom. Really."

"She was very brave," Rudy said.

"Because I found my center."

Ashley smiled at this and nodded knowingly. Then she hugged her daughter. It was the embrace Bárbara had counted on.

Back at the cabin, after changing into dry clothes, Bárbara stepped outside. For a long time, she sat at the picnic table, not knowing where to go or what to do. But then, she heard rustling in a nearby bush. She went to it and found a rabbit giving her its profile, watching her with one eye. She remembered an illustration of a rabbit from her science book. It was meant to show how the eyes of prey are placed on the sides of the head to provide better peripheral vision. She didn't quite understand until now how if you're hunted, you need a wider range of sight. You need to be constantly ready. The rabbit was a safe distance away, but any sound or movement would get it running, so Bárbara stayed silent and still. She wondered how old it was and where it burrowed. She wondered if it was male or female, a parent or child. She wondered if it had a favorite food or favorite color. Finally, she said, "You have a name?" and at this, the rabbit hopped away.

She followed, and that's when she saw a log covered in monarch butterflies. They were packed so close together, crawling over one another. She reached for them, and they flew away, brushing against her. One landed on her arm. It didn't weigh anything. She softly blew on it, and it disembarked, flying off in a wild zigzag. How much distance would it cover in its lifetime? Ten miles? Five? One?

Suddenly, the significance of the multigenerational relay hit her. It pointed out her own small self. She wasn't the first Bárbara, and she wouldn't be the last. She was only a speck in a long line of the mothers who came before her and of the daughters who would follow. Every insect, every bird, even the trees with their centuries-long lifespans, all the creatures and plants of this world—the world itself—was a speck.

She held out the hem of her shirt and dropped rocks in the makeshift pocket. When she had enough, she dumped them in a flat circle of dirt. She grabbed a stick and stuck it in the ground. It was late afternoon. The locations of the sun and shadows were very distinct. She drew a cross in the dirt and, at each point, made a little tower of rocks. It was tricky to keep them from toppling, but eventually, she managed. Then she buried a rock and, after patting smooth the dirt, placed another rock upon it.

She had never asked for the words her mother spoke that day on the beach, but it didn't matter. She could sing her own poem. It didn't have to be in Spanish or in the language of the people who once lived here. Only the intention mattered.

"To the east, the beginning. To the west, the end. To the north, the ice. To the south, the fire. To the dirt, the darkness. To the sky, the light. To the center . . ." She thought a moment before deciding. "To the center, my heart."

Two days later, they left the cabin near the Frio River. Bárbara's rock piles were still standing. They would collapse eventually, and eventually, she would build another monument somewhere else. She would honor the seven directions. She would sing another song.

Antelope and I

You see me—of course—before I see you.
But then as I walk a sage-fringed trail
up the draw and down, something—
a shared animal presence?—
makes me look west: see you.

Even at seventy-five yards
your bold white chest,
radiant exception to the plains
gone dun, cures my
nearsightedness.

You, on the other hand, can spot movement at three miles away.

Pronghorn, *kwahada*, *Antilocapra americana*,
neither antelope nor deer,
(your closest living cousin, the giraffe)
ancestry assures you persist with
hollowed hairs, your antifreeze for winter,
camouflaged coat, butterscotch stripes and all.

Side set eyes catch worlds in their orbs,
long lashes like sunshades.
Nervous, curious—your Pleistocene genes
still bolt, then stand.
Now this is fossil fuel: at speeds of fifty miles an hour
your ancient bloodline remembers ghosts of grasslands

"Antelope and I" by Shelley Armitage first appeared in *Spiral Orb Fifteen*, special issue of *Spiral Orb*, https://spiralorb.net/fifteen/armitage.html, accessed 20 May 2023.

chaparral cacti. You disappear, sliding under on your knees
mocking the wisdom of barbed wire.

But I am exotic am I not?
My old checkered farm coat, sagging sleeves
baggy warm-ups, a whiff of acrid humanness
the unwashed best tolerated upwind.
I am held at a distance by your gaze.

We used to talk to animals—
or was it animals talked to us—
until evolutionary changes in the trachea
made one claim superiority over the other.

But if you were the carnivore
I would offer myself up,
even as you did to the old Zuni
line to the heart

prayer over horns

Instead, I can only say in a stillness
beyond thought:

I would be the grass before you.

ire'ne lara silva

the seedling wife

Claudia

I was fifteen the first time I felt death. I had no language for it. It was an echo, a tremor in my bones. They said *cancer*, and I thought I would die. But it wasn't my death I felt approaching. All those nights I slept in a hospital, I felt things, heard things, knew things. I was never surprised when the next day brought weeping. Distraught mothers. Frightened children. Heartbroken wives. Eventually, I left the hospital. Eventually, they said *remission*. Eventually, the quiet returned and my bones stilled.

Until the air began to vibrate around my mother and didn't stop until she was in the ground. And then with others. Many others. I was never wrong. I could feel their last breaths gathering weeks before they were gone. I felt what remained in houses where someone had died. I stayed far away from cemeteries and hospitals. As soon as I realized that there were places where the ground didn't throb with the blood of the lost, I moved away from the border.

Noxochitzin, I murmur against your hair. You hear nothing, because even in your sleep, you are never completely silent. Always murmuring, as if a river running south or a broad-leafed tree swaying in the wind or a rainstorm greeting the spring lived inside you.

The years do nothing to dull my desire for you. I ache for the scent of you, the feel of you, the heat of you. The softness and the firmness of you. The fullness and the hollows of you and the sweet and salt of you. There is nothing like the sound of my name on your lips.

"the seedling wife" by ire'ne lara silva first appeared in *Apogee*, no. 13, Winter 2019, https://www.apogeejournal.org/series/issue-13.

Ameyalli

The thunder woke me. It hardly took a second to register your arm around me, your soft snoring. You're so still against me, unlike yesterday.

It was thundering then too. The still air and the heavy clouds and the light drawn tight and tense told me rain was coming. I took your hand and drew you away from your garden shed and pulled you down with me to the ground because I wanted you to feel the thunder rippling through the earth. Wanted for your flesh to hum against mine as the earth hummed against the both of us.

Lightning branched across the sky and there was a boom of thunder almost simultaneous with the light that lingered behind our eyelids. Darkness descended—darkness too heavy for day—and then the rain came, stinging and sharp against my skin. I covered your body with my own and then I was brushing against your lips and you exhaled hot hot and your hands were strong on my hips and you made that low guttural sound in your throat that also felt like thunder.

Rain in my eyes, rain on my face, rain in my mouth against your mouth. Your hands firm against my back, on my waist, kneading my thighs, and your hands didn't stop, didn't withdraw, didn't soften. Your hands were on me and my face was against your neck and my mouth was panting against your skin.

You unbuttoned my jeans. Shoved them down enough to slip your hand against me, inside me. And my body bucked against you and your mouth was on my throat and my hands were clawing into the earth. You withdrew your hand and used your whole body to push me to the ground beneath you, and I tasted the rain on your cheek. You tried to pull my wet jeans off until we collapsed in laughter and I had to help you, our mouths filling with rain. Cool green grass against my bare thighs, my hips, my backside. You knelt between my legs, and we pulled our shirts off at the same time, colliding, flesh against flesh. Warmth of you against me.

And, oh, the wild sweetness of your kisses, and the muscle of your arms and thighs under my hands. And the softness of your breasts, your belly, the insides of your thighs. You gasped then grunted as I bit at your collarbone, your ribs, your hipbones. Rain and thunder and the smell of the earth and my body and yours undulating against each other. Your face on my thighs and mine on yours and our mouths sipping and tasting and sucking. I spiraled and thundered and crashed and I could hardly concentrate but the taste of you was so and the feel of you was so and the heat of you was so and I felt your body shuddering and I could not stop. We cried out together and as we collapsed, shivering still and the rain falling still, I thought I smelled flowers. We lay there, breathing and breathing and breathing.

This morning, I went to bring in the clothes we'd left scattered on the grass and saw that where we'd lain, full-grown lilies had sprouted in profusion everywhere, already blooming, the white and gold and pink and peach and tangerine and scarlet of Easter lilies and Asiatic lilies, of sonatas and Sumatras and stargazers.

Claudia

I woke and the seedlings were cool against my skin. Tiny roots raking my legs, my arms, my face. I woke and my hand was in the space between your navel and your hip. The tiny red leaves of a Japanese Maple were curled against my thumb. There was a tiny sound as I lifted it up and pulled it away from you. I laid it in the shallow basin we keep on the nightstand with an inch of water in it.

You shifted in your sleep, turning onto your stomach. From the back of your knees, I pulled the leafless twigs that would become a Texas redbud. You didn't move. I brushed the dark hair away from your face, felt the raspy green of Arizona cypresses behind your ear before I saw them. One. Two. Three. Four of them in your hair. I ran my hand down the center of your back. Without waking, you turned back toward me.

That's when I saw it. It must have begun unfurling before we fell asleep. Six leaves, green, rounded but slender, glossy. A lime seedling. The first of its kind. In all my years with you, you'd never released a lime seedling. Its roots reached from your neck to the corner of your right eye. As if tears had pooled in the hollow of your neck. Grown solid, grown green, grown into leaves. When I pulled it away, it released the scent of sweet, wet earth. I dug my face into your neck, breathed you in. Tightened my arms around you, sighed, and fell asleep again.

Ameyalli

I don't know what alchemies you perform. Only that every morning while I am making coffee, you take the seedlings out to your workstation beside the deck. Sift soil and sort the tiny pots. There are shelves and shelves and bins and bags with different kinds of soil, with river pebbles and sand and moss and bark and perlite and other things I still can't name. No moments of hesitation, no wasted movements. You find each seedling its best home, placing each one in the sunlight with care, breathing on each one as if you were kissing me. Even watering them, you are tender and careful, as if you wish you could be the morning dew.

In our first years, I thought you would tire of me, tire of them, tire of all the work—this work of plucking and sorting and potting and watering and weeding and sunning and growing and feeding and planting and tending. But you are as delighted now as you were then and you emanate peace as if you were the earth itself, breathing in the sunlight.

Claudia

To love leafing things is to know how life flows into death and back again. How many seeds have I planted and never seen emerge from the ground. How many tiny green limbs lost to the sun. Lost to cold and frost. Lost to darkness. Lost to too much or not enough water. Lost to pests. Lost to bitter soil. Lost for no discernible reason. Each green life that flourishes eases the ache of those that were lost. The ache of all the tiny, yellowed things I held in my hands. Shriveled and brittle and breakable.

But every budding flower, every unfurling leaf, every new green-tipped limb is a whole new miracle. From earth and sun and rain, they make and remake themselves. It seems impossible. The journey from leaf to seedling to tree. Incandescent. All the green life furiously alight. Death kept at bay.

This is what you are. Sunshine in my hands.

* * *

It's impossible to count four hundred rabbits, but I know that's who they are. All of them white and slightly iridescent. Their eyes look at me intelligently. They possess no fear. They came in ones and twos at first. Then in threes and fours. They come into our yard at dusk, emerging from the magueys that grow along the east side of the backyard. Sometimes the magueys are there, the flower spikes unbearably tall, twenty feet high and more. Sometimes the magueys are only shadows.

I created a second garden just for them. Right at the very edge of our yard. Where the grass gives way to the woods. I planted everything they seemed to like most there. I don't know when it came to me that they were your brothers. They give me a solemn look, knowing that I watch them as they emerge from and return to the magueys as if the magueys were a doorway to another world. Sometimes they call me sister-in-love. All their ears twitched furiously the one time I was brave enough to say the names of your real mother and father. When I asked the four hundred rabbits, they told me you were what the old gods chose to make when they decided to make something new.

Ameyalli

The first time it happened, I didn't know what to do. I was only thirteen. First, there was the hint of red in the water streaming from my body in the shower. I touched myself and thought it was so strange to bleed and yet not hurt. And then I felt tiny leaves brush against my hand, and a sharpness pricked my fingers. I reached in further, took a hold of it gingerly, and pulled it slightly. It didn't come free. I pulled harder. Panicked a little bit. But finally it came away from my body. I wasn't sure what it was but the leaves looked like the leaves on the trees we had had in the backyard. So green, so green. The roots were twice as long as the little tree. A baby mesquite.

I didn't know what to do with it. I wrapped it in a hand towel and put it in my backpack. On my way to school, I tossed it into the creek when I passed over the bridge. Every morning, a single new seedling tossed into the creek.

Until the morning that there were three. The night before, I'd made myself come for the very first time. My friends and I had whispered about it, I'd read about it, had even talked to my mom about it, but I knew somehow that my body was different. I tried so many things, tried touching myself soft and hard, quick and slow, here and then there, tried fingers inside. Tried thinking, not thinking, and finally it happened. Like nothing I could have imagined. Leaves and roots erupted from my body.

The next morning I found three seedlings instead of one. Other times there were two or four. Every morning I launched them into the creek. On weekends I rode my bike and found somewhere to leave some of the seedlings. So many different kinds, sometimes in my hair, from the corner of my eyes, from my nostrils, my lips, my underarms, my navel, my hips, my thighs, from between my legs, from behind my knees, from behind my ears. Most of the time, I didn't know what they were called or where they were from or what they needed. I just knew I couldn't keep them. Knew my mother would ask me questions I couldn't answer.

I learned to lock my door at night and to search my body first thing every morning. It was hardest my first year in college when I had a roommate. I learned to wear concealing pajamas, to always sleep under covers, to wake several times in the night to check myself. I never allowed anyone to fall asleep in my bed, and with every lover, I feared a seedling would emerge and leaf under their hands. I was afraid to see fear in their eyes, and it wasn't long before that fear turned my body inward. Blunted my desire.

Claudia

Sometimes it feels like I've spent my entire life waiting to hear that word again. The doctors are oddly careful. They won't say it. They'll say, *no signs of reoccurrence*. Strangely, I believed them more when the tests were more invasive. What they do now, decades later, is too easy, too quick.

I don't know what I'd do if you weren't there holding my hand. If you weren't there to stay up with me the nights before I go in for the results. If you weren't there the nights I wake up gasping for air. And I tell you my dreams. I'm in the shower, always in the shower, running my hands over myself, checking for lumps and tenderness and worrying over the flesh that in its fifties is no longer as smooth as it once was. I feel a small bulge in my side and press my right hand over it. It throbs under my fingers and then I'm holding it with both hands as it pushes and pushes. And I can feel my insides being overrun, my organs swallowed, and it grows and grows while the rest of me crumbles. And no one hears my cries and no one can help me.

I wake up because you're calling my name. You're already pressed against me, kissing my wrists, the palms of my hands.

Ameyalli

It's not enough to thank you. And I know I can't ever really know what it costs you. But I'm grateful. And my parents are grateful. And of course, they're grateful too.

Mom and Dad started taking me with them when I was ten or eleven. They wanted to teach me that action was necessary, that compassion was never wasted. We worked with a group of people that left water and food and clothing along the border. They wanted no more deaths. Each life saved was a victory. They'd seen too many dead bodies, starved and desiccated, killed by thirst, hunger, and the heat of the sun.

For years, we hardly saw anyone when we were out there. And then you and I went to visit my parents on the border. You came with us. That changed everything. We learned to go where you told us to go. You'd tilt your head to the side, with that faraway look in your eyes and your hands clenching into fists. How many did we save once you joined us, arriving when things were at their most desperate?

Your Spanish is like mine. Like my parents'. North of the border Spanish. Enough to make ourselves understood. But we could speak to them and help them. Though sometimes we had to say, *lo siento*, because we were too late.

Mom and Dad weren't too late for me. They've shown me the retama where they found me. Golden blooms falling in cascades. They said I was humming and smiling. Not starved, not thirsty. Lightly swaddled in the early morning heat. No signs of a mother or a father or other people. No diaper. No bottle. No toys. No name. Wrapped in a length of sky-blue cotton.

Claudia

On a summer day so long ago, you took my hand when I asked you to dance. Our friend Leticia was throwing me a welcome-to-Austin party. Tons of food. Sangria and margaritas served by the pitcher. Cumbia and salsa and rock en Español playing in the backyard. You were the first woman in Austin I asked to dance. The first and the last.

We danced. We laughed. We drank. I followed you back to your place. We talked till the sun rose and when I kissed you our mouths tasted like coffee and dawn. You were the most beautiful thing I'd ever seen. The morning light golden on your dark skin. Only traces of eyeliner and lipstick left after so many hours.

I woke before you and found the seedlings in your hair spread across my face. I didn't question them. I had tasted you. Earth after rain on my tongue. I'd smelled the green behind your ears, behind your knees. And the first time I made you come there were colors blooming in your eyes. Your skin itself sang *life life life* under my hands, under my lips.

When you woke and saw me, you smiled—and then rose in a panic, rushing to the restroom. I caught your arm, waved toward the seedlings I'd placed on the nightstand. *It's OK. I'll take care of them. Come back to bed.* Your eyes were wide and you bit your lip, but you came back to me.

In that first week, only flowered trees were born from you. Small things. Barely more than twigs and roots and a leaf or two. I pored over the leaves, tracing their fragile edges with my fingers. In my mind, their future colors bloomed. The soft pinks of magnolias and redbuds, purple bauhinias and jacarandas and mountain laurels, blue paulownias, white manucas and dogwoods, yellow huisaches and retamas. All the fruits—orange trees and grapefruit trees and apple trees and peach trees. Crepe myrtles of every color. I plucked each one from you with wonder.

Morning sunshine streamed in from your bedroom window. I brought soil and bark and string. Made tiny baskets for each seedling, setting their roots in the soil and bark. I cut the string to different lengths, hung each seedling so that it would receive as much sunlight as possible. I wanted to delight you.

You cried and told me about all the seedlings you'd tossed in creeks and parks and other people's yards. *Never again*, I said. *I'll take care of them.*

And I have. Trees grow slowly, but there are at least two hundred potted seedlings in our backyard at the moment. I've donated at least five hundred trees that were at least seven feet tall to local parks. There's a twenty-five-mile stretch of highway outside of town which we supplied with native drought-hardy trees. Every now and then, I'll take a few into the forest and plant them where I think they'll flourish. I've dedicated twenty acres on the other side of the house to growing fruit trees.

All the time, I am surrounded by your leaves. Your flowers. Your fruit. Your seeds. Your scent.

Ameyalli

I've dreamt it, you know. I know what will happen the day I die. You'll need to stay close to me. You'll need to be there before I take my last breath. There won't be much time to carry me out to the empty land beyond the fruit orchards. In the moment I take my last breath, leaves will start emerging from every part of me, from every pore. Tendrils and branches. Leaves and blossoms and fruit and seeds. All of my flesh, all of my organs, ruthlessly rooting and seeding. You'll try but you won't be able to pluck them from me fast enough. They'll fall from my body and take root as soon as they touch the earth. You'll have to run, my love, you'll have to run as fast as you can. As soon as you lay me down, run. Without hesitating. It'll seem as if my body's exploding—entire tree trunks and branches bursting out of me. The green will spread in every direction so quickly that the earth will shudder and roll, heave and sigh. All of me, my eyes, my skin, my limbs, my blood converted into flowers, into vines, into a green river shot through with sunlight.

I've dreamt this, my love. I've dreamt this and your tears, but you'll never be alone. I'll always be with you. You can sleep among the roots of my trees. You can touch each blossom to your face and feel my kisses. You can eat any fruit and taste me. Live in my garden after I am gone.

It will take years, perhaps decades, but a strange flower will bloom—and you'll see a seed, pearl white and the size of your fist. Take it to the desert where I was found—take it when you feel your days coming to an end. Embrace it and you'll be embracing me.

Claudia

Age hasn't slowed your parents down at all. They're flourishing in the heat, attending protests, registering voters, translating for refugees, fundraising for various nonprofits, still trekking out into the empty spaces to leave water and dry foods. I'll come along too and do what I can.

And then we'll come back here, our home, our garden, our little forest away from the city. To days and days with you. Nights where we have dinner on the patio and the candlelight causes the first few gray hairs on your head to glimmer like silver. Mornings when the first thing you say is my name. My hands will harvest the seedlings from your body. I'll wonder at how they emerge from your skin. How they multiply in number each time I make you come, again and again and again. And they're not always trees nowadays. I've been surprised by tiny orchids from your thighs, passionflower vines from your feet. I went to nibble at your neck and followed the scent of roses until I found them rooted behind your ears. I want to know what else your body will learn to make, what else will emerge—will there be little succulents on your back, green thumb-sized balls of cactus on your legs, bougainvilleas branching out of your hair? Will I see plants that have not grown in the Americas in centuries, in millennia?

We live in a paradise of our own making. We are still a long way from goodbyes, my noxochitzin. I hear no whispers in the wind. Today is not our last day. Tonight we'll sleep in each other's arms. And tomorrow morning, I'll find pots for the new seedlings.

The Round-Roof Hooghan

The round-roof hooghan is like a woman's tiered skirt.
It is said that the mother, amá, is the heart of the home.
It is said that there is beauty within,
when a home is as it should be.
Beauty extends from the hooghan.
Beauty extends from the woman.
Beauty extends from the woman.
Beauty extends from the woman.
Beauty extends from the woman.

"The Round-Roof Hooghan" by Luci Tapahonso first appeared in *A Radiant Curve: Poems and Stories*, University of Arizona Press, 2008.

Laguna y Río Carry Me

In memory of Roxana Hernandez, a transgender woman who was part of the caravan of Central American migrants. She died in ICE custody at a hospital in Albuquerque, New Mexico, on May 25, 2018. *En memoria a Roxana Hernandez, mujer transgénera quien fue parte de la caravana de migrantes de Centroamérica, el cual ella murió estando en la custodia de ICE en un hospital de Alburquerque Nuevo México, el 25 de mayo 2018.*

Rain river ocean stream
run beside me
until my legs tire
take me with you
carry me home

Ocean water
I bathed in your waves once
with a white bar of soap
because I didn't understand Spanish
so much back then
"Cuando entras el mar" the seer said
"Limpia todo tu cuerpo"[1]
and she slid her thick black hands
up and down her arms, legs, neck
and in circles over her eyes
I used soap cuz she told me to wash myself
and you cleansed me

1 When you enter the sea, cleanse your whole body.

you pushed her along the banks, water
up onto the streets
behind a dollar tree
and we found her
still breathing

dad said you pushed
him over to the side
against a nest of Montezuma cypress roots
he climbed
met my mom
now there's me

Rain river ocean stream
run beside me
until my legs tire
take me with you
carry me home

When Tía brought me bags of oranges
from the valley
on her trips to visit abuelita
'Buela said
        your water fed the fruit
        the ocean burst into waves
        when I crushed the pulp
        between my teeth

I saw her
tossed on her side
red fingernails
scars softened
lips still touched with pink
hands and arms hanging off the edge
of grandma's sheets I inherited
hair soaked with you
after a cold bath

Rain river ocean stream
run beside me
until my legs tire
then take me with you
carry me home

After he *made me*
I woke up to dry tears of river on my shirt
and mocos[2] in a puddle of ocean   with a fistful of flood and stream
    dripping
out the edges of my palms

When the cold came
you,
river
swelled
silenced
told the people to leave your waters
that you would freeze around them

Rain river ocean stream
run beside me
until my legs tire
then take me with you
carry me home
where I don't have to run
anymore

"Just add water and it will grow into whatever you want"
I put the little pink capsule in my pocket
and rushed home
hoping it would grow into a cute girlfriend or invisible cloak

When the rain came
I did too

2 Mucus.

opened by the undertow
sprayed out into the ocean

I drove four and a half hours to see you
laguna, mi madre
but when I got there
I met a girl
and she felt just as good
on my skin

"Water" I whispered
because I didn't want my friends tanning behind me on the sand to laugh
"Water, the curandera[3] said to come here and ask for you to clean the memory
of him away"
the water had already rose above my belly button
and I started to pee
"Water, wash his taste from my mouth"
I asked
and you did
and he drowned

Back then
when we saw a sombrero float by—
Rosi and I—
we laughed
made up stories about how the *panadero* must'a let their hat fly off their head
we didn't know
their spirits sunk to the bottom

When her body landed on the river
her brown hair floated to the surface
took a lick of azure-stained sky
and painted ribbons of silver and blue
ringlets around each of her fingers and toes
to hold her afloat as she goes

3 Traditional folk healer who practices Indigenous medicine.

Rain river ocean stream
run beside me
until my legs tire
then take me with you
carry me home

"There's nothing concrete about water" I said
"Only movement, melting, freezing, floating, expanding, running
If you want to understand me
understand water"
"I don't get it" she said
You won't
I think to myself
I don't even get me sometimes

"I need to go to the water" she said
and left

She walked on the Mexican side of the river
chased uñitas[4] flowers
their hats swayed back and forth with the wind
she pretended they were people at first
dancing
then used the spit from her tongue
to stick their petals to her fingernails

"When I used to see bodies in the river" she said
"I used to think that the river had taken them home"

"All she knows how to do in the kitchen is boil water"
her tía mocked
and the others laughed around the kitchen table

4 Flower petals that look like little false painted fingernails when licked and stuck onto a baby's nails.

she was doing her best
and water for tea was the best she could do for herself
at that time

"It's cause I'm a water baby"
and my ex looked at me with dry creases between their eyes
I don't want to dry up like you
I thought
and we broke up

Rain river ocean stream
run beside me
until my legs tire
take me with you
carry me home

"Drink six eight-ounce glasses of water every day"
"Mija, six or eight glasses of water?"
the doctor repeated herself again
"No" she said
and wagged her finger at Mama Grande
"Señora, you have to drink six eight-ounce glasses of water"
"I do already" mija
Mama Grande was confused
"Dame un baso de agua,"[5] she ordered me

River flowing through her
open up into the bay
take her to laguna madre
wake her
shake her
quench her
but don't ask her to stay.

5 Give me a glass of water.

Rain river ocean stream
run beside me
until my legs tire
take me with you
carry me home

Summer Music

Cicadas sing—
thrum and wheeze
from the mulberry trees
a row of knotted trunks hugging the fence
between pole beans and dandelion lawn,
the highest, greenest leaves dusty from weeks
of our passing back and forth on the gravel drive.

I stand on our unpainted, sagging porch,
holding the baby's cup and her dress,
clean and crisp as Chinese poppies
flaming in a summer portrait.

Cicadas begin their song again
singing again
as if they had stopped
when the screen door slammed,
stopped and breathed in,
their eyes like orange beads
and their wings like chaff.

They sing even within the walls
of my human chest, they sing
in the rooms of my eyes and lungs,
in the struggling chambers of my heart,
and the trembling of the blood in my wrists.

"Summer Music" by Diane Hueter Warner first appeared in *SWWIM Every Day*, 8 February 2021, https://www.swwim.org/swwimeveryday/2021/2/8/summer-music.

When I stand in the sweet humid air
holding a cup of water and a red dress,
I foresee their bodies' husks
emptied, clinging to the trees,
shells of lace,
I wonder what it will be
for my fragile daughter and me
to shrug our dresses, our skin,
like linen from our shoulders
confused or blessed by music of our own.

Diane Hueter Warner

Two Women Talking on a Winter Morning

A pearl gray car stalled
catty wampus[1] in the street.

The policeman cruising by
waits to see if it can get going again,

while the snow-crusted school bus lets down
the handicap track for two coatless boys in wheelchairs.

I'm sitting this one out—trapped in my driveway,
morning coffee steams the inside of my windshield.

I run the wipers with fluid,
scraping off last night's runnels

of bird droppings. I love the birds, even the black
grackles, but especially the cardinal

calling "pretty boy, pretty boy." I see my breath,
I see two women, neighbors down the street

standing on a brown and dormant lawn.
One wears a blue house dress with pink roses large as hands

clapping in the wind. Her short hair gray as concrete
and curly as clouds. The other woman wears a black coat,

1 Crooked, or out of alignment.

patternless and belted. On her way to work,
her car idles in the driveway, pluming past the leafless trees.

Her white hair pinned in a bun—
I see little tendrils coming loose, framing

her head like dandelion fluff or eider down.
Together, their breath comes out, ribbons

linking them as surely as hands on shoulders.
I don't believe they are talking about the crisp morning air

the newspaper boy, the moon,
dogs that bark and whimper all night.

They look into each other's eyes
as if the world was not twirling busily around them

ricocheting past in yellow buses and red or ebony wings
or indeed as if they recognized its erratic path

and knew they had to be
the steady calm center of it all.

An impulse took her by the lake
instead of down the highway
directly home

Among the trees
the sky fell like cotton

And where one winter they had skipped stones
clanging and echoing across solid ice
now mud-caked fence posts trace
the faint ruts of a driveway

"It's a sweet dream," sang the radio
the water so low she could see

the farmhouse foundation
the cistern's cement lid
and corroded handle
shingles scattered like doll clothes

She could point to where she knew
the lilacs should stand
and the elm tree with the swing
                    She knows

there was never a promise made here
that was not broken

Anel I. Flores

Una Hojita de Buganvilla: A Parable

Six-year-old Solitaria listened to her knees crack into the cement floor by the force of her brother's heavy hands of sand on her shoulders. She never really developed a green thumb after that.

Her mami said, "Your hermano has a branch, mija, *y* tu, you have una hojita de buganvilla."

Even after trying to ask her mami in the morning, at night, in the kitchen, and even once out in the yard, Solitaria never had the stamina to move her lips to the shape of the real words she wanted to say: "Why does hermano make me put his branch in my dark pink buganvilla flower, mami?" Solitaria believed she was the pretty purple buganvilla flower and her place down there was the small leaf mami told her about.

Her mami rubbed the thin hojita, growing long like a trestle of flowers and leaves around their front door, against her cheek every morning. "Buenas," she'd speak to her plantitas and sigh at the pleasure of their coolness against her skin on hot valley mornings.

Hermano had a dirty dry branch and with it he tore the sides of her Solitaria's moth. She knew it was almost over when hermano pressed his hands against the chipped cemento bathroom walls. Her stomach plummeted onto the ground along with mint green paint flakes from under hermano's nails. She didn't know the taste of his branch would one day grow into a phobia of all plant foods and an addiction to breaking her teeth down on pen caps while writing furiously against all big dry branches and dirty brothers.

a veil

read the future in sizzling
yolk   on the hot sidewalk
          between our homes

how many times can we
survive   the crack
not sure who it was
                         that broke

i collect the parcels of shell
rinse them in vinegar and
rosehips bake them in desert
heat crush them paint my
body in their salty yeast
          anoint with sunday oil

my upper lip my third
eye   the spot that hinges
open and close like a cage
          door on my chest

smoke curls upward
from the adobe horno
outside my window

i lift the hem
          of the shadow
which is long and flat
like a wedding veil

and disappear
inside of it where
the pressure of
everything is
immense

Lisa Lee Herrick

Part 1: Bête Noire, a California Extinction in Five Walks

I. Fresno: Trespassers Within

If you walked in a straight line for eight hours a day at a steady pace, every day for three years, you would traverse the equivalent of the earth's circumference at its equatorial bulge (or twenty-five thousand miles, more or less) and return to find your self-same footsteps, the little cupped domes of earth molded into the shape of your body, as you once were. Walking is one of the simplest and most liberating movements. It seems that our bodies evolved simply for this activity: to stand upright and canvas the world and map its contours by the measure of our feet. To walk and explore, to meander and daydream without purpose or destination, to escape ordinary sights and leave some residue of ourselves behind—an eyelash here, a bead of sweat there, a burl of loosened hair clinging to a ponytail elastic band—is to imagine that the landscape clings to us, too, and recognizes our belonging. But is the earth truly so seamless that it has no edges? No vistas that are difficult to reach, no canyons or oceans impossible to bridge? A world with no edges has fidelity to no nation, no constitution, no tribe. It is a place of limitless freedom. If we *were* able to walk the earth for three years and meet the artifacts of our old selves again, would we still recognize each other or be utterly estranged from ourselves?

When I am walking where I live, in Fresno, California, I cannot find myself in the landscape. When I am walking through other cities, other towns, or crossing a neglected field of tall, dry weeds, I also *feel* a world with sharp edges. It is in the hard, flinty looks warning me that I am about to approach a cliff. *Danger*. It is the stern stare that lasts a second too long

An abridged version of Lisa Lee Herrick's "Bête Noire: A California Extinction in Five Walks" was published online in *The Bold Italic*, 18 September 2020, https://thebolditalic.com/the-sad-story-of-the-bear-on-californias-state-flag-8077ba11846f?gi=cded96bfd508.

and the pursed lips that spit out the question, *Where are you from, originally?* (Never mind that I am from here, the United States, originally.)

My Asian- and female-presenting body is not always tolerated in urban spaces, but I choose to walk, sometimes in solitude, because I want to feel the forward motion of my body stomping on these false limits. I am neither a petite woman nor am I delicate, although I was advised many times by my Hmong community members to make myself as small as a quail's egg cupped in the palm because people cannot help but want to protect beautiful, tiny, breakable things. But a quail's egg lives in secret, suffocated by feathers and hidden from view. I did not want to be an egg. I wanted to celebrate my animal body. When I feel my sweat cooling on my golden, tanned skin and the thick skirt of my black ponytail whipping the backs of my shoulders—each thudding footstep rippling little earthquakes upward through bone to the base of my skull—I feel strong. My legs are as thick as tree trunks, with thighs that kiss and ropey calves spilling over the tops of my boots. My legs and arms are dusted in soft black fur because I haven't shaved in a long time. I am not like those Asian women on TV commercials and period piece serials, thin as sparrow bones and flaccid like spring bamboo, prone to fainting. I am sun toasted, like many people who live here in Fresno, so I blend in as someone who is not white. I am an *other* walking through neighborhoods with my hands outside my pockets and a quick smile ready to disarm suspicions. An *other* who remains unreadable, unknown, and unfamiliar. I am an *other* walking neither too slow (appearing to loiter) nor too fast (appearing to be criminal). Someone who walks the line between friend or foe, a proxy for any other person or thing or idea that is disliked or even hated. I am a dark stranger, someone potentially monstrous behind my polite mask of civility; someone perhaps less human, less dignified, less deserving of the freedom to simply exist in the world. I cannot blend into the landscape. When I am walking where I live, I sometimes feel like I am seen as a black nightmare beast, a bête noire. Because I am treated like I could be concealing a monster behind this smiling facade.

The other day, as I was walking my dog through the neighborhood, an elderly white man stepped out of his house and demanded to know if I lived here, even though we had shared the same backyard fence for over a decade and I regularly walked along this street near daily ever since. "Well," he said, "*I've* never seen you before." I told him that I felt the same: I had never seen him face-to-face before either, so who had been the longer resident? Who had more right to tread this public walkway? Who gets to be seen as the main character of the universe, or even the city block? (It reminded me of the time I hiked the Portland Rose Garden Loop at Washington Park, Oregon, and paused to admire a view of Mount Hood, and an elderly white woman in a black velvet tracksuit and dyed purple hair—elbows pumping—nearly hip-checked me into the blackberry bushes as she huffed past, yelling at me to *Move!* before disappearing around the bend.) It's ridiculous to think of hypervigilance as a side effect of citizen surveillance in the name of public safety. The hypervigilance is mine. I am the one constantly scanning the landscape, constantly observing my environment as I pass through it, constantly watching the weather for sudden changes like the greenish air of an oncoming tornado, because who will protect me? Hypervigilance is an ugly coat that I cannot get rid of because it is now part of my skin. And because I am a woman and I often walk alone, hypervigilance reminds me that, all too often, I am also seen as prey. A toothless creature of easy surrender. I don't see myself as a victim waiting for the inevitable. This is why feeling the heaviness of my body—my feet pounding the concrete into submission—and taking up public space are my rebuke to the idea that I am not a natural part of this landscape. You see me? I am here to stay. And where does a woman choose to walk? She walks until the land, or her wonder, ends.

It's hard to parse what that means, though—a woman walking with purpose (or for leisure). A popular image in the American imagination that comes to mind is John Gast's infamous 1872 painting of a giant white woman enrobed in a diaphanous ivory dress scattering dark-skinned and bare-chested Indigenous peoples, wild dogs, buffalo, stags, and bears away with her glowing body. She is centered in the painting, suspended midair in her westward sprint, and her bosom is modestly concealed by contrived draperies. She phosphoresces. Her white dress billows behind her blond tresses like angels' wings as she gazes serenely beyond the horizon. She is beatific because it is all so easy for her to go wherever she pleases. Behind her, the totems of the modern and civilized world, according to Gast, trail her: electricity wires, trains, wagons, white men, ox-driven agriculture, and fair and sunny weather. The allegorical painting is *American*

Progress.[1] And the giantess's name is Columbia. She holds a schoolbook in one hand for enlightenment and a loop of electrical wires in the other for industrialization. The Indigenous peoples, wild dogs, and bears snarl as they gaze upon her face because they know that she is unstoppable: She is the personification of manifest destiny and a shibboleth for the expansion of American democracy founded on white supremacy, and I am nothing like her.

For one, Gast would have painted a woman like me ducking from Columbia's pale ankles. Was I supposed to turn around on the sidewalk and scamper back home with my tail between my legs when I was questioned by my elderly white neighbor whether I actually lived in the area? Was I supposed to simply "get out of the way" for that elderly white woman in Portland who saw my body as an impasse? Too often, nonwhite people like me who take up any public space, albeit temporarily, are demanded to relinquish it immediately as though we were caught trespassing. This game of chicken plays out on sidewalks, stairwells, doorways, and even inside our own homes: Who gets the right of way? Who will step aside first? Who will avert their eyes and cower, and who will stare ahead and charge forward? This idea that you are either an insider, one of us, or an outsider—an interloper, an invader—is too facile a binary to form a national identity based on proximity to whiteness. Societies are composed from interlocked networks and systems that are inherently nonbinary and fluid themselves, and shifting values determine deep cultural changes; the idea that racial whiteness can be authenticated as a congenital privilege ignores the fact and history of its own malleable social definition. I am not white. I am not Columbia treading where she is uninvited, floating above the mud with uncalloused toes. Further, I have no interest in shaping the world to suit my tastes. The world is far too interesting, too round, too full of wonders and contradictions for me to compress it all to fit only my narrow point of view. The world is not flat, and my feet have already made a covenant with this land as one of its many curious creatures.

When I walk from east to west, following the arc of the setting sun, I notice that the seams between human and nonhuman worlds are simply

1 John Gast, *American Progress*, 1872, Picturing US History, https://picturinghistory.gc.cuny.edu/john-gast-american-progress-1872/.

illusions formed by cascades of microevolutions too minute for us to track. What little residue I leave behind in my walks does not matter as much as knowing that where there once was a bear, pink azaleas now bloom in its memory. From a distance, all trees look similar until you hold a leaf to the sun and recognize that you too are knit from the same fine netting. To an insect, I must appear a giantess, too, but I am constantly scanning the ground underfoot to step lightly so I do not flush them from their homes. And that makes all the difference.

II. San Francisco: Dreaming at the Western Edge of the Continent

The first time I walked from the Embarcadero, in San Francisco, to Ocean Beach at the western edge of the peninsula, I was surprised that I had been able to accomplish the walk in less than half the day. Perhaps I had underestimated my body's strength or ability to endure pain and monotony because I was living with a man who constantly commented on how I had grown flabby since the early months of our relationship. Once, he reached out and palmed the flesh of my soft belly between his thick fingers, lifting the handful and giving it such a strong shake that my breasts and thighs shivered. He made me feel embarrassed of my aging body: it had failed his inspection, thus its current state was undesirable. I had decided to walk the length of the city to "clear my head," and I marched steadily toward the lacy fog softening the sky into shades of pigeon gray. When I reached Ocean Beach, I dug my toes into the chilly layer of sand, and I felt the pulsing ache of my legs at rest. I knew the truth: my body was amazing, and I didn't need anyone's approval or admiration to exist. I watched the sun blink its burnt orange eye below the horizon, and I knew that our relationship was over.

When I dream of San Francisco, now that many years have passed since that first walk to the sea, I dream of earthquakes. After all, it was the dark churning of primordial fires that lifted the peninsula up from the depths of the ocean floor eons ago. San Francisco is a hallucination of diatomaceous chert with pointed houses glittering salt white like rows of jagged teeth along the three-mile sandbar of Ocean Beach. The water's edge was once the lip of the New World, and the sun still dips below the heartless immensity of the oily Pacific waves each evening. Every time the earth shakes, I return to the place where California was born. I feel the ghosts of the past buzzing like mosquitoes near my ear, humming secrets in the dead languages of the vanished world, telling tall tales of dark, nut-brown warrior women with golden arms and heroic white men from the east. Tales of when California was an island, the ultimate unknown horizon.

San Francisco was once a barren seaside desert tufted with dune grass. It was claimed before the Pilgrims landed on the Atlantic shore. It existed before the Declaration of Independence, before the emergence of rival American nations, and the cages that would detain animals and men alike at its contested borders in the twenty-first century. In the ancient world, a walled city marked the boundary between orderly, man-made civilization and the stateless empire of wild beasts. Today's cities still offer shelter and refuge, but the walls have since disappeared as forests receded. Only the scavengers—pigeons, gulls, rats, raccoons, roaches, and squirrels—thrive in abundant numbers. Humans are the most successful and resilient scavengers of all because we will recycle any resource found in the environment. But unlike the other beasts, the world as it is will never be enough. We must engineer new ways to ensure that our cities are designed in the vein of imagined utopias for the civilized and impenetrable fortresses against the undesired.

Last night, I dreamt that I was walking through my old neighborhood at Fifteenth Street and Guerrero Street in the Mission District. I had lived there in the early 2000s during those unsteady years after the new millennium but before social media corporations pulverized and rebuilt the city as a giant mall food court for their tech workers. Actually, I should say that I dream of my *neighborhoods* because I bounced from one Craigslist apartment to another so often that I left little pieces of myself all over the city. All of San Francisco belonged to me back then, starting at the third-floor walk-up where I house-sat for a friend while she visited family on the East Coast. Valerie was an avant-garde sculptor with bright blue eyes and flame-red hair who smoked cigarettes for breakfast. She had fled Florida for the West Coast to earn both an MFA and the freedom to "fly her freak flag" without her relatives' constant surveillance. I had done the same, too, in a way—only I hadn't traveled nearly as far. I escaped California's Central San Joaquin Valley farm region about two hundred miles inland to reinvent myself and, ultimately, disappear in the city as one of its many undernourished, underpaid, and underemployed writers.

We sat at Valerie's gold-flecked, vintage Formica kitchen table during those damp mornings, tapping cigarette ashes into stale coffee, and watched the pink walls of the Valencia Gardens housing project crumble outside the sole window. It was an exciting time: the planet had white-knuckled through the Y2K scare, the economy was beginning to recover from the dot-com crash, underground raves ruled the nightlife industry, rent was dirt cheap and artists flooded into the city wherever the landlords turned a blind eye to housing code violations. The neighborhood was changing fast. We were part of that change, Valerie and I. We watched cannonballs arc through the pink walls of Valencia Gardens, the inner guts of its former occupants spilling from the walls like grubs tumbling out of beehives. Plumes of asbestos mushroomed into the air. At lunch, our kitchen table and chairs jittered against the linoleum floor as the bulldozers' teeth scraped broken furniture and weeds from the pits. Our coffee mugs jumped each time a hammer punched rebar into deep pits. Valerie's apartment vibrated all day and night. Once, amid the dust, we saw a thin Black teenager dart through the rubble. His elbows pumped as he charged forward like an exclamation mark. He seemed to be searching for some lost thing in the trash heaps, something forgotten or irreplaceable. He disappeared behind a fallen wall. "Should we call the police?" asked Valerie. She dangled her cigarette over her cold coffee and gazed at me. What would we say? *Hello, police? There's a young Black teenager walking around a construction site. No, he's not messing with the equipment. No, he hasn't taken anything, but he does look suspicious.* And if they asked us why he looked suspicious? No, we wouldn't call the police. After a few weeks of rumbling, I felt my back molars slightly loosened. My bones felt looser. My blood vibrated with pins and needles. I felt restless. I had to get out of the apartment.

I started exploring San Francisco on foot because I didn't know how to drive. This was how I came to know the pine-green street signs with names, like headstones, dedicated to five centuries of conquistadors and city founders. All in English or Spanish. All men. All *rich* men.

Before this city was christened San Francisco, it was *Yerba Buena*, or "the good herb." Yerba Buena was the terminus of *El Camino Real* at the *Misión de San Francisco de Asís* in the 1700s, a.k.a. Mission Dolores.

The Mission District and Mission Dolores—that house of pains[2] where the Spaniards goaded bulls to gore chained grizzly bears[3] and a blood-red rose garden bloomed atop nearly five thousand First Californian corpses[4]—were right around the corner from Valerie's apartment. But the *El Dorado* pilgrims and prospectors who followed the Doctrines of Discovery, seeking Queen Calafia's mythic treasures in San Francisco, found mostly fool's gold and mud.[5]

When the city needed to expand further to accommodate the new settlers, the marine boundaries on the eastern side of the peninsula were extended by creating floating barges of garbage and shipwrecks[6] and building atop them until it was indistinguishable where the land ended and the floating garbage began in San Francisco. As the myth of Yerba Buena spread, so did the influx of global fortune seekers. They were made to live in a city within the city, caged by street intersections and restricted from leaving their zones—for example, Chinatown. Tens of thousands of indigent and immigrant—mostly Chinese—laborers were buried in unmarked graves near the rocky crags and under the shadows of mansions in the northwest corner of the city. Today, their bodies form the firmament for both a posh art museum and a private golf course for the nouveau riche.[7]

Watching the ballet of demolition and dust each morning deeply affected me. The thought that *It's only a matter of time* before my view from Valerie's third-story kitchen window would vanish, too, ribboned

2 *Dolor* is the Spanish word for pain. Plural *-es*.

3 *San Francisco Chronicle*, "When Bulls Fought Bears in Brutal Mission District Matches," 3 March 2017, https://www.sfchronicle.com/bayarea/article/When-bulls-fought-bears-in-brutal-Mission-10975827.php.

4 Culture Trip, "History of the Mission San Francisco de Asís," 2 November 2016, https://theculturetrip.com/north-america/usa/articles/history-of-the-mission-san-francisco-de-asis-mission-dolores.

5 KCET, "California, Calafia, Khalif: The Origin of the Name 'California,'" 15 December 2015, https://www.kcet.org/shows/departures/california-calafia-khalif-the-origin-of-the-name-california.

6 National Geographic, "New Map Reveals Ships Buried Below San Francisco," 2 June 2017, https://www.nationalgeographic.com/history/article/map-ships-buried-san-francisco.

7 Alta Online, "Buried Histories," 26 September 2022, https://www.altaonline.com/dispatches/a40981186/hidden-history-san-francisco-graveyards/.

through my mind. I wondered how many unaccounted bodies were still buried under her Valencia Street apartment and whether there were poltergeists we simply hadn't noticed because the only noise haunting was the ceaseless construction of a city constantly rearranging itself like a living collective organism. But wasn't impermanence the unfortunate truth of a place? Every city is a graveyard. Every building will eventually be digested by the soil beneath it.

Even time wears away the face of a mountain.

***

If the earth is constantly rearranging itself, then what is a frontier? Is it a true margin, as in, the space between the world as it was before versus the world to come? Or do we only imagine that such liminal spaces exist because we fear the impermanence of our own cultural institutions, our own mortality, and the face of alternative viewpoints?

Is a frontier a wall that delimits those who live inside as human and those living beyond it as *other*? And if a person lives outside of a wall, are they no longer human and no better than a beast? Perhaps even cursed to be a monster whose sole purpose is to be destroyed?

Do the violence and destruction done to Indigenous people and local flora and fauna, in the pursuit of a fantastical "Promised Land," only reveal a failure to make sense of new interactions within a world in perpetual flux?

And why is it that when predominantly male American conservationists spoke of preserving critical habitats for endangered species in the twentieth century, they spoke of the land as though it was made of ideal female flesh: pure, virginal, untilled, and untouched by man? Didn't they know that they were already too late to reset the world back to the previous ice age? What of the past ten thousand years of complex biotic networks managed by two ever-present apex predators—humans and bears—each shy and hesitant to war with the other, and the abundant habitats sustained by their distant encounters. Did that not count as conservation biology knowledge?

When is a wall not a frontier or a refuge but the perimeter of a cage? If walking is a democratic demonstration of freedom, containment is its opposite. How is it decided—who lives in palaces and who lives in prisons?

It all seems so obvious. When we dehumanize people unlike ourselves and indiscriminately destroy habitats that efficiently support complex systems of interdependent organisms, we engage in the savage violence that we secretly fear may be our true nature. It is a vice we gladly persecute in others but deceive in ourselves. When we meet the gaze of our perceived enemy and recognize our own faces, it is an unbearable mirror of our own ethical and moral failings. Making monsters of *others* makes them easier to destroy. An *other* can be an animal, a person, a thing, a gesture, even an idea that is judged inferior. I am always checking that box on forms: *other*.

> Each time I look into the eye of an animal, one as "wild" as I can find in its own element—or maybe peering through zoo bars will have to do . . . I find myself staring into a mirror of my own imagination. What I see there is deeply, crazily, unmercifully confused. There is in that animal eye something both alien and familiar. There is in me, as in all human beings, a glimpse of the interior, from which everything about our minds has come. The crossing holds all the power and purity of first wonder, before habit and reason dilute it. The glimpse is fleeting. Quickly, I am left in darkness again, with no idea whatsoever how to go back.[8]

Respectability is the mask of the wild man trying to deny his own inner violence.

It is because of this that I think sometimes, a bear is simply a bear.

8 Ellen Meloy, *Eating Stone*, Vintage Books, 2006, pp. 15–16.

Part II

Landscapes

> Even though some Western landscapes practice a trickster's habit of presenting themselves to newcomers as if they were fresh, untouched, vacant spaces, nonetheless, stories have become quite literally something in the Western soil. As well as rock, soil, plants, animals, water, and air, the American West is composed of layers and layers of accumulated human activity and thought . . . I have kept oriented by reckoning with these strata of memory.
>
> Patricia Nelson Limerick, *Something in the Soil*

Our Abuelos, the Trees

Our Abuelos, the trees, stand guard,
their bark-lidded eyes, tired from too much wisdom,
have seen a thing or two.
They sometimes sit so still
we don't even see them
Always, they see us
squint those wooden curandero eyes
at foolish grandchildren so so
young they think that they
discovered this place
discovered history
discovered life.
Los Abuelos laugh among themselves
shake their heads, leaves tossed like graying locks
tremble in a deep breath
settle in for another siglo or two
and hope the grandchildren
won't tear up the place too much in the meanwhile

Our Abuelos, the trees, hum low lullabies around us
whisper words of warning beside us
hope we'll eventually grow up enough
to learn to speak the language
or at least learn how to behave
when spoken to

"Our Abuelos, the Trees" by Carmen Tafolla first appeared in *Sonnets and Salsa*, Wings Press, 2004.

El Desierto

When I was young, I loved our family car trips to California. I marveled at the rhythm and abundance of the Pacific Ocean, *swish, swish.*

I've lived much of my life in the Chihuahua Desert, my home landscape. There is much I love about its bare, majestic mountains, its sky.

Since I was little, I've written about this dramatic landscape and have now written desert poetry for adults, teens, and children. From *Chants* (1984), my first book of poetry, to *Encantado: Desert Monologues* (2018), the desert, el desierto, has been a theme.

I am a desert woman.

Spring

Longer days,
    warm breezes
        quicken our steps—
trees and cholla bloom
    hot pink and yellow.
Birds build scraggly nests.

    Our feet float

Stephanie Elizondo Griest

The Activist and the Ordinance

Suzie Canales was cruising the back roads of Corpus Christi with her sister Cindy when something sinister caught their eye off the side of the road. They pulled over and retraced their travels, walking against traffic. Though still within the city limits, they were far from any residential neighborhood. Down the knoll and beyond some trees, they could make out a pond-size body of darkness. Cindy ran back to lock the car. *Don't go down there without me!* Naturally, Suzie did.

The water was thick as sludge and the color of scorched coal. It exuded an odor Suzie couldn't place. Like tar, but danker. Cautiously, Suzie stuck a foot upon the mud bank surrounding it. Her shoe sank a few inches, but it seemed firm enough to hold her. What could it be? Given all the oil refineries in the area—Citgo, Flint Hills, Valero—the possibilities were endless. It could be crude oil. Hydraulic fracturing fluid. Drill cuttings. Petroleum waste. She took another step. It could be a benzene bath. A carcinogenic stew. A toxic—

Suddenly, she was submerged in it. Chest high. A scream escaped. Sludge filled her open mouth, and in her panic, she swallowed. The darkness slithered down her throat. She flailed her limbs until they found something solid beneath. A pipeline of sorts. She clenched it between her feet.

Seeing her sister struggle, Cindy half-ran, half-tumbled down the knoll toward the bank. Finding a grassy spot, she extended her hand. Little sister to big sister. Growing up, these women weren't especially close. Suzie had been the baby for seven years, until Cindy wailed along. Suzie had resented her ever since. Only now, in their forties, were they starting to connect. Now that they had lost their older sister, Diana. Now that they had formed a coalition to fight what might have killed her.

"The Activist and the Ordinance" by Stephanie Elizondo Griest first appeared in *All the Agents and Saints: Dispatches from the U.S. Borderlands*, University of North Carolina Press, 2020.

The sisters locked eyes and gripped hands. *On the count of three. One. Two.* But Suzie's hands were too slick. She slipped deeper into the sludge. Cindy screamed with frustration before reaching out once more. Again, she lost her grip. Suzie sank further into the murk. The third try. *This is it.* They stared hard into each other's eyes. *This is too much!* They burst out laughing. That's when Cindy's adrenaline surged. Clutching her sister by both wrists, she yanked her from the swamp. The two stumbled backward onto the mud bank where Suzie lay in a heap. *I swallowed some. I swallowed some.*

As baptisms go, Suzie's was gruesome but fitting. Here was a woman who had dedicated her life to fighting oil companies—and she nearly drowned in one of their pits.

* * *

Oil refineries are the first sight to greet you upon entering my hometown. They line both sides of the interstate, a city unto themselves, sprawling across hundreds of acres of land as they rise in towering mazes of pipe and steel, looking both antiquated and futuristic as they emit plumes of smoke into the sky. Their storage tanks are mostly painted hospital green or tenement cream, though some sport murals of dolphins and sea turtles and say things like "Sharing the Earth with Responsibility: CITGO." Powdery black hills of the petroleum by-product known as "petcoke" abound.

Because they backbone our economy, criticizing these refineries makes you a polarizing figure. If someone doesn't work for a refinery themselves, their tío surely does. So city officials tend to wince when Suzie Canales comes knocking at the door. They dispatch their secretaries to stonewall her. Industry reps are even less diplomatic: they reach for the phone and dial security. The media love her, since she's a reliable source of opinion. She appears on the evening news so often, though, she can seem like a zealot. When I mention my plans to have breakfast with her one morning, a friend asks, "You mean, the crazy one?" But that's why I want to meet Suzie. Like the other Tejanos I've been admiring lately—Santa Barraza, Lionel Lopez, Sister Maximina—she appears to have transcended the typical preoccupations of family, career, and self and channeled her fervor into something greater.

In her early fifties, Suzie has cropped black hair, a prominent nose, olive skin, and melancholic eyes. Her earrings are shaped like bunches of grapes; beaded bracelets adorn her wrists. She has the air of a guidance counselor from an at-risk high school: deeply empathetic, yet a little wary, too. At the Town & Country Diner, she orders the bacon-and-egg special before saying, more to herself than to me, "Where should I begin?"

Suzie grew up on the west side of Corpus Christi—the part of town where multiple generations gather each Sunday for backyard barbacoa, where sons tinker beneath their trucks while their fathers shout encouragements from the front step, where young moms put on lipstick before pushing strollers down the street, where every taqueria with a hand-painted sign should be frequented. Suzie's father mostly worked as a construction supervisor, but he also picked up shifts as a security guard at the refineries. When the girls were little, their mom would pack an ice chest full of chicken, rice, and beans and the family would spread out on a knoll overlooking the industrial park for dinner alfresco. At dusk, the refineries lit up like Christmas—a soft glow of golden lights, the red ones occasionally blinking. Rounding out their neighborhood was a municipal garbage landfill called Greenwood. Though unsightly, it only bothered them when it rained and made the air reek of spoiled eggs. The family would dart about the house sealing windows whenever the sky turned slate, despite the soothing winds.

Suzie fostered two dreams as a child: becoming a nurse and moving to New England (because it sounded regal). She ditched the first plan during her second semester of nursing school when she glimpsed a patient in a hospital bed with a tube stuck up one nostril and bile spilling out the other. That left New England. She married a Navy man who promised to take her there. Together, they lived in places like San Diego, Hawaii, and Washington, raising two children along the way. By early 1999, her husband was primed for retirement. They planned to move to Pennsylvania for the millennium.

It happened one morning in February. The kids were late for school. Suzie was watching her son Jason tie his shoes when a vision took his place.

"A vision?" I interrupt.

"I don't know if you believe in this kind of thing," she says, then hesitates.

"I do," I say, more forcefully than intended.

She studies me for a moment, then describes how her sister Diana appeared before her, face up and frighteningly still, "as if she were in a casket, but there was no casket." The image lasted just a second before vanishing. For two weeks, Suzie wondered what to do about it. Then her mother called to say that Diana's breast cancer had returned. It was now stage four and had metastasized to her brain. Diana was forty-two years old.

Suzie had to make a decision. Should she move her family back to Corpus to help her sister through this? Or should they continue on to New England as planned? Her husband was game for either, but Suzie couldn't shake the feeling that returning to Texas would wreck their marriage. *If I move back home, we'll be over within a year.* This haunted her to the core. Twenty years they'd spent together. Twenty years of seizing each new duty station by storm—camping in the Olympic Mountains, visiting Amish markets in Ohio, and on quiet nights, playing board games with the kids.

Yet home has a gravitational pull like no other. They returned to Corpus in September. Diana died that December, two days before the millennium. Friends descended upon them, rosaries wrapped around their wrists. *Aye, so young. You know, my niece has breast cancer too.* Neighbors she hadn't seen in years. *My sister died of breast cancer last year. She was even younger than Diana, only thirty-five.* Former classmates from Cunningham Middle School. *I heard three of your sisters got hysterectomies. Me too, and I'm just thirty-eight.* The services blurred into a fog of grief. *Remember my little brother? He's passed. My big brother too. Pues, they had cancer, both of them.*

Before departing the funeral home, the family gathered in a huddle. *Did anybody notice all that talk of cancer?* They had. Someone started compiling a list of the dead. The names quickly filled two pieces of paper. By the time they grabbed a third, they vowed to investigate. First, they ran an ad in the *Thrifty Nickel* and *Adsack*, asking Greenwood residents to contact them if anyone in their family had cancer. Within days, they were fielding calls about teenage girls undergoing hysterectomies. The local CBS affiliate noticed their ad as well and rang them for details. Though nervous about public speaking, Suzie agreed to a slot on the evening news. Soon, her telephone was ringing incessantly. Suzie typed up a health survey she found on the internet, ran off hundreds of copies, and distributed them to her brothers and sisters.[1] They fanned out in their old neighborhood,

1 Activism runs strong in this family. One of Suzie's sisters, Juanita, is married to Lionel Lopez, who directs the South Texas Colonia Initiative. "Must have been in the water,"

knocking on every door, and returned with stories not only of cancer but of birth defects and immune deficiency diseases as well. People complained of migraine headaches, asthma attacks, nosebleeds.

Meanwhile, Suzie started researching the history of the area and learned that it used to be littered with oil and gas production companies.[2] Pipelines ran right beneath their old neighborhood. She combed through property records. She searched through city planning archives. She flipped through volume upon volume of minutes from meetings of the railroad commission, the city council, and the school board, not even knowing what she was looking for until one afternoon at the Office of Planning Commission, when she found the minutes from a 1942 meeting devoted to the topic: "What to Do with the Negroes?"

I suck in my breath; Suzie closes her eyes and nods.

Their solution: race-zoning ordinances that placed the city's African American population in neighborhoods adjacent to the ship channel, right where the refineries were being built. Tejanos, meanwhile, were zoned by some oil waste dumps that had been repurposed as landfills, including the one bordering Suzie's old neighborhood. Greenwood, it turned out, had been built atop a forty-seven-acre hazardous waste dump. When Suzie and her classmates marched around during band practice after school, they were hovering over covered oil pits.

Although those ordinances have long since been outlawed, many of the families remain. Heavy industry, meanwhile, has proliferated. By the millennium, Corpus Christi was home to six oil refineries plus a slew of chemical manufacturing plants and gas processing units, all located along a fifteen-mile strip called Refinery Row that is surrounded by impoverished neighborhoods of color. These are the borderlines that lurk in every community: class and race.

After city officials dismissed Suzie's health surveys as "anecdotal evidence," she plunged into activism full time. In 2000, the family founded a grassroots organization called Citizens for Environmental Justice (CFEJ) with Suzie as director. Though she'd never received formal training in college, she learned basic toxicology and epidemiology as well as bureaucratic

Juanita jokes.

2 According to the Port of Corpus Christi's website, back in the thirties, Nueces County was home to "3,760 wells in 89 oil fields, within a radius of 125 miles of the port."

legalese. She typed up reports. Sent out press releases. Conducted community meetings. Organized press conferences. Appeared on television and radio shows.

Meanwhile, her husband struggled to readjust to civilian life. The kids—now grown—were making their own friends and leading their own lives. Nobody needed him anymore. His days stretched like putty. He sulked in the doorway while Suzie pounded on the keyboard.

You're ignoring me.

What do you mean? I followed you around for twenty years. Kept your house; raised your kids. It's my turn now.

Eventually another woman caught his gaze: twenty-eight years old, with two little ones of her own.

You want another baby? All right. I'll give you one.

You can't. You're all messed up.

Contaminated, he meant, from living so long atop a toxic waste dump. They'd always wanted a third child, but after their son, Suzie had a miscarriage. Then another. Then a third. Then a fourth.

Suzie's marriage dissolved nearly a year to the day after returning to Corpus. Stirring her cup of diner coffee, she softens her voice. "People often ask if I could do it all over again, would I have moved back? But I already had that choice. And I decided to do it anyway."

Suzie maintains certain military privileges such as health insurance, but she is on her own financially. CFEJ has received a few grants and she's won some major awards[3] over the years, but nothing to subsist on. Office jobs sap too much time; she needs a flexible schedule so she can attend meetings and press functions and rallies and parent-teacher conferences.

"Parent-teacher conferences?" I ask.

3 Some of Suzie's accolades include the Congressional Hispanic Caucus Institute's Award for Outstanding Achievement in Environmental Justice, the HERO Award from the University of Texas Medical Branch National Institute for Environmental Health and Sciences, and the *Texas Observer*'s 2012 People's Friend Award. The honor she finds most gratifying, however, is a 2015 "trailblazer" award from the Corpus Christi League of Women Voters. "Locally, I am considered a pain in the ass, so to be recognized here, well, I just can't believe it. I'm supposed to be the troublemaker!" she told me.

"Oh yes. I'm raising one of my daughter's sons too, so I'm a single mom on top of everything else," she says, shaking her head. "What can I say? It takes a village."

Lately, she's been working at Luby's, a family-style cafeteria. For $7.25 an hour, she dons a blue uniform, tucks her hair inside a net, and scoops salads and gelatins into a tower of bowls that she proffers one by one to an unceasing line of customers. It can be humbling at times, particularly when she gets yelled at for dropping the occasional bowl, but it allows her time to think.

Suzie feels certain that industrial contamination poisoned her sister. The problem is how to prove it. There are plenty of reports about the high rates of birth defects, cancer, and respiratory illnesses in fenceline communities (that is, neighborhoods bordering heavy industries). The refineries themselves admit to releasing millions of pounds of hazardous air pollutants each year. But there has yet to be a widely accepted scientific study that establishes a direct correlation between the two—and attempts to do so have proven contentious. In 2008, for example, CFEJ helped secure funding for a pilot study by the Texas A&M School of Rural Public Health that discovered blood and urine samples collected from residents living along Refinery Row contained 280 times as much benzene[4] as samples from other US residents and fourteen times as much benzene as a sample taken from gas station attendees in Mexico. A toxicologist hired by the Flint Hills refinery quickly discounted the study, however, concluding from state data that there was not enough benzene in the air circulating the refineries to produce such results. After months of getting bombarded[5] by industry personnel questioning the legitimacy of his research, the lead Texas A&M scientist, Dr. KC Donnelly, died of esophageal cancer before he could complete it. His colleagues eventually released a new study revising his figures downward (although a quarter of the people tested

4 Benzene, a natural part of crude oil and gasoline found in petroleum products and cigarette smoke, is a known carcinogen. Short-term exposure can cause drowsiness, dizziness, and unconsciousness; long-term effects include leukemia and shrunken ovaries.

5 In an email to Suzie dated December 9, 2008, Dr. Donnelly wrote, "I am having to dodge a number of consultants to CITGO & other refineries who want to shred our study."

still recorded elevated benzene levels). A 2011 federal study then showed "normal" levels of benzene in the community.

But while the correlation between refineries and ill health is considered "ambiguous" in Corpus Christi, the connection between refineries and power is not. Citgo alone has a $345 million annual impact on our local economy. Flint Hills, meanwhile, is owned by Koch Industries, whose majority stakeholders—Charles and David Koch—have a collective net worth of more than $100 billion and whose political action committee bankrolls scores of ultraconservative campaigns and causes.

It didn't take Suzie long to decide she was better off conducting her own studies. After learning how to monitor air quality herself from a nonprofit group, she loaded up some buckets, air pumps, and collection bags and started driving around Refinery Row at night and on weekends with her sister Cindy, collecting air samples. Every refinery operates a fleet of security guards with whom the sisters quickly got acquainted: practically every other weekend, one pulled them over for interrogation. Reminding themselves that their father once did this work, the sisters answered their questions respectfully. After all, the guards probably lived in the neighborhood too.

No, sir, we're not terrorists. We're activists. We're here to monitor air quality.

No, sir, we're not with the TCEQ, but you can give them a call. They know who we are.

In March 2006, Suzie and Cindy piled into their jeep and spent the afternoon monitoring Citgo, which refines upward of 165,000 barrels of crude oil a day. Suzie hoped to photograph Citgo's coker unit, which she says releases a cloud of heavy particulates every eleven hours. CFEJ was on the verge of publishing a new report, and she thought a belching coker would make a good cover. Cindy drove slowly down the public road, snapping photos, while Suzie filmed the facility with her camcorder. A few miles into their venture, a security guard from Valero pulled them over. They explained their project and he permitted passage. Assuming he would notify other guards in the area, they sped on.

Suddenly, the coker unit erupted. A cloud burst into the sky like a demonic firecracker, maybe four stories high. Within seconds, blackness coated the jeep, reeking of hydrocarbons. Grit swept into the sisters' eyes, their ears, their noses, their throats, their mouths. Cindy frantically flashed photos while Suzie rolled the camcorder.

Are you getting it, are you getting it?

I got it, I got it.

Lights flashed behind them. Another security guard, this time from Citgo.

Hello, officer. We just got stopped by Valero five min—

Driver's license?

The port police arrived as the security guard called in the sisters' information and detained them. While waiting at the station, Cindy started feeling queasy. She wiped particulate matter off her face. Ten minutes passed. She blew particulate matter from her nose. Another ten minutes passed. She coughed particulate matter from her lungs. Ten more minutes passed. Particulate matter churned in her belly. Twenty minutes passed.

At last, Citgo security returned.

Look, you know who I am. We've got to go. My sister is sick.

Oh no, you're not. You ladies are waiting right here.

Detaining us is illegal and you know it. We're going.

This isn't over.

Days later, the US Coast Guard gave Suzie a call. Apparently, she had been reported to the National Resource Center for conducting "suspicious activity." The FBI wished to interview her: When could she come in?

Suzie stares at me, still incredulous years later. "And I said, bullshit. I'm not going anywhere. They need to come to my apartment full of doilies and see I'm just a little old grandma."

The Coast Guard and FBI arrived on her doorstep, a two-bedroom apartment in a seven-hundred-unit complex on the south side of Corpus. She welcomed them in, turned on her tape recorder, and started pulling down the plaques from the walls that recognize her community work. She told them about babies born with holes in their hearts and little girls dying of leukemia. An hour later, they thanked her and left. It seemed prudent to share her side of the story before Citgo beat her to it, so Suzie made a few calls. The front page of the *Corpus Christi Caller-Times* soon featured her headshot beneath the headline "Activist No Terror Threat, FBI Says." Once again, her telephone started ringing. She tried to laugh off the "terrorist" charge, but the headline truly haunted her.

"And those readers' comments," Suzie says.

And those readers' comments. They were vicious:

> GiveItUpLiberals writes, "Suzie is an environmental wacko."
>
> Basilb writes, "Suzie Canales has done nothing but bring attention to herself for years. She is using these people for her own cause. . . . I wonder how Suzie changes the color of her hair without chemicals."
>
> Citizen2000 writes, "If I had to choose between hydrofluoric acid and Suzie Canales, I'd have to go with the acid because it's much less corrosive than she is."

Activism has invigorated Suzie's life, giving it focus and meaning. Yet she thinks this work might be shortening it too. She has high blood pressure. Tension ripples through her limbs. Like her brother-in-law Lionel, she sometimes looks in her rearview mirror and swears she is being followed. Infamy might be a blessing in this regard: "I've been in the media so much, it would be obvious if something happened to me."

When I ask how she maintains her fervor, she reflects for a moment before citing her spiritual practice. Prayer has become especially rejuvenating for her. She prays for courage. She prays for endurance. She prays for words. "I don't see myself as a smart person. I have no degrees, and so often I am arguing with people who have PhDs."

What Suzie does have is rage. Not just at the refineries, but at the government: "They are supposed to be there to protect everybody, and they're not."

So when she received an invitation to attend the first-ever White House Forum on Environmental Justice in November 2010, she rejoiced. At last, a chance to hold the truly powerful accountable. Then she read the fine print: no travel assistance provided. She dialed the White House Council on Environmental Quality to explain that, by definition, environmental justice activists are low-income people of color. How did they expect her to fund the trip? *If you can't afford it, you can always watch it on your home computer, via live stream.* Suzie resigned to do that—until word leaked out in the local activist community. Someone offered her frequent flier miles; another pledged to cover her hotel. That December, Suzie took a few days off from Luby's Cafeteria, arranged childcare for her grandson, and jetted off to Washington.

The forum was set to begin at 9 a.m., but Suzie was so excited, she arrived at 8. Denied early entrance, she was shown to a café across the street where a coffee cost half her hourly wage at Luby's. Once inside the White House, she was directed to a water fountain in another building when she asked for something to drink. For lunch, she was dispatched to a cafeteria, where she had to buy her own ham sandwich.

"There is no way they do that to all those movie stars and celebrities always visiting!" she mutters.

One hundred activists had gathered that day from across the nation. The sessions, however, featured only cabinet secretaries and other top Obama officials. The first batch devoted ninety minutes to reprimanding the Bush administration for failing to prioritize environmental justice. Not the Obama administration, they crowed: their Plan EJ 2014 would apply cutting-edge technology to study fenceline communities around the country.[6] This revelation made Suzie squirm. "I kept thinking, that's how they're going to help us? Another study? They're already studying us to death!"

At last, a question-and-answer session began. Many of the activists' hands shot in the air, but only two were permitted to speak before coordinators announced the arrival of the attorney general. Suzie checked the agenda. Only five minutes of discussion had been allotted for dialogue. She looked around the room. The other activists were shaking their heads, clearly upset, but no one was speaking out. Rising to her feet, Suzie maneuvered to the front of the auditorium and stared into the crowd.

Hi there. My name is Suzie Canales. I traveled here all the way from Corpus Christi, Texas, but I didn't come to be talked to.

The activists turned to her. The White House aides turned to her. The reporters turned to her. The cameras turned to her.

I came here because I thought I was going to be able to voice concerns. Plans like EJ 2014 are just bureaucratic words on paper. They do nothing for our communities.

6 Indeed, the EPA soon awarded $7 million in grants to researchers to study how low-income communities are impacted by pollutants.

The activists nodded in agreement while the aides scrambled about. Suzie concluded her remarks and sat down, trembling. A reporter darted over and crouched beside her. *Ma'am, can we interview you?* Suzie scribbled her phone number as an aide asked to escort her outside. *I hope you're not kicking me out*, she said, loud enough for everyone to hear.

People craned their necks as she was shown to the door. The first person she encountered outside was Attorney General Eric Holder. Extending his hand, he asked Suzie how she was doing. *Not very well, sir. I didn't come here to be talked to.*

The aide hurried her along to the Eisenhower Executive Office Building next door, where EPA chief Lisa Jackson awaited on a love seat. Patting the space beside her, she asked Suzie what the EPA could do to help. Suzie handed her CFEJ's newest report: "Why EPA's Attempts to Achieve Environmental Justice Have Failed and What They Can Do about It."

Instead of giving us more documents that have no value to us, you need to roll up your sleeves.

She asked Jackson to prioritize the needs of communities who live in the shadow of industry, relocating them if necessary. And if the federal government was unwilling to shut down polluting factories, at the very least, it should stop protecting them by conducting endless risk assessments and studies. When Jackson rose from the love seat, Suzie asked if she would hear from her again. Jackson promised so.[7] An aide escorted Suzie back to the auditorium. For the rest of the day, conference attendees stopped to thank her, even in the bathroom. Soon after, Suzie generated yet another headline: "Environmental Justice Activist Urges EPA Chief 'to Roll Up Your Sleeves' at Tense W. H. Forum." Only it wasn't the *Corpus Christi Caller-Times*. It was *The New York Times*.

"I know, I know," Suzie says, laughing for the first time this morning. "I can't believe me sometimes."

7 Although Suzie has, as of July 2015, never heard directly from Jackson again, she did receive a follow-up from the EPA chief via Al Armendariz, a scientist who briefly held the position of EPA regional administrator in Texas. Beloved by activists and scorned by industry personnel for publicly supporting the idea of relocating fenceline communities (among other things), Armendariz took a job with the Sierra Club after causing a scandal for comparing his enforcement strategies to Roman crucifixions.

Norma E. Cantú

Soundscapes along the US-Mexico Borderlands

I am who I am because I grew up on the US-Mexico borderlands—more specifically, between the states of Tamaulipas and Texas and, even more specifically, at a time and place where the Río Grande / Río Bravo marks the division between Nuevo Laredo, Tamaulipas, and Laredo, Texas, between modernity and what some are calling postmodernity.

My ancestors who lived along these borderlands shaped me via DNA. The border shaped me via the formative experiences, the lived and embodied notions of what a border is, of the history of the place, the geography, the climate, and the flora and fauna. But more so, the soundscapes that fall within these landscapes shaped me. Nature is a veritable cacophony of sound, and the sounds in South Texas are particularly emotive.

One of the last times I slept in my family's home before we sold it in 2019, I was pleasantly awakened by a rooster greeting the day, as I had been so many times in my youth and young adulthood. The sound of a faraway train whistle served as a lullaby, and the braying of the donkey our neighbors sometimes tied to the mesquite tree in our yard was a reminder that we share this world with other beings.

The sounds of life—especially animal life—along the border have remained the same even as other sounds have changed or vanished altogether. We still hear the crickets chirping, the cicadas' evening call, a creek's water rushing, the river, the cenzontle,[1] the dogs barking, and in many communities along the river, roosters and horses. The urracas,[2] the grackles, blue-black birds with beady yellow eyes, continue to plague the locals as they swarm en masse each evening to roost on the branches of whatever tree or telephone wire they can find. Some even perch on rooftops and the electric and cable wires. Despite their impressive appearance—black satin feathers with a sheen unlike any other bird's—the urracas' cawing,

1 Mockingbird.

2 Magpie.

squeaking, whistling, and croaking can be annoying. High-pitched clear whistles and the calls, when together, remind me of the chatter of teenagers in a crowded high school cafeteria; its intensity and level can be deafening.

In the borderlands, the sound of animals, the sounds produced by nature—such as wind or thunder—along with the sounds that rushing waters or rainfall produce, constitute a backdrop for all kinds of outdoor activities. The cooing of the doves in the afternoon, as well as the sounds of rushing water, provide a background playlist that rivals the most sophisticated soundtrack. The soundtrack for life on the border in the mid-twentieth century was rich and complex, and because we lived in the outskirts of the city, almost en pleno campo,[3] we were privileged to hear cenzontles and other wild birds alongside the pigeons and doves that roosted on the pirul tree.

The sounds in nature on the border aren't necessarily unique to this region; cicadas, crickets, owls, frogs, and snakes exist in other areas, but they acquire special meaning for us as we decode the messages inherent in these borderlands sounds. The chicharras and the owls, lechuzas, are still acknowledged as omens. The lechuza's ominous presence and its hoot portends death, and the other birds also have messages for those who can interpret them, such as the soft murmur of doves in the afternoon heat or at dusk: Coo coo. Coo coo. Mom claimed they were communicating a message: pequé, perdóname—I have sinned, forgive me.

I am pretty sure that the wind has a similar function in other places blessed with palm and banana trees, but I distinctly remember the ones in my yard when I lived on campus housing in the old Fort McIntosh officer quarters, at what is now Laredo College. The wind blowing so close to the river carried sounds unlike any I've heard elsewhere. The palm fronds and banana trees swishing back and forth and the cedar ash—those giant trees with their blue-gray leaves—whooshing, seemingly alive and serving as windbreakers, true to their name in Spanish, cubreviento. It didn't even have to be a strong wind, a gentle breeze would blow, and I could hear the trees whispering, reminding me of the cubrevientos of my childhood.

Rainy season was short and sometimes came with swift violence. Thunderstorms with the impressive culebras, our term for the lightning—snakes splitting the sky—and the earth-trembling thunder that shook our world.

3 In the countryside.

Once, I was teaching a summer course, and as we ended class and stepped outside the building, hail the size of golf balls began to fall. The sound of the vicious winds, un ventarrón, and the torrential rain, un chubasco, we could hear while inside, but the granizo hitting the walkways sounded the worst—and it was.

The rushing waters of the Río Grande or the creek near our house could be gentle and swift but also fast and rushing, especially after one such storm. The rare stormy nights were the perfect time to hear the croaking of the frogs, cantarranas. When I was a toddler, we lived in the cantarranas barrio, aptly named, as we lived near the river and the singing frogs kept us awake late into the night. The perfect setting for my grandmother Celia's stories of la Llorona, the wailing woman who roamed the riverbanks to snatch mischievous children, mistaking them for her own. Another tale she told involved a couple of disobedient sons who got into all sorts of trouble and were invariably punished.

Beyond the sounds from nature, perhaps the most prolific and most identifiable as Tejane are the people themselves. Arguing, greeting each other, celebrating or mourning, singing, cussing each other out, or merely telling stories, many Tejanes resort to the linguistic register that has been forged over centuries of blending English and Spanish. A language that exists somewhere between a Texas drawl and the campesino Spanish of northern Mexico with an upward tilt at the end of certain phrases and the use of a special lexicon and phrases like "¡Quihúbole!" that can be found in both rural and urban talk. Saying "Ay" when in agreement with someone is a good example. Or answering "Mande" when we miss a point or when someone calls our names. Moreover, the soundscape includes a complex and raucous medley of sounds found in our musics, voices, and other human expressions like gritos, those exuberant spontaneous yells that punctuate many a ranchera, mariachi, or tejana song. Unique expressions of an unnamed feeling that the music elicits.

Tex-Maniacs-Marisoul Grito Example 1
transcribed by Cruz, R.

Other sounds found in the borderlands soundscapes that come to mind are mechanical or technological, especially the sound of traffic on the international bridges with a cacophony of running motors—cars, semis, a motorcycle now and then. These are a constant and constitute an urban vibe, a marker that many posit is a sign of progress and prosperity. "Don't complain about the trucks," a friend said once over dinner, "it means money for the city and for many who work in import/export offices." We had always been a busy port of entry, but when the North American Free Trade Agreement (NAFTA) was signed in the 1990s, the change was noticeable. It was obvious that things were never to be the same along the US-Mexico border, especially amid the influx of new technologies that sought to handle the outrageous growth in traffic. The increase in import/export businesses and the proliferation of maquiladoras brought increased activity and thereby increased the noise levels of our earlier tranquil and peaceful community. Although, decades earlier, in the 1950s and '60s, that tranquility was often shattered by the roar of planes piloted by young lieutenants from Laredo Air Force Base and other recruits training for service in Vietnam; the landscape of my youth was forever changed.

I am certain these sounds occur elsewhere, but for me they convey a specific place, the border. So the wind rustling the palm fronds, or the owl hooting, or the Mexican American English and Mexican American Spanish that meet to form a third language—the language of the border, with its disappearing caló and localisms—all these signify an identity and a particular way of looking at the world. My world.

||||SOVERYEMPTY||||

||||the wall is not a wall||||

there are language holes in the wall||||
wall, walled, walled in |||| are references ||||
to US systems, structures|||| enforcing the en masse numbing |||| that is,
the wall||||is a caging ||||, posing as a prison|||| implying we are criminals ||||

but like Texas prison history||||
refers to criminalizing Indigenous dissent |||| to |||| land theft |||| illegal
dispossession||||
"sovereign" impunity |||| immunity |||| to justify |||| state sanctioned |||| abuse ||||
violence||||and hiding ongoing genocide||||

||||capitalism is key||||cheap
Brown and Black labor||||gas and mineral extraction||||cattle||||barbed
wire||||and||||willful mythology||||the wall||||is religion||||specifically||||
profit||||on innocent civilians||||by the regime||||

Elders said ||||there were other walls before this wall||||the numbed
conflate||||domination with existence||||
R&D and shareholders made this wall||||and triangulated |||| made fungible||||
material conditions|||| between Vietnam, Gaza, and El Calaboz[1]||| to will walls
on the wailing||||

The||||wall||||is a spectrum and a tell||||-
a spectrum of wars on perennial resistance||||The walled

1 El Calaboz is a colonia in Texas that lies south of San Benito in Cameron County. Colonias are residential living areas, generally unincorporated, that lack basic necessities, including potable water, sewage systems, electricity, and paved roads.

El Calaboz||||“the dungeon”||||coils|||| past||||present|||past||||no future
Indigenous earth imagined||||
by American storylines||||

||||The wall is forensic architecture||||the wall is||||a
family||||a girl||||a woman||||a man||||a boy||||a school||||a dump site||||a
cemetery||||a classroom||||a landfill||||a gang rape||||a laboratory||||a universe||||
a bank||||a holiday||||a tourist excursion||||a hobby||||a game||||a

trick||||a treat||||a job||||a paycheck||||rent||||debt||||credit||||a date||||a
holiday||||a secret||||a murderer||||a victim||||triage||||ER||||a highway||||a
labor camp||||a decision||||a promise||||a dead end||||a blur||||a microfocus||||
a noun||||a verb||||a subject||||a predicate||||a possessive||||a

dispossessive||||a singular||||a plural||||a now||||a then||||an obsession||||
a thing||||alive||||created||||undone||||lived||||disbelieved||||owned||||denied||||
known||||unknown||||inherited||||contiguous||||claimed||||acknowledged||||
recognized||||dismantled||||smoked||||

sovereignty||||Sovereignty||||empty lines||||so very
empty||||SOVERYEMPTY||||
world||||we are awoked||||waked||||we are
waked||||soveryempty|||sovereignty|||
is so very empty in shadow of the wall||||sovereignty||||is
soveryempty||||walled in||||
Sovereignty|||empty lines||||tries to extinguish us|||to unalive us||||to force
us|||into||||

Obscure footnotes||||the graveyard of social death||||sovereignty||||empty lines||||
so very empty|||| they got nothing||||for us||||but||||dungeons||||
and||||for the nonsurrendering||||knowing||||sovereignty is soveryempty|||
is freedom||||

Cordelia E. Barrera

Shadowing Butterflies in the Monte

Monte

I grew up in the suburb of Del Mar Hills in north Laredo in the early 1980s, where I spent my summers exploring the endless monte[1] that encircled our home. Ours was one of the few houses scattered about the developing neighborhood, which dissolved into thickets of native chaparral—what my father called Tamaulipan scrub. Battered tennis shoes on hot pavement and armed with string and maybe a tool or two pilfered from one of our dads' toolboxes, my friends and I would set out "adventuring." In two short blocks, we'd be off the pavement, cool in the grassland dense with wild acacia, prickly pear cactus, spiny hackberries, and honey mesquite.

I recall one summer when our dreams teemed with life as copious as our thicket sanctuary. We had a bag full of electrical wire we'd "salvaged" from one of the inexplicable metal boxes that always seemed to spring up overnight on some new corner; our fantasy of building the perfect fort was in reach. We combed old trails where the sticky brush was thick with disuse—overhanging lazy brambles and thorns sweeping our legs—in search of mesquite limbs snapped by families of wild javelina (we could not break big limbs ourselves). Wildness inhabited by native jackrabbits and armadillos and horned lizards stretched as far as our young imaginations, and when we tired of fort building, we waded to our armpits in natural ponds and fished for crawdaddies. In prowling the senderos and exploring miles of untamed monte fed by natural creeks and reservoirs, we learned by touch and experience (and maybe instinct?) how each thing that shot up from this arid but so-alive place of parched earth stuck, prickled, or

1 Scrubland.

Portions of "Shadowing Butterflies in the Monte" by Cordelia E. Barrera first appeared in *The Haunted Southwest: Towards an Ethics of Place in Borderlands Literature*, Texas Tech University Press, 2022.

punctured the skin. The thorns, spines, and rattlesnakes that thrived here compelled us to look and step closely.

Rushing through the brushland is not just dangerous; it is impossible.

Feet on the Ground

A few years ago, after my father's unexpected death, I was at our old home in Laredo wading through legal documents when I came across an unpublished essay titled "On Middle-Age Running: 'And Miles to Go Before I Sleep,'" written by my father in 1985 when he was forty-four years old. Dad taught life sciences and kinesiology for over forty years, mostly at Laredo Community College, where he was also a basketball coach. In the piece, he details the '80s "running boom" and the pleasures of competitive sport. But I was gripped by what came later, by how he described his runs as a "privilege" and form of effortless contact with the earth beneath his feet. He wrote that a bonus to being an "old runner" was the presence of "the old earth itself. Becoming ever more intimately acquainted with the surface of the earth," he continued, is "probably the most powerful pleasure of my running in middle age. The sense of contact must have always been there; however, now I love it." How incredible, I thought. My father's best story about himself was enmeshed, was bound in kinship somehow, by an interconnectedness that emanated from what he *felt* as the old earth itself, from a stillness that gives in perfect quietude.

On the surface, the essay is about the private rewards and public benefits of staying in shape through middle life. His runs were never "workouts," he wrote, as there was nothing of work in running—no punishment or unwelcome pain, just something he called "purposeful fun." For him, the circular pulse and pace, the yielding gait of his feet in motion over the ground (affecting with his body and having his body affect the earth) was his artistry. But it's also about the aging process itself, and maybe a kind of knowledge that comes with age—and reflection—as the "miles to go before I sleep" of the title is meant to evoke our human need for connection, kinship with the earth, soil, and dirt beneath our feet. How running, like adventuring through untamed thickets of briary shrubs, is more than a state of mind. Feet on the ground is a practice of balance and equilibrium. Feet on the ground is to occupy space, move and progress through it, all the while trusting that the earth, the soil, the place our bodies occupy will correspond. Limbs moving in a circular motion, leading the legs as feet land under the knees, breathing easy . . . all these movements are in synergy with the ground beneath our feet, reminding us—if we step mindfully—that we are land creatures alive to and in constant cooperation with an overlapping, corresponding form of energy.

In *Being a Beast*, naturalist Charles Foster begins with the idea that animals, specifically those he studies—badgers, otters, red deer, swifts, and foxes—are in a "rolling conversation" with the land from which they come and of which they consist. And by this he means that animals are indebted to and embedded in a genealogy of experience shaped by landscape. For example, swifts spend months at a time in the skies living on insects caught in flight and sleeping on the wing; they are part and parcel of the air in which they hover and soar their entire lives. Badgers subsist on a diet of over 85 percent earthworms; they are the ultimate soil animals, almost entirely made out of the land they inhabit. He reminds us, too, that humans are "soil things." We are soil things connected to a vertigo of time that stretches beyond *human* time. Soil things alive to some origin that filters up from the earth itself and is as overgrown and obscure as the boundless monte that once encircled my childhood home.

Coming Home

By 2023, the wild brushlands surrounding my childhood home have been overtaken by new suburbs, strip malls, industrial parks, and a conglomeration of unsustainable forms of economic and social development. With the 1994 passage of the North American Free Trade Agreement (NAFTA), Laredo burst the small-town seams it indulged since its founding in 1775, its population nearly doubling between 1990 and 2010. 2020 census reports indicate a population of 265,761, but this does not include the Laredo–Nuevo Laredo metropolitan area, which has an estimated population of over 636,000—a number that may or may not incorporate those who live and work in the area without official residency papers. Although the city is today recognized as the largest and most important inland port on the US-Mexico border, Laredo's infrastructure is notoriously disorganized, and the new wealth and substructure created by NAFTA have wreaked havoc on the ecological limits of this once sleepy border place of overwhelmingly Mexican and Hispanic origin.

In the nineteenth century, Laredo entered a developing American capitalist modernity based in the trade of southern cotton. Today, pervasive industrialization that favors speedy human profits over conservation or preservation exhausts the city and threatens the dwindling monte's sheen of life. A *New York Times* article from January 2023 describes how upward of $800 million worth of products ranging from auto parts, clothing, dog food, petroleum products, and avocados pass through Laredo every day, necessitating the quick construction of several million *more* square feet added to its present thirty-six million feet of warehouse infrastructure. Evidence of hydraulic fracking along the Eagle Ford Shale scars the I-35 corridor in an endless procession of semitrailer trucks, oil tankers, groundwater treatment trucks, wastewater treatment trucks, hazmat trucks, and trucks full of sand, steel pipe, casings, and drill rigs. Methane plumes mark the escape of dangerous gases into the atmosphere on Old Highway 83 and forgotten country roads on Laredo's outskirts—little towns like Asheron, La Pryor, and Carrizo Springs. Driving through these areas reminds us how quickly land erodes after being cleared. But what else erodes and crumbles?

***

I remember conversations about my family's history and my great-great-great-grandfather, Manuel Barrera. We had these around the dinner table during my high school years. Sometimes, we talked about how my father was a supposed heir to a Spanish and Mexican land grant (now called the Texas Land Grants). Presumably, he was a descendant of the original grantee of a tract called La Tinaja de Lara, which comprised over a thousand acres in Jim Wells County, Texas. I remember asking why and how our family came to Laredo and why we were not rich landowners. Could anybody really *own* the land, I asked. For that matter . . . what did it mean that our family had Spanish and Mexican and Indian blood and lived on what was once Mexican soil but was now the United States?

In the early 1980s, my father and others in his position made claims with the Asociación de Reclamantes, which brought legal action against Mexico for the alleged taking and conversion of tracts of Texas land lost to reputed heirs of original grantees during the US-Mexico War of 1846–48.

After years of pushing through the proper channels in Austin, Dad gave up the ghost that was La Tinaja de Lara. I don't think he ever believed he'd *actually* acquire rights to any land or receive any compensation. But he recalled stories tied to the place, took great pains in tracing our genealogical line, and developed relationships with others in similar predicaments.

A born storyteller who loved to recount cuentos about earlier days on the borderlands—folktales and legends full of battles, curses, curanderas,[2] and rain gods set in Mexico, Old and New Spain, and along the Río Grande—his words conjured a collective past for me and my brothers. Embedded throughout his stories about Pancho Villa, la Adelita, la Llorona, and the chupacabra was a land ethic attuned to recognizing the claims others—our ancestors—have upon our bodies in the present. For him, the sweat, blood, and tears of generations of our descendants filtered into the soil and made it sacred; South Texas' wild topography of thorny thickets and spiny cactus was our cultural heritage. Honey mesquite chaparral, Spanish dagger, Yellow huisache, retama, and cenizo—native brush that sometimes disappeared overnight in the name of federally funded land clearing programs or when ranchers or farmers became "oil men"—this was not just setting, but a cultural and historical network that framed his stories. His worldview recalls Devon Peña's observation that Mexican Americans are inclined to define "nature as homeland" as opposed to nature as "natural resources or wilderness."[3] A biophile, lifelong outdoorsman, and a marathoner well before it was trendy and fashionable, Dad was infatuated with the Tarahumara of Chihuahua,[4] who, he reminded me and my brothers, relied on their aboriginal knowledge of the land, water, and agriculture for their survival. I now see how the lost foundations of so many of his anecdotes and reminiscences veered from an abstract faith in modern values and the immediate promises of power and profit—values of little worth to him—toward preconquest, native modes of knowledge and being-in-the-world.

2 Traditional folk healers who practice Indigenous medicine.

3 Pp. xxxii.

4 Also known as the Rarámuri; a group of Indigenous people living in the state of Chihuahua in Mexico renowned for their long-distance running ability and believed to be descended from the Mogollon culture of the American Southwest.

After I found "On Middle-Age Running," I often dreamed of my father. I would wake with an image of his solitary figure running off into the distance, his back to the world. In my mind's eye—awake, or asleep and dreaming—I see him running. Running always and forever toward a place where he could put incentive and satisfaction into his life, and so the world, without an element of violence, power, manipulation of others, or harmful aggressiveness.

Wheels on the Ground

Laredo's wild spaces, like those of South Texas and the greater Southwest, are vanishing. In *Adios to the Brushlands*, Arturo Longoria laments the systematic clearing of native chaparral in South Texas by large-scale ranching and dry farming practices that exploded in earnest in the 1970s and '80s. A trained biologist and former investigative reporter, Longoria describes a vanishing habitat that once covered four million acres of the Río Grande Valley. He links the loss of landscape to the death of his grandfather and describes private policies and public actions that reduced the brushland to less than 5 percent of its former extent. But this was only the beginning. Today, the devastation of the chaparral in the name of oil and gas exploration and unbridled corporate interests is choking the lifeblood of the monte that tejanos hold as a sacred heritage. Continued talk of erecting border walls along the Río Grande, unceasing immigration debates, and a spillover of Mexican Narco violence along this desiccated stretch of earth further imperil the future of this unique biosphere. More malignant is the dark shadow of an ever-increasing military presence and additional threats wrought by the building of detention centers to house asylum seekers and refugees on the borderlands.

* * *

While in college, and for years afterward, I'd sometimes meet my father at my uncle's ranch off Highway 359 in Laredo to ride. After knee surgery, he gave up long-distance running in favor of road or mountain bike riding—a sport he enjoyed doing alongside me and my brothers. My greatest solace, my most perfect moments of peace, come when I ride through the senderos and overgrown ravines on the old ranch. I have never been a runner like my father, but like him, I require those connections with the old earth itself to feel grounded in a landscape that is more than terrain, more than property or real estate. The last time I visited Laredo, I took my mountain bike with me; I don't need an excuse to ride at the old ranch. My brothers elsewhere and my dad gone, I usually ride alone these days. Some things don't change, though—like the little colonia[5] (complete with its own ballroom) I pass on the way to the ranch. I feel rooted, grounded, on the ranch. What grounds me is the sameness of the dusty gravel under my feet, the constancy of the syrupy, bitter smell of mesquite. From the high ridges of this place, I see the mountains of Mexico, but I also see the new landfill and several new fracking sites. If I use my binoculars, I can spot a new detention center and ICE facility.

It had been a couple of years since I last rode here, and I found a new lock on the gate. Determined to ride, I suited up and rode along the barbed-wire fence. I knew what I was looking for. After riding east for about half a mile along the southernmost fence line skirting the ranch, I found it: a crawl space where the fence had been loosened and lifted carefully to permit entry. I crawled through and dragged my bike after me. I've seen these crawl spaces all my life; immigrants traversing the landscape in the dead of night make them. The ranchers fix the cuts in the fence, and Mexicans and Central Americans pursuing the American Dream, or a job, or a chance to reconnect with family members who have successfully made the journey, cleave through them. It's all part of the same cycle. Sometimes I find evidence of their journeys along bleached paths and gulleys: discarded wrappers, balls of foil, empty water bottles caked in dirt. When I make my way to Frog Pond and the little cabaña where my uncles like to cook fajitas on Sundays, I sometimes notice that Epifanio, the rancher, has surreptitiously left several gallon water jugs by a grove of mesquite trees. One day I asked Epifanio, who was born in Nuevo Laredo but who has legally lived and worked on the ranch in Laredo for over twenty years, about the jugs. A quiet man of few words, he smiled and softly said, "Están para los que cruzan el río, los que tienen tan poco" (They are there for those who cross, for those who have so little).

5 Along the borderlands, colonias are residential living areas, generally unincorporated, that lack basic necessities, including potable water, sewage systems, electricity, and paved roads.

The sun has baked the sandy loam firm on the ungraded path that slopes above Frog Pond. But as I round a bend, I lose traction and skid down a rocky embankment. I land on my back, my head swimming. Dazed but not too stunned, I take stock of my limbs, head, and immediate surroundings. No broken bones and no rattlesnakes. Excellent, I think, as I unwrap myself from around the spiny undergrowth of palo verde that has broken my fall. I lie there for a few minutes to allow the pain in my back to subside.

I open my eyes and am astonished to see a kaleidoscope of monarchs swirling high over my head, just beyond the overhanging canopy of mesquite that skirts the shoreline. Half a million monarch butterflies enter Texas every year in early September on their annual migration to Mexico; they arrive in the forested highlands of Central Mexico by early November. Monarchs hold a special place in Mexican culture, as their coming is thought by many to represent the souls of their ancestors returning to visit them for Día de los Muertos, traditionally celebrated on November 1 and 2. Day of the Dead is a joyous, highly spiritual celebration with roots that date back thousands of years, before Spanish colonization of Mexico.

I lie on my back, the smell of sweet sage—huisache—and dust and sweat hot in my nostrils, and think of butterflies and their seeming magical transformations, how they so obviously symbolize change, renewal . . . and growth. The Tarahumara believe that when humans (and animals) die, their souls become butterflies that visit the living, no longer soil things but things of the air and the cosmos. Tarahumara anthropologist Enrique Salmón has described how certain butterflies are Iwí—which translates as "soul"—or that which sustains the body with the breath of life.

I lie on the parched dirt for some time, lazily watching the butterflies circle and swirl, and think about the monarch's long migration—and their uncertain longevity. Climate change, illegal logging, widespread use of herbicides and loss of habitat, among other factors, have pushed the monarchs to the brink of extinction. But like the scrublands, they carry traces, hopes and history alive to an energy that sometimes feels dormant but somehow triumphs over global forces of modernity that, on the surface at least, appear to favor profit and economic growth above all else. Just as scrubland is *more than* sun-parched eroded desert, overgrown and briary, the butterflies are *more than* insects: they are cousins, connections attuned to worlds and ways of being beyond the immediately visible, beyond human time. Humans are soil things, and as soil things, we build fences. We also sometimes tear them down or cut holes through them.

Wheels on the ground, I dust myself off, pluck a few prickly pear thorns from my socks, and pursue the butterflies' path for a bit. Rushing through the brushland is pointless when shadowing butterflies.

Works Cited

Foster, Charles. *Being a Beast: Adventures across the Species Divide*. First Edition. Metropolitan Books, 2016.

Goodman, Peter S. "How a Texas Border City Is Shaping the Future of Global Trade." *The New York Times*, 5 January 2023, https://www.nytimes.com/2023/01/05/business/us-mexico-trade-laredo.html. Accessed 20 June 2023.

"Monarchs and Día de Muertos in Mexico." *Monarch Joint Venture*, 2 November 2020, https://monarchjointventure.org/blog/monarchs-and-dia-de-muertos-in-mexico.

Peña, Devon G. *Mexican Americans and the Environment: Tierra y Vida*. University of Arizona Press, 2005.

Salmón, Enrique. "Kincentric Ecology: Indigenous Perceptions of the Human-Nature Relationship." *Ecological Applications*, vol. 10, no. 15, 2000, pp. 1337–32.

la hija de la llorona

a pack of coyotes
dragged a drowned
child from the river

yelping
          yapping
                    yips

they licked the salt
from her eyes shocked
open drank from the dark
well of her mouth

scattered by the rattles
 wrapping her
in undulating
 scales

hissing water
from her lungs

uncoiled
breathing
sleeping
child

"la hija de la llorona" by Petra Salazar first appeared in *Coffin Bell*, vol. 5, no. 2, April 2022, https://coffinbell.com/volume-5-issue-no-2/.

warmed by sand
& sunset blood
on red cliffs

listen
your mother
  wails upriver

roused
she stood
& ran far

in the other
direction

borderlands

los alabados blow across empty desert this
grief place between mother and child

ancestors keep vigil over larvae-shaped depressions
her death would be easier than this no-man's-land.

Christine Granados

Parable of the Weeds

Karen Klein felt more at home among the reeds that were ruining the Guadalupe River tributary at the back of her ranch than sitting on the cushioned wood bench her husband Danny built for her, under the two-hundred-year-old live oak, out front. The historic tree compelled drivers to pull over, get out of their cars, and snap photos of its girth and grandiosity. She drove her truck to the back of her forty acres, away from the highway to the fence line where the sand turned to rock and opened to a creek bed that was overrun with *Arundo donax.* The giant reed was ten feet high—perfect for hiding. She slipped down from the driver's seat onto the sand and walked with her laptop to a makeshift limestone seat. She called this her sweet spot, a prayer spot, the only place besides the inside of her house where her wireless reached. The view amid the rolling hills, dotted with red poppies and bluebonnets, was obscured by the giant reeds. Like an armadillo burrowing in for the day, Karen settled into place. Her scalp shone in the spring sun, and her cherub-like cheeks glistened with sweat as she opened her laptop and scrolled through pages and pages of paragraphs culled from books filled with what she believed to be pornographic scenes. Her internet friends sent these paragraphs from books like *Beloved*, *The Handmaid's Tale*, and *The Perks of Being a Wallflower* daily. This prayer spot was also where she could get some peace from Danny, who kept asking her to come into the bedroom and read aloud from the pages in the books as he lay in bed. She swept her thinning hair, the color of the limestone home she recently purchased, behind her ears as she read. She didn't look up when she heard the familiar crunch of sand as a truck approached her fence. It wasn't until she heard her name that she lifted her gaze.

"Karen, I've been trying to call you all morning," Patricia jumped down from her F-150 and tiptoed over to the seat so her heels wouldn't sink in the sand.

"I saw," Karen said as she stared at her screen. "I had to get out of the house, 'Tricia."

"Danny?" Patricia checked her heels to be sure they weren't buried in the soil.

Karen nodded without taking her eyes off her computer. "You won't believe the filth I found today."

"I know. I've started my own list, thanks to you," Patricia pointed toward the truck. "You think that river cane is going to give me a flat?"

"River cane doesn't have stickers, silly," Karen looked up from the screen and smiled.

"Well, how would I know?" Patricia laughed. "My daddy is always setting it ablaze on the ranch. He says once those stalks take hold, they're like Mexicans. You'll never be rid of them."

"He doesn't have to worry. I think they're originally from China," Karen ran her fingers across the touch pad of her computer.

"I don't know if that's any better. I just know those reeds grow quick, but I didn't come all this way this morning to talk about grass," Patricia laughed.

"You started it," Karen stuck her tongue out at Patricia. "And I like these reeds. They keep people from peeking at our land."

"That reminds me of why I wanted to see you," Patricia watched Karen scroll on her computer. "To tell you Mary is furious."

Karen looked up.

"She said Noah got sent to the principal's office because of some girl who was holding that book . . ." Patricia looked up at the cloudless sky. "It's called . . . it's a girl's name . . ."

"I know it. I've seen it. Moms in Utah told me about it. It's called *Juliet Takes a Breath*," Karen spit out the words like she'd been holding her breath. "Mrs. Connor assigned it as extra reading in her English class. There was no way I was gonna let Joseph read that filth."

"Yes, that's the one," Patricia bobbed up and down on her toes. "I didn't know Betsy Connor was trying to indoctrinate our children. I went to high school with her, when she was Betsy Garza. She went to the Spanish church, but I think she's a good Christian, or she was. She *did* go off to school in California, though, and she's kin to that Lupie Alfaro with the funny son."

"Really, 'Tricia?" Karen said. "I didn't know that."

"Yes, they're sisters," Patricia said. "Give yourself a break. You've only lived here a few months. How could you possibly know everyone?"

"Well, what I *do* know is the people in Alamo City need to wake up," Karen said. "Apparently, they're passing the book around at the school, and the teachers don't care. That Lupie and her son are leading the charge."

"Apparently, the girl with the book kicked Noah in his privates, according to Mary." Patricia placed her hands across the crotch of her jeans.

"And I'll bet the girl got off scot-free," Karen squinted. "It's one of the books on my list. Pure filth."

"Oh, don't you know it," Patricia looked like she was doing calf raises trying to keep her high heels clean. "Mary said she was going to press charges with the police against the gal for sexual harassment."

"Good for her. She should," Karen scooted over to give Patricia room on the rock. "The child probably got the idea to be violent from what she was reading. If that's not a shining example of what we've been telling the school happens when kids get a hold of these books, I don't know what is. Look here. This is what that little assaulter has been reading."

Patricia tiptoed to the rock and seated herself. Karen set the computer on her lap, then Patricia read from *Juliet Takes a Breath*:

> And I'm supposed to be ashamed of being gay, but now that I've had sex with girls, I don't feel any shame at all. In fact, it's pretty fucking amazing.
>
> "I said you lookin' mad good," he repeated, his breath harsh on my neck.
>
> My back tensed up. I cracked my middle knuckle with my thumb. Every way this group of man-boys could possibly assault me flashed through my head. A bolt of fear snaked up my spine. I squeezed the can, wishing I was bold enough to clock him with it. I shrugged hard and turned around. His friends had moved in closer, forming a little semicircle around me. Fucking dudes, man.
>
> "Whassup? You too good to say hello?" he asked, smiling.
>
> "I'm gay and not interested," I blurted out.
>
> My whole face went hot. Why did I say that? Jeezus. With fluorescent lights above me, stained white tiles under my feet, and

> a circle of machismo incarnate around me, there was nowhere to run.
>
> "That's a damn shame. Maybe you just need this good D right here," he said as he grabbed his crotch. He stared at me and gave himself a good up and down stroke. His eyes had a hard glint to them.

"This is totally inappropriate for middle schoolers," Patricia turned to Karen with an open mouth. "You're right, these so-called teachers are grooming our children. It's like they want them to be queer and hate America."

"This is why we have to protect our children," Karen took the computer from Patricia. "And they are calling *me* an extremist for wanting this sexualization of children to stop!"

"That's also got that critical race theory. It's an issue we've identified in the schools. We need to educate ourselves and think about how we're going to tackle this. I'm ready to roll up my sleeves and take this on," Patricia mimed pulling up her sleeves.

"The public school system is not what it once was. Gone are the days of quaint Americana . . ." Karen sat up straight.

Patricia took Karen's hand in hers. "You're right."

Karen placed both hands on her heart and whispered, "We are witnessing the complete indoctrination of our precious children with the very list of sins Paul warned adults about two thousand years ago."

Patricia sighed aloud and leaned in so close to Karen that their lips almost touched. "This is the radical left agenda. We conservative, Christian parents have to step up."

Karen's lips parted, "Right now, we're trying to make our schools a safe place again for our children."

Patricia's eyes narrowed and she brushed back the near-translucent strands of hair along the side of Karen's neck.

"Not so much physically, but spiritually, emotionally, and mentally," Karen said, her face the color of an evening primrose. "We care about each other. That's why we're taking on this fight, right?"

"We do care," Patricia continued to run her hands across Karen's neck. "We care about each other, our children, about our town."

"I know you love our children," Karen said, and as she moved Patricia's hand to her breast, her laptop slipped to the ground.

The two women were entangled together as if taking root. Shouts coming from the house stirred them out of their embrace.

"What's all the fuss about, 'Tricia?" Karen looked toward the house and saw Danny waving.

"We'd better go see," Patricia stood and buttoned her blouse.

Karen searched for her laptop and found it nestled in the river cane shoots. She got up and walked behind Patricia, who was tiptoeing to the truck. Karen opened the driver's side door for her and watched as Patricia slid in, then followed suit. Karen turned the key hanging from the gold Jesus Fish keychain in the ignition and revved the engine. A raft of gadwalls fluttered out of the creek and Patricia laughed. The tires kicked up the pale brown loam as they drove toward the house. Patricia's manicured maroon nails shone bright as the silver toggle switch that she pressed to roll down the passenger window so they could talk to Danny.

"Hey there, 'Tricia. You are looking mighty fine," Danny bent down to make eye contact. "I'll bet you still fit into your high school cheerleader uniform."

Patricia tucked a Big Red–colored ringlet of hair behind her ears and giggled. "Danny, do your boots have holes in them?"

He looked down at his bare feet, at Patricia, then at Karen. "She's funny."

"I know. She made me laugh the first time we met, remember?" Karen looked at Patricia. "In my sandals of readiness."

"Like the apostle Paul said, we need to stand firm with our feet fitted with the readiness that comes from the gospel. How can I ever forget Danny's big city bride at the stock show?" Patricia turned her head away from Danny and winked at Karen. "I never thought my words would be so prophetic."

"I told her not to wear them strappy sandals, but she don't listen," Danny laughed. "She's stubborn as a mule."

"It was too hot to wear anything else," Karen rolled her eyes at Danny and frowned. "What is all this fuss about, Dan? Why'd you call us over?"

He pointed behind him toward the house. "The school called and said we need to pick up Joseph again."

"Why didn't you just text?" Karen snorted.

"You know I don't do that phone stuff," Danny stood and waved his hand. He straightened his blue baseball cap with a white letter *T* stitched into it and said, "Want me to ride with you? I can go inside and put on some shoes."

"No, I've got 'Tricia," Karen pointed at her passenger. "You stay here in case the school calls again."

Danny saluted the two women, took a step back and watched gravel fly from the truck wheels as they drove down the driveway toward the gate.

"Wonder what he could have gotten into this time?" Patricia moved to the middle seat and searched for the seat belt buried in the cushions.

"I know those teachers don't like him." Karen turned onto the highway. "The belt should be by those lovely heels. If you're not gay, Black, or brown, the school doesn't want to help you."

"Ah, found it." Patricia pulled the belt up from between the floorboard and cushion then over her stomach. "I didn't think you noticed."

"Girl, I always notice what you got on," Karen's smile made her look like Wilbur the pig when he won the special prize at the fair.

Patricia giggled, then stopped abruptly and straightened. "You think that Spanish lady's son is provoking him again?"

"Lupie. Lupie Alfaro," Karen said. "She's pure evil. She's helping the school district *groom* children."

"My only question is why?" Patricia put her hand on Karen's thigh. "What exactly is she advocating for?"

* * *

With Joseph in the buddy seat next to her, Karen couldn't stop smiling. She was going to use his suspension from school in her next talk at church. She wanted everyone to know how radical the school district had become.

"It's bad enough that he's a cheerleader, but he also wears girls' clothes," Joseph looked at Karen as he watched the cars in front of them. "He was asking for it, Mom."

"The school and teachers are trying to normalize deviant behavior," Patricia said. "It's not right, and so it's not your fault."

"Yeah, exactly," Joseph looked at Patricia and nodded.

"I don't understand why they didn't talk with the both of you. You were *both* involved," Patricia said.

"Because all of them—teachers and principals—they're trying to normalize that deviant behavior just like you said, 'Tricia," Joseph straightened the red cap on his head. "They just told *him* to go home and get some rest."

"I get it, Joey. You had to do what you thought was right to be heard," Karen tried to suppress a grin.

"I was making a point, Mom," he waved his arms so wide and aggressively that Patricia had to duck to get out of the way.

"What point was that, hon?" she asked, tapping the steering wheel.

"I could be as obscene as he was," Joseph crossed his arms.

"Point taken," Karen said and nudged Joseph's midsection with an elbow and a smile. "I gotta stop for gas at the QuickStop."

As Karen pulled her truck next to a gas pump, Lupe and Alex Alfaro walked out of the convenience store to a Prius parked next to a fuel dispenser in front of Karen's idling dualie.

Karen opened the truck door, slid down to the pavement, and said, "Hand me my phone, will you, Joey? It's on the dash."

"Who you gonna call? Dad?" Joseph tossed a rhinestone-studded phone to his mother.

"Why would I call him?" Karen said as she looked through the card case on her phone. "I need my credit card."

Lupe glanced at Karen, then whispered something to Alex, who ran a hand down the front of his tunic, lifted the hem, and placed the book he was carrying underneath it. Lupe leaned against her Prius after placing the nozzle in the tank.

"What did you say, 'Tricia?" Karen asked as she turned to face the gas dispenser. "I can't hear you over the music."

Karen frowned when she noticed Alex and Lupe. She sneered after reading "Save Our Forest, Plant a Tree" on Lupe's T-shirt.

As Lee Greenwood's "God Bless the USA" blared from the QuickStop speakers, the two women gave each other the evil eye; the air between the two vehicles was thick and hot as a honky-tonk just before closing.

"I thought those foreign cars didn't need gas," Karen said as she placed her plastic in the card reader.

Lupe looked Karen in the face and straightened. "Excuse me?"

Alex stood still next to his mother like a buck caught in a beam of oncoming headlights.

Lupe rubbed Alex's arm, and he coughed and took the book *The Love and Lies of Rukhsana Ali* from under his tunic and set it inside the car through an open window.

"I *said* I thought those foreign cars didn't need any gas," Karen punched at the pump's keypad.

"Oh, yes, yes it does. It's a hybrid," Lupe crossed her arms and glanced at the truck. "It gets great gas mileage."

"My blender doesn't need gas either," Karen chuckled as she flicked open the tank door.

"How original. I haven't heard that one before," Lupe felt Alex's hand on the nozzle, and she whispered "It's OK" before she let it go.

"I prefer my 3500HD," Karen opened the door to the tank.

"It is . . . big," Lupe faced Karen as Alex pumped gas.

"What did you say?" Karen looked up.

"The truck. Your truck." Lupe pointed to the bed. "It's big. Huge, in fact."

"Do you need any help, mama?" Joseph hung his head out the driver's side window.

"No, hon. I'm fine. It just stinks to high heaven out here," Karen shoved the green nozzle into the tank.

Joseph laughed and poked his head out the window even further to gawk at Alex. Lupe stepped in front of her son, and Joseph frowned.

"It must be all the gas fumes from your truck," Lupe smiled at Joseph.

"What's your problem, Lupe?" Patricia yelled from inside the cab.

"Oh, hello, Patricia," Lupe said as she kept her gaze on Joseph.

"What *is* your problem, Lupe?" Karen stopped pumping gas.

"I don't think you want to know." Lupe said. She stopped looking at Joseph and turned to Karen. Alex stopped pumping.

"I would seriously like to know." Karen let go of the gas pump nozzle and took a step toward Lupe.

No one noticed that a sheriff's patrol car had parked on the other side of the pump from the still-idling truck.

"I can't believe that you'd let your son wear that dress to school," Karen said, as she took another step toward Lupe and Alex.

"It's not a dress . . . it's . . . it's a kurta," Alex whispered as he stopped pumping gas and placed the nozzle in the dispenser. He mumbled, "She'd know that if she read a book once in a while."

"It's a kurta, not a dress," Lupe angled herself between Karen and Alex. "Indian men wear it."

"Oh, so you're not Spanish anymore," Karen shook her head and looked back at the truck.

"We're Mexican American. Who told you we were Spanish?" Lupe kept her eyes on Karen's.

"You know what I mean," Karen chuckled. "No Indian I've ever seen has worn a dress."

"I don't know where you get your ridiculous ideas," Lupe added, suppressing a roll of her eyes.

"Well, I know where you get yours," Karen took a step and pointed at Lupe's face.

"What is that supposed to mean, Mrs. Klein?" Lupe opened her hands, palms facing the sky.

"You think I'm ridiculous for not wanting my child to read pornography?" Karen's face flushed and her shoulders hunched. "I seriously don't understand why you are fighting us. Why you side with evil."

"You are mistaken," Lupe put up a hand.

"The books I have identified at the schools have sex in them," Karen's small eyes widened.

"Yes, and so does the Bible, but you're not trying to ban that one," Lupe held her hands in fists at her side as she watched Sheriff Schmidt get out of the patrol car.

"I'm not banning any books," Karen crossed her arms. "I simply want them removed."

"It's the same difference," Lupe shrugged her shoulders. "Those books, all seventy of the ones you want to ban, were written by educated people from different backgrounds who have children and a story to tell."

"Yeah, how to have sex with adults," Patricia startled Karen when she stood at her side.

"Again, you're being ridiculous. That's just not true," Lupe gestured like a conductor prepping an ensemble. "If you would bother to read . . ."

"I read those pages and they were disgusting," Patricia pointed at Lupe.

"That's the problem. You only read a few pages . . . take scenes and stories out of context . . ." She took a step toward Karen and Patricia as Alex screwed the cap onto the tank, then closed the tank door.

"Mom, don't," Alex said in a low voice. "It's like talking to a melon."

Lupe looked down at the ground, trying not to laugh because she'd never heard the Spanish phrase "ser un melon" translated to English.

"You need to read the *entire book* to understand the bigger picture, why writers put in the scenes you all find offensive," Lupe said and took another step toward the women.

Karen also took a step forward, so the women were a foot apart. "It's not just us. Anyone in their right mind would find those scenes offensive."

"There's the problem. Who are you to decide what's offensive?" Lupe hissed through tight lips. "You can decide what's right and wrong for Joseph but for my—"

"Shut up, you dumb bitch," Joseph yelled out the window.

"Hey now, there's no need for that language, Joey," Sheriff Schmidt smiled as he walked toward the women.

"Joseph, be quiet," Karen said.

"Why should I? She's slandering my name," Joseph said to the sheriff.

"You're doing a pretty good job of that yourself," Lupe looked at Joseph and clinched both hands into fists.

"Don't talk to my son," Karen said.

"Someone should." Lupe stood tall as a live oak with a ten-foot taproot.

"I take my role as a parent seriously," Karen said.

"Are you implying that I don't?" Lupe said as Alex gripped his mother's upper arm.

"I'm not implying. It's obvious," Karen pointed at Lupe.

Lupe laughed, "Oh really? How?"

"Well, just look at your family." Karen pointed toward Alex with her phone.

"Yes, we volunteer, go to church, help at the food pantry, register people to vote—" Lupe held up four fingers.

Karen shook her head. "Well, your son. He's, he's, he's . . . a cheerleader."

"Yes, he is. We're very proud of him. He has a lot of school spirit. He has a lot of friends and knows how to get along with people," Lupe said as she took a step toward Karen and looked right at Joseph. “He’s not the kind of person who exposes himself to his classmates because he can’t control his hate.”

“Ladies, ladies, what’s all this going on about?” Sheriff Schmidt stood between the two women, who looked like boxers getting instructions from a ref before a fight. “What’s the problem?”

“Gary, the problem is Lupie here keeps calling me names,” Karen looked at Sheriff Schmidt.

“That’s not true,” Lupe’s eyes widened. “I did no such thing.”

“You called me ridiculous,” Karen put her hands on her waist. “Now you’re calling me a liar.”

“Hello, Alex,” Sheriff Schmidt said. “Lupie, are you calling Karen names?”

“Hi, sir—” Alex waved.

“Of course not,” Lupe shook her head. “I said Karen’s ideas were ridiculous.”

“What’s the difference?” Sheriff Schmidt looked first at Lupe then Karen.

“I was just explaining to Lupie here that all the pornography she wants our children to read is harming our children, and it encourages deviant behavior,” Karen’s eyes teared up and she raised a hand toward Lupe. “She may be OK with boys being cheerleaders, but I sure don’t want my son to wear a dress and cheer.”

“For goodness’ sakes, Karen, these ideas of yours are toxic,” Lupe looked behind her at Alex and thought, even frightened, he looks composed and handsome.

“Lupie, come now, that’s not a very Christian thing to say to your neighbor,” Sheriff Schmidt said. “You know Karen is only trying to help. At church, she’s been letting us know about all those filthy books at the school and how they can corrupt our children.”

“Corrupt?” Lupe lifted her arms and raised her palms to the sky. She thought of the alligator weed and river cane that Karen allowed to grow wild on her ranchette, reeds that suffocated native species, reeds that established residents of Alamo City regularly committed to dig burn so that native species could thrive.

“Yes, Lupie,” Karen said. “Those books are a corrupting influence in our community.”

"Oh really?" Lupe smiled wide. "Does Joseph read any of the books on your list?"

"Of course not," Karen said. "We don't read filth in our household."

"Sheriff, has Mrs. Klein told you why our children are not in school this morning?" Lupe crossed her arms. She thought about how Karen's influence was just as damaging to the natives of Alamo City as the giant reeds Karen allowed to take root in her creek. "Did she tell you what her son, her uncorrupted son, the boy who doesn't read those *filthy* books did at school today?"

"What's she going on about, Karen?" Sheriff Schmidt looked at Karen.

"Joey just got carried away, Gary," she said.

"How so?" he looked at Joseph. "Joey, what did you do, son?"

Joseph pulled away from the window and slumped in the passenger seat facing forward, "Alex kept eyeing me like he wanted a date or something."

"And?" Sheriff Schmidt said.

"You know he's a homosexual, right?" Joseph flicked the brim of his cap with his middle finger toward Alex.

"I asked you what you did, son." Sheriff Schmidt rested his hands on his utility belt.

"I was just playing around," Joseph looked down at the floorboard. "Trying to make my friends laugh."

"Did they?" Sheriff Schmidt said.

"Well, yeah, I showed him my junk," he smiled and peeked up at the sheriff.

Sheriff Schmidt shook his head. "You know you could get arrested for doing that—it's called indecent exposure."

"Gary, Joey was just being a boy," Karen took a step toward the sheriff.

"Karen, boys his age don't expose themselves in public," Sheriff Schmidt pointed at Lupe and Alex. "You see Alex over there. He's a good kid. Funny too, and I'm not talking about that dress he's wearing or the fact that he's a cheerleader. He makes people laugh, like Joey was trying to do. But I know that he has never once made anyone laugh by doing what Joey did."

"I've heard enough of this nonsense," Karen turned and walked to her truck with Patricia following. She pulled the nozzle out of the gas tank and shoved it back on the fill port as Patricia screwed the cap on and shut the gas tank door. "I'm not going to stand here and be told that my boy is less than a, a . . . homosexual."

"Karen, you're not understanding—" Sheriff Schmidt said.

"Oh, I understand perfectly," Karen's cheeks glowed neon pink.

Karen and Patricia parted like synchronized swimmers as they marched to their respective truck doors. In unison, they opened their doors and stepped up and inside. Karen drove off before Patricia's door was fully closed. When the passenger door shut, the Chevy left skid marks on the pavement as it turned into the street. Sheriff Schmidt, Lupe, and Alex watched river cane sprouts dislodge from the truck's tire treads into the bar ditch and a puddle of water.

"By next week that irrigation ditch is gonna be overrun," Sheriff Schmidt looked at the Alfaros.

Lupe, Alex, and the sheriff walked toward the ditch to clean up Karen's mess.

Diane Wilson

Monkey Wrenching My Way Home

In normal times, I'd be fine, but it hadn't been normal for 180 days—the amount of time I had spent in Victoria County Jail. The jury that sentenced me made the comment to the judge that they wished it could have been way longer. Yes, in 2002, my country cousins did not appreciate the fact that I had climbed Union Carbide's chemical tower and chained myself to the top for an environmental issue related to the people of Bhopal, India.

They said, "India, for God's sake! Who cares? Where's it even at?"

Anyhow, I was out of jail and in my little dump of a trailer sitting on four cinder blocks in Gulf Coast rattlesnake country. I was washing dishes and singing a sad song. Willie Nelson, I think. I looked at my soapy hands stuck in a dirty tub of dishes and went straight back to a bad memory in my cold cell. No, I didn't nearly drown in a shower, drink pee from a toilet, or have my head shoved under the sink. It was just the all-around pounding you get in a Texas jail. It was abuse, alright, but it was standard abuse. Everybody in that cell got a dose or two. That's why, after 180 days in jail and with the skin on my hands the ripe color of the gritty cement floors I'd just left, I decided to go back fishing. Commercial fishing. None of that rod and reel recreational crap.

Fishing would clear out the jail cobwebs and the steel bars that anchored my soul. A boat on the water would do it! Problem was, I didn't have a shrimp boat anymore, and a fat lot that would have done me because Texas shrimping was shot to hell and all the shrimp boats at the harbor were up for sale. Seadrift, Texas was dying. Or dead. Three fish houses were shut down for good. One was bulldozed and the cement foundation blazed in the hot sun like a ruined mirror. And no fishing. Not with nets, anyhow. That was illegal and would send a local fisherman to jail quicker than if he had shot a game warden. One local fisherman and his son got caught by a game warden and spent three years in Huntsville for using a gill net to catch a washtub of red fish.

But I *could* legally string a trotline along a reef. That was an OK thing left to do in the commercial fishing book. So I went to my local bank, put my Chevy truck with a dead battery and 150,000 miles on it up for collateral, and bought a twenty-two-foot skiff, a 120 Johnson motor, and a thousand stainless steel hooks. I went into the trotlining fishing business that fast.

So for the next few weeks, I strung a thousand stainless hooks on hundred-feet lines in my front yard and steered my new skiff into San Antonio Bay looking for the telltale signs of submerged oyster reefs. A poke here, a prod there, and bingo! Some wet oyster shells poked their heads out of the water. I was in black drum heaven. Black drum were the only fish that a commercial fisherwoman like me was allowed to catch, and black drum loved to crunch on the tiny oyster spats growing on a reef. So I strung my trotlines along the edges of that reef, and the next morning as the sun came up, the great wide chocolate-colored bay rose up to greet me.

My fishing days were a lot different from my shrimping days, which began when I was ten years old. Back then the first thing my boat captain daddy needed was a deckhand, and I was it. So I was borrowed from Grandma, where I was helping her dry out chicken feathers in a pillowcase. Every time Daddy headed for the store, I hopped over the net we were working on and made a mad dash for his truck. He did this six times before he was satisfied.

At three the next morning, he stood with his hands on his hips and gave me exactly three minutes to move. Recent experience had wised Daddy up to the fact that some of his girls wouldn't work no matter what he did or how many RC Colas he had bought for the shrimping trip. My sisters weren't in the mood that day. They were ticked off from the day before because Daddy wouldn't allow them to go swimming in the bay. And they had new swimsuits. It was no big deal with me. I couldn't swim a lick. I wasn't about to go swimming in the bay.

So I was the lucky dog that rolled over and fell out of bed. Not unusual. I was good at anticipating orders and did ever' cotton-picking thing I was told.

I was his deckhand, and now that this problem was fixed, he walked into the kitchen and gave Momma orders. Three bacon-and-egg sandwiches with mayonnaise and white bread! And the coffee! Don't forget the coffee! And his change of clean clothes!

Next, I got *my* order. “Let’s check out the nets in the barn,” he said.

Daddy’s nets were hanging in the rafters, and not one sat in the dirt or was exposed to the sun. He was nice to his nets. His motto was, treat a net right and it will treat you right. His nets were so clean that I could sleep on the webbing and not once wake up with my head clogged with shrimp juice. Daddy had a method. He shook every croaker and ribbonfish out of his net after he pulled it in, and when he was done with that, he dragged it an extra mile to wash the seaweed and mud out of it. Mud was why some nets worked and others wouldn’t. Nets got moody when careless shrimpers drug them through a muddy dredge hole. Mud from a dredge hole took the hide off your fingers, and everything your finger touched left a trail of blood. Mud would eat a net, too. Leave a muddy net in the sun for two days and it might just disappear.

The minute we hit the docks, Daddy revved the dead engine alive, nosed the bow into the wind, and kissed that dock goodbye. The wind howled and whipped the rigging, but he didn’t slow down. He was playing catch-up with the wind, and according to his calculations, we would enter Mesquite Bay just as the morning sun spilled across the water. In the meantime, I went below and slept on a quilt that smelled of salt water and sea lice.

At daylight, Daddy yelled at me that the sun was sliding over his left shoulder and shrimp were begging to be caught. A few hours later it was sun sun sun. I culled shrimp with the sun to my back, and when the boat turned, I culled with the sun on my face. The deck was hot, and the shrimp quickly went dead as a hammer. I culled and cleaned off the deck twice, washed two baskets of shrimp, triple-iced them in the homemade ice box (once on the bottom, once in the middle, and once on top), pulled in the try net ten times, and only stabbed myself twice with a hardhead.

I straightened up and looked over my shoulder at Daddy, who was sitting in the captain’s chair with his foot on the wheel. He was pretty good with that foot. He could turn the boat in a complete circle and not take his foot off the wheel once.

I wasn’t any slouch either and never minded the insane orders. If he said to jump overboard and grab a buoy, I’d do it even though I couldn’t swim a lick. If he said to climb out on the end of a ten-foot pole and untie the messed-up try net, I’d think, “Just watch me!” I did ever’ cotton-picking thing he said, and sometimes that carried over into the truck and clear into the house. *Get my smelly boots and take them outside! Go fetch my pliers! Unload that deck bucket of crabs and clean them for your momma!*

I was Daddy's best deckhand.

But those shrimping days were over—mine and his—and mine were now Huck Finn days of trotlining. Later that summer, things changed. Man-made things. Things nature had nothing to do with. A seismograph team from a heady group of petroleum hunters, including Pennzoil, Shell, and Phillips Petroleum, showed up on the bay with a long string of boats. They were on their never-ending search for oil and gas deposits. The bay was already pockmarked with their oil and gas wells, and the shrimp nets and hulls of our boats found them easily enough. In those early shrimping days, when I was learning the bay by myself, I spent entire mornings cutting my net off rusted pipes, gears, and broken pilings from abandoned gas wells. Some boats ripped holes in their hulls from the oil trash and sank. Then I had a sunken shrimp boat to watch out for.

So on the arrival of the seismic team, I sat in my skiff and, without an ounce of surprise, watched the boats string long lines of dynamite charges up and down the north end of the bay, skip a reef, and then hop over to the middle of the bay. There were five of us trotliners in the bay that day and we pulled the noses of our skiffs in a tight circle and discussed the disaster happening in front of us. A few of the fishermen were talkers, and the rumor mill went something like this: the seismograph team had just moved out of the Corpus Christi Bays where the dynamite had destroyed the fishing, and now these same guys were setting up shop in San Antonio and Espirito Santo Bays and who knows what other bay. Matagorda Bay, most likely. And the story went that dynamite blasts did enough damage to the trotlining in Corpus that it set fishing back all year. In the aftermath, the seismograph company with ties to powerful oil and gas companies like Exxon and BP and Phillips Petroleum threw those dumb cluck fishermen in Corpus some dollar bills to shut them up. After all, the seismo crews couldn't quit setting off dynamite just because the blasts were blowing fish out of the water and rocking their seismic skiffs and tearing little corners out of the oyster reefs. Dynamite equaled shock waves equaled newly found gas deposits. Now how simple was that for a bunch of dumb cluck fishermen sitting in San Antonio Bay to understand?

Well, the fishermen in San Antonio Bay didn't think it was gonna be that bad for them. Surely not. But the next day when I went fishing, I lifted my lines, and instead of black drum, I found a long string of dynamite charges hanging off the hooks. I wasn't the only trotliner with problems. One fisherman pulled his skiff near a reef and coils of black wire loaded with dynamite charges got tangled in his prop.

Now, everybody knew what the seismo teams were doing was illegal. Rules were being broken, reefs were being destroyed, but heck this was Texas! Big oil could do anything it was big enough to get away with. When some of the trotliners complained that they had witnessed dynamite charges blowing fish out of the water, the seismograph team hired three airboats to run up and down the bay to scare the fish out of the bay. Their thinking was "You can't blow up fish if they're not there!" The airboat idea was pretty ingenious. Airboats are like low-flying jet planes. They sound just like them, too. So every fish in the bay left, and there went the fishing business.

* * *

I'm a fourth-generation fisherwoman in a sea of fishermen, and it's a well-known fact that fishermen don't quit even when there is nothing to fish. Fishing is what their daddies and their grandaddies did. They couldn't quit. And if one did quit, he never fully recovered. He was like a dead man walking. I was no different. I couldn't imagine a time when salty water didn't fill my days. At times it pained me watching the granddaddy waves and the great-granddaddy waves. My old great-grandpa on Blackjack Island fished on top of those old waves. I never knew him, but I knew the waves. They were back in time somewhere but here today as well. So even if I didn't know where I was going, I sure knew where I came from. A direction *from* rather than a direction *to*, which, I suppose, was the reason why every time the water dipped me and my trotlining skiff in her warm salty sea, I was closer to home than I had ever been. This was also the closest thing to dreaming while being awake that I have ever known. I was drunk on the sea, an additive, a thing that was ever poured from a bottle.

So I tracked down the phone number of the seismic company that was printed on the dynamite charges and told the receptionist over the phone that I was hiring a lawyer and suing them on behalf of all the fishermen in San Antonio Bay. Their dynamite had ruined fishermen's lives. Well, that got me a meeting with a coy lawyer who was pretty much bluff for my bluff. The lawyer said commercial fishermen didn't keep records of anything, so they couldn't prove they had lost anything. And I said, "just watch me prove my loss." The lawyer gawked at me for a long minute before he said, "OK, but we're only giving a thousand dollars per fisherman, and there's a gag order on this. If those fishermen say a single word about any of this, then they have to pay back the thousand dollars."

"Sure," I said, "The fishermen won't squeal."

And they didn't. The trotliners lined up at the bank two days before Christmas and cashed in their seismic checks. I got a thousand dollars, too, and five kids to spread it around with, so all of my kids got cash for Christmas except Crockett, who was autistic and just starting to talk to people. I bought him a digital calculator with colored flashing lights and he was happy.

Two months later I was barreling down a highway in my truck when a man called me on the cell phone. He told me Formosa Plastics on the Texas coastline had a wastewater problem. He talked about a big mix-up between the expansion plant and the vinyl chloride plant and said ethylene dichloride was backed up in all the workplace units. There was some bad crap that was going down into the storm ditches and out into the bay. Workers were walking through the stuff like nothing.

I asked, "How long have you been working at Formosa?" and the guy didn't pause a second. "Hell," he said, "twenty-five years!" Then as fast as he started talking, he slammed into reverse. He didn't know if he could trust me. Could he trust me? Could he? He went back and forth on that awhile like he was a two-year-old on a teeter-totter. I didn't bother to ask him why he had called me in the first place if he thought I was so got dang untrustworthy.

I was used to this type of insane, blind-ended conversation. Half the time chemical workers were midway in the conversation before they realized they'd picked up the phone and called a former shrimper.

"Hey," he said. "I hear talk at the plant. Are you working for Formosa?"

"Where on earth do you guys get these stories? Don't you know I'm a broke ex-shrimper?" I answered.

"Don't know, don't know," he said. "I've just heard talk. You know those guys out there. They're just like a bunch of old women. Hanging 'round the pipes and gossiping."

Then my caller backpedaled again. I wouldn't give his name away, would I?

"Hell nope," I said. "I don't give away names. Certainly not to dang Formosa lawyers or the EPA. Those EPA criminal investigators are worthless. Last one I talked to told me to investigate the complaint myself!"

He agreed. "Oh no, you can't trust 'em. A bunch of stinkin' SOBs holding hands with the company." Made him sick thinking about it, he said. Every time he drove his truck past Formosa's gate he had to stop and throw up, he said. Had I ever heard of such a thing?

"Yep," I said. In Taiwan, where Formosa came from, there was so much of that upset stomach and throwing up feeling from Formosa's engineers that they called it the "Formosa Syndrome." Got a whole disease named for what Formosa did to its workers.

Well, the caller wasn't a bit surprised. Formosa was driving him slap dab crazy. He was retiring. He was quitting. He didn't know what he was doing. He needed to do something. *Wanted* to do something! Man, oh man.

"Well, that's good," I said. "What did you say your name was again?"

He never said his name, and he knew it and I knew it. It was just a parlor trick I used to get a worker to slip up and give his name, because lots of times, that was the last I heard of that worker. So it was good to get a first name. But no siree. No name from this guy. He'd tell me later, he said. After he got his insurance settled. After he exited Formosa in mid-October.

Mr. No Name called in September, again in October, and by November he said he was "for real." He was giving me his name and talking. So I went scrounging for the spiral notebooks where I took notes from the thirty or forty whistleblowers I had talked to over the years. Where did I put them? I certainly didn't file them. I went out to my truck and found them under some wadded-up trotlines.

Yes, Mr. No Name was official. He was ready to show me his documents. He had a briefcase with lots and lots of documents. Ambient air monitoring reports. Vinyl chloride releases that were never reported. Ethylene Dichloride in the ditches. Things like that. Violations!

Bob was his first name and the last name started with *D*. He wasn't ready to give the last name. Bob said he'd promised the guys when he left (he called it "exiting out") that he wasn't just leaving. Lots of guys did just that. They hit the pavement running and left skid marks on their way out. He wanted to make things better for them. Safer. But at the same time, he had a sick, chronic worry about the trouble it was gonna land him in to tell me the truth. He said he couldn't even tell his wife that he and I were talking.

I finally talked Bob and an old ex-worker he was bringing along "for protection" into meeting me at a little fishermen joint in Seadrift. I got there first and sat at a screened window so I could watch the comings and goings of shrimpers. Then Bob drove up in his white truck, parked in front of the café, and we just looked at each other through the window.

After years of knowing who to trust or not, I knew how to spot a paranoid guy—and Bob cornered the market. He was scared out of his wits by a well-dressed man sitting at the middle table in the café. Yes, the man spooked him, and Bob turned and nearly ran over his ex-worker bodyguard getting out of the café. I grabbed his arm and pulled him back in.

"Oh, don't mind that fella," I said. "He's just the Baptist preacher. Dresses real fancy, but he's a nice fella. And those fishermen over there? Don't mind them neither."

I explained to Bob that there was no escaping the eagle eyes of the fishermen. Nothing slipped by them. They could spot a water bug on the snout of a trout twenty yards away. So just get used to the idea that we were going to be watched.

"Why, I know every one of them fishermen on a first name basis. And I know their wives and their kids and their grandmas," I said.

Bob wasn't impressed and neither was his bodyguard, so I said, "Why don't we all sit next to this screened-in window and get some fresh air?" But nope. Bob and the bodyguard made an immediate beeline for a booth in the far corner with hot vinyl seats and very little legroom.

Bob spilled his guts promptly. He was a twenty-five-year veteran of the old vinyl chloride plant at Formosa in Point Comfort on the east side of Lavaca Bay. He had seven operators under his shift and his job was to keep the PVC unit up and running, troubleshooting when there were problems, writing logs about what all they were doing out there, and sending out operators when the alarms went off in the control room indicating that there was a vinyl chloride leak in the field.

Vinyl chloride was the bad boy and the most common chemical floating around their PVC unit. It was a primary ingredient in the plastic process and very toxic. It'd cause liver cancer if you weren't careful (angiosarcoma was about the only thing that a vinyl chloride manufacturer like Formosa would admit to), but that would be twenty years down the road and after lots of exposure. Heck, the workers could worry about it in twenty years. Yep, the workers had no idea they'd be coming down with all those ailments and all that sickness.

Bob knew of four cases of cancer in his own unit. He knew two guys who had died of brain cancer. Recently. One man's widow wrote to Formosa and said that if they dared set foot on her property after they'd shown him so little concern while he was alive, she'd kick them off her premises but good.

There was so much talk about brain cancer among the workers—worrying over knots forming on their necks or having to drive to Houston to take a biopsy (and what would happen if they did)—that upper management got wind of this and sent a memo to all the vinyl division employees saying that they were bringing in a third party to discuss cancer with the vinyl workers to answer all their questions. "Let's just have a little seminar to explain this," they said all polite. So a doctor was brought in from the University of South Florida. He told the workers that *anything and everything could be toxic if you got enough of it*. Heck, even water could kill you! (If there was enough of it.) The number-one and most important rule of toxicology was that all substances were toxic. The dose made the poison.

After the lecture, the workers were given a copy of a scientific study that was sponsored by the American Chemistry Council, which said that brain cancer excess was unrelated to vinyl chloride exposure. Who knows what the true culprit was. It remained uncertain. It might be eating all that barbecue with all those nitrates.

* * *

If Formosa knew I was talking with their workers, they'd have a conniption fit. Talking with workers threw Formosa management into a tailspin and made their executive heads spin. They *hated* activists talking to their workers. I had a cousin named Wally who was a lifelong commercial fisherman and spokesperson for all the fishermen in the county: it was probably due to this that Formosa hired him to keep tabs on what *I* was doing—and pass that information on to them. And if he didn't mind, he could also stand up at a permit hearing and say a good word about Formosa. Talk about how good they were for the fishermen and how we'd never be as successful without them.

Wally came to the fish house where I worked and chatted with me all the time. I had no problem with Wally. He was always the first guy who went to bat for the fishermen, and he had been doing it a long time. And he was tired, beat down, and had a fish house going broke. Wally had a lot of shrimpers who depended on him, so he figured if one chemical company would pay him to watch me, then maybe another one would too. Wally wasn't entirely wrong.

"What do you want from Union Carbide, Diane? Here, write it down. I'll go talk to them. These guys like talking to a man. They don't want to talk to a woman," he said.

My cousin said nothing threw Formosa's management into a tizzy more than bad press. When a reporter called with questions, the Formosa executives would sit around a conference table half the evening, saying things like, "Now, how do we answer this question? Now, what do we say here?"

And reporters got their tips from me, and I got them from the workers. Or Wally. So that's why a worker talking to me was such a big bad deal. It led Formosa to places they'd rather not go—such as frontline headlines in the *Houston Chronicle* accusing them of kickbacks, extortion, worker injuries, and chemical releases.

This was the name of my game: I was a got dang environmentalist when I wasn't going broke trotlining for black drum that had disappeared because some oil company had thrown dynamite in the bay.

But I had spent the better part of my life on a shrimp boat, so after the episode with the fish getting blown out of the water, I kept my toes in the fishing business even though the shrimp boats were gone and the fish houses were bulldozed. I'm a Seadrift native, a Bay Rat, and so I remain. These days, I spread my net under a canopy of ash trees in my momma's front yard while she sits in an aluminum lawn chair on a sunless front porch and observes me with the detachment of day-old roadkill.

Flesh and blood mean one thing to her these days. Daddy. She hasn't seen him in a while. I don't tell her he is dead.

"He's in Mesquite Bay," I say.

* * *

Ahh, Mesquite Bay. I missed my breakfast as Daddy's deckhand a lot of times on account of that bay. Mesquite Bay was (and still is) a shallow bay with salt grass around the edges and endless flocks of white birds that drag their feet across the muddy water just for the thrill of it. But mainly it was famous for being a big pain in the butt and a long haul for commercial fishermen like Daddy who had to get up early and run their boats full throttle for three straight hours to get to that bay—when normally it took forty-five minutes to get where they needed to be—in San Antonio Bay, pitching their nets over at sunup for that first drag.

That run across the bay for my daddy meant a lot of extra nonsleeping hours and extra diesel burned and extra ice melting and probably a new net sewn, hung, and dipped the evening before just so he could try the net out on those sneaky shrimp in all that grass.

For all that trouble, Daddy would get a brand-new back strain and bleeding hands from all the culling he would have to do if he didn't get one of his lazy flesh-and-blood kids on board as a deckhand. That was me, 'cause Sheena wasn't coming, and neither was Pearlina.

My sister Sheena was fifteen and had a boyfriend who gave her a real Mexico velveteen painting of spilled wine and a smoking gun, which she crammed under our bed, and heck no, she wasn't stepping on a smelly shrimp boat. On Mesquite Bay mornings, she'd turn over lazily and go back to sleep.

On Mesquite Bay mornings, my sister Pearlina wouldn't even lift her curlered head off the pillow. She'd stick a finger down her throat and gag. Pearlina was ten and hated anything to do with shrimp because Sheena had told her that shrimp crawled out of the bay to skitter up sewer pipes and toilets and stick people on the butt. Those nasty shrimp!

Daddy would stand in our bedroom's doorway and I'd do a slow roll over my sleeping sisters, fall out of bed, and haul on my elastic-band shorts with the frazzled edges and a crop top. Then I'd pull up Daddy's cut-down-three-sizes-too-big rubber boots onto my kid's feet so I could wade into a knee-high pile of shrimp, crabs, and hardheads. This way, if I fell over the boat I wouldn't drown; I'd just kick off those boots!

If I expected a big thanks, I got none. Daddy didn't believe in thanking kids who should be doing what he believed they should be doing anyhow, and he certainly wasn't gonna thank a twelve-year-old kid who had drunk an entire case of RC Colas on his last trip out—before the shrimping day was even finished!

Yep, I was that twelve-year-old, and RC Cola was my drink of choice because Daddy never bought Dr. Pepper like the rest of the shrimpers. Daddy bought RC Cola because it was cheap—and by the case it was even cheaper, especially when it came from Mexico like Sheena's Mexican velveteen painting. Maybe they came from the same guy, but even as a kid, I didn't think so.

Regardless of my RC Cola drinking problem, I was trustworthy, and so I was Daddy's best deckhand. I didn't run around with boys like Sheena did, and this made me a truly great kid. I sure thought so, anyway. I could stick my hands in a pile of shrimp and stinging jellyfish for hours on end, burning my arms till they were brick red, and not even cry. Yup. I was a great kid.

* * *

I jump into Daddy's truck and he pitches a mason jar of coffee covered in newspaper into my lap and says, "Don't drink it."

I wasn't about to drink it. Daddy's number-one rule was Daddy drank the entire jar of coffee all by himself. Later on, he'd brew cowboy coffee over a tipsy three-legged Coleman stove on the catchall. I could drink that all I wanted. He had no problem with a twelve-year-old kid drinking a gallon of coffee.

We don't say nothing the entire ride to the bay. We are both non-talkers. If Daddy had wanted a talker he should have waited on my sister Pearlina, who could talk the hide off a fence post.

It is early morning and the moon is full, so Daddy doesn't put on his truck headlights. There is another reason for no headlights that even a twelve-year-old like me knows about. Game wardens. We don't say the word, but we are thinking of game wardens. No sense stirring up trouble. Make no mistake about it, shrimpers lived in a world where game wardens and regulations were the sticky glue that tied fishermen to trouble, and that was a fact and would be a fact as long as the game wardens and their Texas Parks and Wildlife bosses in Austin—who gave them gas money to chase commercial fishermen—stayed on the bay. And the game wardens weren't leaving. Oh no. The shrimpers would leave first.

So we just coast on moonlight. Daddy doesn't need floodlights or even a compass; he is a born navigator. Just the moon and the wind and he can arrive at the exact spot he needs to be every time.

The minute we get to the boat, Daddy says he is changing shrimp nets. That old chain net won't work, he says. Too much grass in Mesquite Bay. What he needs is his secret bottomless net that is rolled up on the back deck of his boat. It is called a bottomless net because it has no bottom to speak of and it sneaks up on shrimp like a cat on a freshly dug gopher hole. And that is rule number two: sneak up on shrimp before they know which way is up. (Rule number one is Don't Drink the Coffee.) So for thirty minutes we work like crazy in the dark, counting lengths of chain and unhooking and rehooking thimbles so many times that I get confused which side is right and which side is left, and besides it is dark as heck and I can't see anything, so Daddy comes over and reworks the end of the net I am working on.

It is one of those steamy mornings and the bay is slick as trout vomit. Daddy isn't the only shrimper out. I listen to another shrimper griping on the radio about the weather. He sure hates the heat. He sure hopes a norther would roughen up the water. He sure hopes some bad weather will send the shrimp stampeding to his shrimp net. Too much talk, Daddy and I think.

We make it to Mesquite Bay for that early morning drag, and Daddy kicks over the bottomless net as the sun spills across the water like banana-colored Kool-Aid.

I love the empty space on the back deck after the net and shrimp doors are shoved off the stern and into the water and the ropes that previously held the net are now coiled and rehung on a rusting hitch. It is like a house flipped on its side where sofas, coffee tables, beds, and kitchen stoves are tossed on their ears out the front door. The boat dances. Or maybe it is just that the wind blows harder and the bow shifts into the waves and we take the wind full on. Another dip and the wind comes through the side window and I make myself a bed with one of Momma's old quilts and sleep through the entire first drag.

When I wake, the boat has stopped. Daddy sits in his dilapidated captain's chair smoking a Camel cigarette, and his eyes are strangely lit. He pulls me by my arm and says, "Put away that quilt. Time to pick up!"

I imagine wall-to-wall shrimp on that first drag. A dream catch! And Daddy would have to restrain us both from ecstatically jumping with excitement because, likely, another captain with binoculars is watching us pull in the net. And who needs another shrimper dragging a net in our gold mine. But also, in our excitement, Daddy might trip over a rope or a deck bucket and fall over and drown with the back deck loaded with shrimp. That would be a crying shame. Such a crying shame.

* * *

But that was long ago, and my home on the back deck of Daddy's boat—and mine later—was something I never saw again. The shrimp houses are gone. The boats are gone. All that remains are the watery routes of industry outfalls—pipes carrying gases and metals and lethal fluids that could kill every shrimp embryo within a ten-mile radius.

So now it's just me and my momma. She's in the later stages of Alzheimer's and believes my daddy is alive and in Mesquite Bay making a lot of money.

When he gets back from the bay, she says, he's gonna buy her a brand-new red car.

Carried by Seeds

Carried by seeds, by people with eggs and sperm, carried by need, by hunger, carried by legs, fueled by frijoles y tortillas, composed of water and stars—without water and stars and a birthing mother we don't exist. Transformed by myths that cradle us to sleep well in the chaos of empire.

* * *

Do I make a daily metaphoric commute from Santa Ana, California, to El Valle, Texas borderlands? 1,500 miles each way? Did my grandmother from Mata Ortiz, Chihuahua, to Ysleta, Texas? Did my grandparents from Guanajuato to Brawley, California? By the time we arrive, a day or so has passed just to turn back again. Mine is the furthest and easiest migration. One abuelo[1] spent most of his sixty-two years in Ysleta two miles from the colonial border. For me, ancestral Mexico is right here too, and just across international bridges, but truly inaccessible as a place in my daily life.

* * *

Don't ask me where I'd like my remains to be buried or scattered when I die. It doesn't really matter, but it does really matter.

I belong to the dirt wherever I land. And in the meantime, don't hate me if I move through it and write about a flower or a bird or a river that is beautiful and deadly. Deadly because of militarized borders. Many of our ancestors' remains are in cemeteries no one tends anymore.

* * *

If decolonization means land back, how am I helping Native nations, some without federal recognition? My writing doesn't help a damn thing. If I were wealthy I'd buy a bunch of land to gift to local nations, including

1 Grandfather.

the Esto'k Gna,[2] whose tribal chairman says they belong to the land, not necessarily the other way around, even as they care for the land here up against Elon Musk and SpaceX, the border wall, and more.

* * *

My father didn't want some of my mother's ashes scattered where she was born and raised in Ysleta. He also didn't want them in his childhood community of Brawley, where my mother was also raised after she was ten. Though my mother spoke of her childhood with great affection, he knew her poverties and childhood pains deeply and refused to return her to those earths, as if she or he would not be at peace in those places that I hold so dear to my identity because of them, though I was born and raised in Santa Ana—Acjachemen and Tongva[3] land—where my parents lived for nearly sixty years (and where my father continues to live).

* * *

Do we ask permission of the stars, the ocean tides
to exist? Do they stamp us with their locations?
Does a shark or a starfish?
Do we apologize to the grass for matting it?
The peach for eating it?
When will *our* lives begin?

* * *

My mother said she was *Mexican* as if it were the essence
of her being. *I'm Mexican.*

* * *

Do I have a home now that my mother is gone? *Gone.*
Like the Diné say in English. She's *gone.*

My father who also calls himself Mexican
continues preparing their house in Santa Ana,

2 Carrizo/Comecrudo of Texas; Esto'k Gna translates as "the Human People."

3 Indigenous peoples of California.

readying for his eventual departure, says he should have gone first.
Sometimes I think *they* are the only place I am from.

***

If I tattoo my mom's nickname on my arm
will I be copying my dad? Dare I include his name too?
Would the names have to be on separate arms?
Where would I place my children's names?
The birds of paradise? Chuparosas?[4] The pink bottlebrush leaves?
And an owl for my grandmother, who called them tecolotes.

***

Forget paper. *Body* as living headstone, body as altar.

***

If my body is my home, and I *don't* quite carry "home" on my back, am *I* land?

***

This body as moving land. Maybe not this particular land, but a land.

***

Shit, I grew two whole other bodies inside mine. My grandmothers grew nine and ten each—and all of us gave birth in the borderlands.

***

When I walked with Another Gulf is Possible, the group carried a huge sign we painted in consultation with the Esto'k Gna—*Our roots break your walls*—over our heads, walking through a border wall without a gate near the nine-hundred-year-old tree that we watered before returning from "no man's land."

***

4 Desert shrub (*Justicia californica*) of the southwestern United States and northwestern Mexico that has usually red, yellow, or orange tubular flowers.

2022. There's a new concrete wall
at Bentsen State Park's entrance
behind the canal with river water—
the builders are still polishing it
like someone's buttons or cufflinks.
Just beyond it three men in fatigues
ask a brown man in English
if he swam in the canal.
We were sitting on the same kind of solid benches—
he detained with no shoes and his bare
feet were exposed.
One of the men in fatigues and with guns
translated into Spanish.
I wore the blue tag with the state park visit date
Mis papeles para entrar
el parque,[5] not tagged like my mother
in her home a few hours after
she had refused an antibiotic in the Cali hospital
and I rushed to prepare it for her feeding tube
seconds before she transitioned
into dreams, back to stars,
everywhere and seemingly nowhere

* * *

I'm still catching up
to my family's buried histories, reading my tía's writing
about how my bisabuela[6]
whose mother spoke Rarámuri
called my tía "una india pata rajada"[7]
when she took off her shoes
as soon as she thought her abuela couldn't see her
anymore in the streets of Mata Ortiz.

5 (My) papers to enter the park.

6 Great-grandmother.

7 Spanish idiom roughly translating as one who behaves without manners, or one who is "rude" or walks barefoot.

My tía already knew she wasn't quite considered native
but other experiences must have made her consider
the possibility and she took her abuela's awful anger
somewhat as a compliment

***

I'd like my Self back to roam lands
with respect, to experience the earth fully,
a full return from susto[8]
calling my spirit back to my body

***

If I am land, on the move, I am a refuge owned solely by me.
This land is sovereign.

***

Was it bits of tooth enamel in my hands gripping my mother's ashes in *Cali*?

And back in El Valle, the white swirled snail shell packed on the trail, hard like a tooth. My tooth too someday.

That is how our matter will become land even if not massive.

Wherever I go, my body carries me, my homeland with me,[9] until I return to earth and atmosphere.

8 Literal translation is "fright"; in Latin American culture, illnesses from *susto* are thought to result from a shocking or frightening experience that is believed to cause the soul to leave the body.

9 This is a play on the line "I am a turtle, wherever I go I carry 'home' on my back" from Gloria Anzaldúa's *Borderlands / La Frontera*.

Part 2: Bête Noire, a California Extinction in Five Walks

I. Quarantined: The Last Bear King of California

For twenty-two years, Monarch, the last California grizzly bear (*Ursus arctos californicus*) held in captivity, never stopped trying to escape from his cage. The 1,200-pound boar[1] was snared in the San Gabriel Mountains near Antelope Valley in 1889, at the westernmost edge of the Mojave Desert, and he was one of the largest bears ever captured.[2] For twenty-two years, Monarch paced the concrete floors of his enclosure and mourned the vistas from his lost kingdom—that boundless southwestern frontier where his savage existence affronted fabulist mid-nineteenth-century notions of manifest destiny and the limitless western expansion of American democratic ideals. Monarch cared nothing about these human vanities. He wanted nothing more than to return to his desert lair, long neglected now amid the chaparral scrub and golden poppies.

For thousands of years, grizzly bears were worshipped as the shape-shifting guardians of the West by First Nations people. The bear was a sacred gift from the Creator, a shamanic warrior totem symbolizing brute strength, wisdom, medicine, and magical healing powers.[3] Thirty years

1 A male bear is called a boar. Female bears are called sows, and a group of bears is called a sloth.

2 The Monarch Bear Institute, "History and Ritual Honoring of the Monarch Bear," https://www.monarchbear.org/monarch/ritual.html.

3 Native Languages of the Americas, "Native American Indian Bear Legends, Meaning and Symbolism from the Myths of Many Tribes," http://www.native-languages.org/legends-bear.htm.

An abridged version of Lisa Lee Herrick's "Bête Noire: A California Extinction in Five Walks" was published online in *The Bold Italic*, 18 September 2020, https://thebolditalic.com/the-sad-story-of-the-bear-on-californias-state-flag-8077ba11846f?gi=cded96bfd508.

of genocide came soon after the first American white settlers arrived,[4] resulting in the near complete extermination of all of California's Indigenous people by US government agents and local militia. As ranchers and vaqueros occupied Indigenous territories, canvassing the biodiverse habitats with legions of cattle, California grizzly bears like Monarch were demonized as villainous beasts. They were portrayed as ravenous opportunists and pesky scavengers targeted for blood sport and consumption. Monarch was chained and transported to San Francisco, where he became a trophy: a tall tale in the moneyed salons of Nob Hill's manufacturing magnates, robber barons, and lords of industry. At the cusp of the twentieth century, Monarch was no more than a toothless public spectacle, a defeated and dethroned Azazel[5] gazing blankly from his barred cell.

Lately, I can feel Monarch's despair like a restless engine driving my feet to pace the floors of my now too-familiar house. There is the corner where a ball of dog hair has collected and formed a cocoon. There is a spot on the baseboard that will not wash out with soap or bleach. There is the skein of spider silk on the ceiling—it seems to be hanging lower today, and catching on some minute breeze. Perhaps it is my breathing that is the gyre. The air outside my windows feels more *alive*, I suspect, because there are birds and trees moving freely. Because it is simply *outside*. Inside, my toes worry the wooden boards until they groan in protest. My hands (for lack of other things to do) are raw with liquid disinfectant, and the skin around the knuckles is cracked and splitting. I want to claw at the walls and my skin. Both bead with the oily sweat of my own humidity. The days and weeks pass by in irrelevant chronology, a long footnote in an already difficult year.

In June 2021, I have grown accustomed to the deepening crags creasing the broad forehead of our governor's face when he appears on video

4 Benjamin Bradley lecture at University of Southern California, *An American Genocide: The United States and the California Indian Catastrophe, 1846–1873*, 11 October 2016, Yale University Press. Summary and video recording: https://sfi.usc.edu/news/2016/10/12297-benjamin-madley-lecture-summary.

5 Azazel is a celestial figure who resided in Mount Hermon, the home of ancient demons. In the Book of Enoch, Azazel teaches the forbidden knowledge of magic, self-adornment, and weaponry to humans. He is bound and cast into the desert by God, thereby associating his name with the scapegoat rite. His name is also synonymous with "the rugged mountain cliff where scapegoat rituals were performed" and "to be used up, exhausted, or sent away."

to deliver his daily update on the COVID-19 pandemic. It has been over a year now since the emergency quarantines started, and I find the vocal fry of our governor's voice as soothing as white noise now. His voice is the ocean that I have longed to see now for the past year. Governor Newsom looks like a Hollywood actor cast in the role of a state politician: slicked-back hair, unruffled speech, composed and effortlessly cool save for the worried taproot arcing from the base of his nose toward the sharp widow's peak. *My fellow Americans*, he says, *we are living in difficult and unprecedented times*. I have come to detest that word, *unprecedented*, as much as *quarantine*. The word *unprecedented* means that something unknown or unexpected has happened. Our governor's jaw clenches whenever he says this word, as though biting down to crush it. Perhaps, when we say *unprecedented*, we actually mean to say that we cannot recall if something has happened before already because we have lost a sense of time or history. Or *unprecedented* can also sound like we are doing everything by the seat of our pants because we are completely unprepared and, therefore, blindsided. In these sentiments, *unprecedented* is not an anomaly. It is an American state of mind to both panic and flail in the face of calamity.

The global science community is in agreement that COVID-19 is a novel zoonotic disease and only one of innumerable spillover events throughout the long history of human interactions with wild animals.[6] I imagine that the very first spillover event happened the moment a human being left the protection of the walled city and entered the forest. But why is it that I feel like a caged animal today? I feel desperate to be outside. The nagging thought drags itself down my spine as a stream of sweat. *Outside. I want to be outside*. Instead, I gaze past our governor's face and absorb the details of the three flags draped behind him to distract myself from more bad news. Sometimes it feels like the world is dropping away from my feet. I feel estranged from nature, and a bit from myself, too.

Monarch's face dominates the backdrop of these daily televised press conferences from the governor's office in Sacramento. California's official state flag, the Bear Flag, takes center stage. It features Monarch's bleeding maw, captured midsnarl, which peeks out from behind our governor's

6 The Institute for Science Policy, "Zoonotic Spillover and Emerging Viruses: Institute for Science & Policy," 3 August 2020, https://institute.dmns.org/perspectives/posts/zoonotic-spillover-and-emerging-viruses/.

coiffed head whenever he shifts his weight from one foot to the other. For a second, I remember that there is a dark bear painted in the lower left corner of Gast's *American Progress* that has a similar snarl. Maybe it's just a coincidence.

The California state flag is never without the US flag in my memories of childhood, but not once did I ever wonder, until now, if contemporary Californians understood that the illustrated bruin's true story surpassed its cultural mythos. Symbolically, Monarch not only signaled the demise of the Old West and its dream of limitless American expansion, but the spectacle of the bear ushered in the New West: one of the United States' national investments in conservation biology and the geopolitics of public space.[7]

How many times did I pledge allegiance to this flag every morning in the classroom until the end of senior year of high school? How had I so easily placed my right palm against my heart at every school assembly, every sports game, and all those graduation ceremonies? I had no idea what I was pledging to at all.

II. Old Alta California: San Francisco, Sacramento, Monterey

California was once the Garden of Eden (in the American imagination).

By the time Mexico had gained its independence from Spain in the 1840s, California was already a utopia where land was abundant, and the only requirement to receive a land grant in the newly renamed Alta California (North California) was Mexican citizenship. There were only three conditions required to become a Mexican citizen, per *Las Siete Leyes*: be a man, speak Spanish, and earn at least one hundred pesos a year. Mexican citizenship was granted to Indigenous people, European and American settlers, and Mexican nationals. It was all so easy. But if there is one hard truth about Edens, it's that all paradises are eventually lost.

7 Library of Congress, American Memory Collection, National Digital Library Program, "The Evolution of the Conservation Movement 1850–1920," 18 September 2000, https://www.loc.gov/item/00529694/. Overview: https://www.loc.gov/static/collections/evolution-of-the-conservation-movement/about-this-collection/overview.html.

Alta California once embraced its mestizo culture of American and European immigrants, and their Mexican spouses, as *hijos y hijas del país*. Real Californios owned the land beneath their ranches and hunted wild game. This made Californios the new apex predator, while over ten thousand California grizzly bears became outlaw marauders of livestock corrals and the dreaded bêtes noires of every cattle rancher. Each of the black-haired beasts weighed over a ton, which proved too tempting for hungry vaqueros and rancheros. Grizzly bears were trapped and slaughtered. During my visit to the city of Monterey, I was told by Monterey Public Library & Museums Director Brian Edwards that ranchers often slaughtered cattle and left their carcasses out to lure grizzly bears from the forest; the bears were labeled as pests and shot on sight as trophy kills. The bears, whose gray- and red-tipped black fur lent them a "grizzled" look, were once revered as spiritual guides for the native Chumash and Miwok shamans. The bears' ferocious rage and fury and their instinct for self-preservation would later inspire the Bear Flag Revolt. And after San Francisco burned, the grizzly bear spirit would be resurrected as the great protector of a city in shambles.

In August 2023, during my visit to the city of Monterey for a public library event, Library & Museums Director Brian Edwards pulled me aside and whispered that there was a historical trail through the old part of town that would lead to Colton Hall and, if I looked up, I would see a replica of the original Bear Flag. This was exciting, as the only images I had seen of the original state flag were tiny black-and-white photographs, often inset next to an even briefer paragraph, such as in Sutter's Fort State Historic Park in Sacramento. When I had toured Sutter's Fort earlier that spring, I had hoped to find some interesting records locked behind the tall adobe walls. Instead, I marveled at park employees and volunteers baking chocolate chip cookies from scratch using an earthen beehive oven and craft areas designed for young school-aged children with activities like beeswax candle dipping and corn husk doll making. The single flagpole on the dusty grounds displayed both the US and Mexico flags. I had left my visit with only a resin replica of a grizzly bear claw—which proved to be as sharp as the real thing—and a vague idea of what utopian visions drove people to emigrate from the opposite side of the nation.

It's unclear exactly when the Bear Flag Revolt took place because the small band of American militia—the Bear Flaggers—were too drunk after the siege of the Mexican military stronghold in Sonoma to remember. What *is* clear, however, is that no one knew that the United States was already at war with Mexico over the Texas border when a homemade flag declaring California an independent and sovereign republic for Californios shimmied up a flagpole in June 1846. The flag had been crafted from odds and ends: the red flannel petticoat of one of the wives present was used to create a red star, the outline of a bear, and a stripe. The design was inspired by the Lone Star Republic of Texas flag, with the star symbolizing a nation independent of Mexico and the United States, the bear a nod to local militia, and the stripe representing the blood shed for freedom. The original Bear Flag was given to the Society of California Pioneers for safekeeping, but it was later destroyed in the fires following the San Francisco earthquake on April 18, 1906. A replica is displayed at El Presidio de Sonoma and at Colton Hall. But as I walked up the red brick lane toward Colton Hall and stood under the grand white building gazing up at the replica Bear Flag Revolt flag, I thought to myself, *That looks more like a pig than a bear*. I returned to the Monterey Public Library and told Brian that I had seen the flag—and that I was glad it was replaced by a new design much later.

Brian and I talked some more about California's fraught history. "I'm just excited that someone else is as into local and state history as I am," he told me. "I wish more people were interested in the living history that is all around us every day." We talked about how, on July 9, 1846, Commander John B. Montgomery arrived at Portsmouth Plaza—then the central hub of Yerba Buena—and raised the American flag, signifying the official start of the US military occupation of Alta California.[8] I've walked by Portsmouth Plaza many times. It is now the heart of Chinatown, and a plaque permanently commemorates that day. My first job in San Francisco was on Montgomery Street in a skyscraper so tall that, most mornings when I had my coffee in front of the window, the only thing I could see was an endless ocean of white fog below and blue sky above. Brian

8 Plaque commemorating Commander John B. Montgomery erected in San Francisco: https://www.nationalwarmemorialregistry.org/memorials/commander-john-b-montgomery-s-landing-site-memorial-plaque/. Allegations made by Captain John C. Frémont and his wife, Jessie Benton Frémont, claiming to have raised the US flag two days earlier were largely discredited by Bear Flag Revolt participants William B. Ide, General Vallejo, and Harvard historian Josiah Royce in 1884–85.

and I talked about how, in January 1847, Yerba Buena was renamed San Francisco,[9] after that first adobe building was constructed by Indigenous slave laborers and the Franciscan priests. Then came the gold found at Sutter's Mill, the Treaty of Guadalupe Hidalgo, California's statehood, and the greatest human migration and cash grab on the planet at that time. Across the Pacific Ocean, there were whispers in Southern China of a place where the streets were made of gold: San Francisco was *Chiu Chin Shan*, "Old Gold Mountain," and Taishanese immigrants arrived only to be stripped of their rights and excluded from commerce. They went to work on the transcontinental railroad, connecting the two US frontiers as one, but the Chinese laborers were omitted in photos. They were cordoned off in San Francisco and not allowed to live elsewhere in the city. This was how Chinatown was created, near the site of a military occupation and at the edges of society.[10] While *Cosmopolitan Magazine* depicted a wounded but fierce Monarch towering over the smoldering ruins of San Francisco, mouth foaming with rage[11] against the fires, the image omitted the fact that Chinatown was almost not rebuilt. (The real Monarch was never at risk in the 1906 fires because he was languishing in an enclosure inside Golden Gate Park far from the epicenter of the disaster.)

When I asked Brian about what happened to the Chinese immigrants in Monterey, he replied that there had also been a fire. "Their village burned down overnight," he said. "Many believe it was done on purpose. After that, the Chinese left and didn't come back to Monterey. Not too many people know about that history here."

Chinatown remains in San Francisco simply because it refuses to disappear, but a true disappearance is one where no one remembers you were once there at all. The greatest trick about Eden is that it first appears to welcome everyone through its gates, but if you wander too close to the edges of that walled garden, the same doors slam shut behind you, leaving you to disappear into the wilderness beyond.

9 The Museum of the City of San Francisco, "Order Changing the Name of Yerba Buena," http://www.sfmuseum.net/hist/name.html.

10 NPR, "Rebuilding Chinatown after the 1906 Quake," 12 April 2006, https://www.npr.org/2006/04/12/5337215/rebuilding-chinatown-after-the-1906-quake.

11 Poster: The Monarch Bear Institute, "The Monarch Bear," https://www.monarchbear.org/monarch/index.html.

***

On my many walks through San Francisco, I see discreet hints of Monarch's past in the small bronze plaques dotting the sidewalks and the facades of historical buildings. It's difficult to imagine that there were once live animals kept in cages in a basement zoo where now stands a FedEx Office Ship Center at Three Embarcadero Center. These zoos were one of the few places where people could see wild animals performing carnival tricks, and the most infamous zoo barker of all was "Grizzly" Adams.

James Capen "Grizzly" Adams arrived in San Francisco in 1856 and debuted the Mountain Menagerie on 143 Clay Street. It's difficult to imagine how, for twenty-five cents, visitors could see this bizarre man with a dented skull and dressed head to toe in buckskins wrestle with live bears in downtown San Francisco, but that is exactly how it was described in Theodore H. Hittell's 1860 book *Adventures of James Capen Adams, Mountaineer and Grizzly Bear Hunter of California*:

> In the early part of October 1856, while in charge of the local department of the *Daily Evening Bulletin* newspaper of San Francisco, my attention was attracted to a small placard at the door of a basement on the south side of Clay, near Leidersdorff Street. . . . In the midst of this strange menagerie was Adams, the proprietor—quite as strange as any of his animals. He was a man a little over medium size, muscular and wiry, with sharp features and penetrating eyes. He was apparently about fifty years of age; but his hair was very gray and his beard very white. He was dressed in a coat and pantaloons of buckskin, fringed at the edges and along the seams of arms and legs. On his head he wore a cap of deerskin, ornamented with a fox-tail, and on his feet buckskin moccasins.[12]

Adams's menagerie was a private collection of wild animals he had captured and trained, and more of a circus act than a private zoo. The collection included a large female California grizzly bear named Lady Washington that Adams rode like a horse, her cub General Frémont (named

12 Pp. ix–x (full excerpt via Google Books).

after the real John C. Frémont), two male California grizzly cubs from Yosemite—one of whom would become so famous that the bear was given his own obituary as a "Distinguished Native Californian" when he died of old age—and the star of the show, Old Samson. It was Old Samson's promotional portrait in 1855 by Gold Rush watercolorist Charles C. Nahl that would provide the recognizable silhouette for California's most iconic state emblem.[13] Nahl also illustrated Hittel's 1860 biography on Adams. After Adams died the same year his biography was published, Nahl returned to his art studio on Bush Street to continue painting, and Hittel returned to law and eventually played a pivotal role in the creation of Golden Gate Park, where Monarch would spend the remainder of his years locked in a cage.

On May 12, 1869, former California Governor Leland Stanford drove the 17.6-karat Golden Spike into the completed Transcontinental Railroad at Promontory Point, Utah, thereby connecting the Eastern and Western Seaboards. By that time, California grizzly bears had all but disappeared from the state, along with 75 percent of California's Indigenous peoples as a direct result of state-supported genocide. When the Golden Spike ceremony was completed, a "Champagne Photo" was arranged to capture the people who engineered this marvel of transportation. None of the recently freed Black slaves or Chinese immigrants were included in the picture.[14] It would appear that the Western frontier was finally colonized by well-groomed white men, because the photo captured a major achievement of American progress while glossing over the dirty details. In 1872, John Gast would capture this narrative of effortless modernization in his allegorical painting *American Progress*. No recently freed Black slaves or Chinese immigrants would appear in Gast's painting, either.

Nahl's original 1855 watercolor is located in the archives at the Monterey Public Library. Although Brian couldn't let me see the framed watercolor painting in person, he showed me a photo that he took on his phone from inside the archive. The composition is a perfect match: Monarch

13 Grizzly Adams, "It's All about the Bear," https://grizzlyadams.com/history-california-state-flag/.

14 CNN, "Remembering the Migrants Who Built the Transcontinental Railroad 150 Years Ago," 11 May 2019, https://www.cnn.com/2019/05/10/us/transcontinental-railroad-150-workers/index.html.

the bear on the California state flag is actually, technically, a portrait of "Grizzly" Adams's bear, Old Samson. By the time the modern flag design was being discussed, the real Monarch was a toothless and overweight bear in retirement from the zoo. Perhaps, as a last show of mercy or remorse for his long imprisonment, Monarch was revived as a symbol of strength instead of resigned defeat to energize all Californians under the banner of resilience in the face of grave adversity.

Stanford wasn't the only enterprising San Francisco tycoon to stake his claim in the dream of California profiteering and manifest destiny.

In 1887, William Randolph Hearst was a twenty-three-year-old with a lot to prove: his father, US Senator George Hearst, had just handed him ownership of the *San Francisco Examiner* on Market Street, which Hearst Sr. had received in lieu of payment for a poker debt. Hearst Jr.'s first business decision was to add a new motto to the newspaper: "Monarch of the Dailies," much to the ire of his competitors the *San Francisco Chronicle* and the *San Francisco Call*. His next big idea was a publicity stunt: capture a live California grizzly bear. In May 1889, he commissioned Allen Kelly, a writer and outdoorsman with no previous bear hunting experience, to capture the bear. There was only one problem: California grizzlies had gone extinct in the San Francisco Bay Area. Hearst toyed with the idea of simply buying a captive bear and faking the headlines, but Kelly was adamant about capturing a live bear on his own, as documented in Kelly's 1903 book *Bears I Have Met—and Others*.

Before Monarch was captured in Hearst's marketing ploy to outsell his competitors, Monarch was simply a large grizzly bear with a vast territory in Southern California. It took several months, including being bamboozled in Ventura County by a grifter with carved wooden bear print stamps and going broke, then getting fired by Hearst via wire. But in October 1889, Kelly received a lead about a male bear trapped on Mount Gleason near the Sunland-Tujunga neighborhood of Los Angeles. Kelly headed to the San Gabriel Mountains on his burro and met a Mexican syndicate named Mateo who was desperate to get the bear off his hands.

Monarch proved to be a fierce and determined bear, biting and tearing at the logs used in his capture and gnawing at his iron chains to the point of breaking several teeth and leaving trails of frothing blood. He refused to eat for a week and was only interested in tugging against his chains to free himself. The bear even proved to be as smart as a dog and regularly challenged his captors in his transport down the mountain for the train ride to San Francisco.

Even so, Kelly sympathized with the animal:

> Many of my prejudices and all my story-book notions about the behavior of the carnivorae were discredited by experience, and I was forced to recognize the plain truth that the only mischievous animal, the only creature meditating and planning evil on that mountain—excepting of course the evil incident of the procurement of food—was a man with a gun. I was the only really dangerous and unnecessarily destructive animal in the woods, and all the rest were afraid of me.[15]

When Monarch finally arrived in San Francisco, he was a silent and despondent bear. Hearst debuted Monarch to great fanfare on November 10, 1889, inside the bear pit at Woodward's Gardens, a pleasure park that once occupied an entire city block in the Mission District. Over twenty thousand visitors arrived to gawk at Monarch in his enclosure on that day. Among the crowd was Monarch's captor, Allen Kelly, who had formed a familiar and tenuously affectionate bond with the bear during the long transport north to San Francisco. Monarch had allowed Kelly to "handle his chain" and took food from his hand, which led Kelly to gain "genuine respect for his character and admiration for his indomitable courage."[16]

While in his cell, Monarch guarded the shavings used as bedding aggressively and only showed interest when a live animal was placed in his pit for food. He dug, scaled, climbed, and jumped over every cage designed for him. Kelly wrote that Monarch spent three or four years in a steel cell before he was transferred to Golden Gate Park, where he "devoted a week or so trying to get out and testing every bar and joint of his prison."[17] Monarch only gave up when Willis Polk, the architect of the former Flood Mansion-cum-Pacific Union Club on 1000 California Street, designed bars that were entirely enclosed—and impossible to escape. It was Polk's cage design that broke the bear's fighting spirit completely. Kelly wrote, "[A]nd

15 Allen Kelly, *Bears I Have Met—and Others*, 1903, p. 14. Full excerpt via Google Books.

16 *San Francisco Examiner*, November 5, 1889, p. 3.

17 Kelly p. 20.

when he realized his strength was overmatched, [Monarch] broke down and sobbed."[18] Barely anyone visited Monarch while he was at Golden Gate Park. San Francisco was busy shedding its Wild West past as it grew into a global and cosmopolitan city. Of the few people who visited Monarch at Golden Gate Park, in particular, Herbert Fleishhack would design and build San Francisco's first proper zoo. I can only conjecture that Fleishhack was either appalled by Monarch's sad state or energized by Monarch's effective imprisonment. I wouldn't know: I don't enjoy going to zoos and seeing creatures in captivity, put on display like a living curio cabinet. Of all the years I lived in San Francisco and walked its many streets, I haven't been to the zoo even once. I couldn't point it out on a map if you asked me. It seems to me that walking freely and gawking at creatures who cannot be freed is its own brand of psychic torture.

Kelly, for his part in Monarch's capture and lifelong imprisonment, felt great remorse. "He is independent and militant," Kelly wrote. "He will fight anything . . . and permit no man to handle him. . . . Apparently[,] he has no illusions concerning man and no respect for him as a superior being. He has been beaten by superior cunning, but never conquered, and he gives no parole to refrain from renewing the contest when the opportunity offers."[19] Kelly regarded his successful bear hunt as an empty victory and fled civilization to atone in the wilds of Yosemite National Park as a state forester. Like me, I imagine that Kelly wouldn't find any pleasure in gazing at mournful animals either. I find it ironic that a majestic creature like Monarch can be celebrated in a city named after Francis of Assisi,[20] the patron saint of animals, nature, and sojourners and protector of those who die alone far from home.

18 Kelly p. 20.

19 Kelly pp. 19, 21.

20 Francis of Assisi (né Giovanni di Pietro di Bernardone) was a twelfth–thirteenth century Italian mystic, friar, and founder of the Franciscan order in the Catholic Church. He believed that nature was the mirror of God and that all nonhuman creatures were brethren. In the book *Fioretti di Santo Francesco d'Ascesi* (1864, pp. 39–41), he singlehandedly tamed the man-eating Wolf of Gubbio. The wolf accompanied him and was given an honorable burial after its natural death; a church of peace was built atop the wolf's remains.

Monarch was euthanized in 1911, and his body was buried in Golden Gate Park. Perhaps Franciscan brotherhood just doesn't apply to bears.

When Joseph Grinnell, director and cofounder of the University of California's Museum of Vertebrate Zoology in Berkeley, found out that Monarch had been buried in Golden Gate Park, he tasked one of his students to secretly locate and exhume the bear's remains. Grinnell then taxidermied the bear and gifted it to the California Academy of Sciences. The following year, he would lead the charge for the preservation of "critical habitats" and seed the foundational philosophy of American environmental conservation movements. Grinnell studied microevolution using his own methods—that is, the Grinnell Method,[21] which advocated for local and regional studies of flora and fauna instead of capturing specimens abroad. He would appeal to the morality of habitat destruction, stating, "It is now generally recognized as ethically wrong to jeopardize the existence of any animal species"[22] and that "it's a curious perversion when 'conservation' is appealed to justify destruction."[23]

That same year, 1911, would also see a series of events to memorialize the life and death of Monarch, the last California grizzly bear held in captivity: Charles Scribner and Son reissued the 1860 edition of Hittel and Nahl's illustrated biography of "Grizzly" Adams to much acclaim, the Bear Flag was redesigned with Nahl's 1855 postcard portrait of Old Samson as a model for the bear, and the bear on the newly redesigned state flag was named Monarch. Thirty years after the last wild California grizzly bear was shot and killed in Sequoia National Park and the last Yelamu Ohlone people passed away, bearing away the residue of the Old World and all its magic with them, an artist in Marin County named Donald Graeme Kelly would illustrate the modified design for the California state flag and transform Monarch into his final form: a symbol of perseverance despite his own extinction. Thus, a simple bear who was once monstrous, then defanged, became California's official state animal in 1958.

21 UC Berkeley Museum of Vertebrate Zoology: https://mvz.berkeley.edu/history/the-grinnell-method/.

22 Joseph Grinnell, "Bird Life as a Community Asset," *California Fish and Game*, vol. 1, no. 1, October 1914, pp. 20–22.

23 Joseph Grinnell, "Editorial Notes and News," *The Condor*, vol. XXXIII, May 1931, pp. 131–32.

III. Returning Home Step by Step

Woodward's Gardens was already long gone by the time I moved to the Mission District, over a hundred years later. Gone were the entire collection of animals, sculptures, plans, exhibits, and theme park rides; local business tycoon Adolph Sutro, of the famed Sutro Baths, purchased everything for his vast estate near the western bluffs of Land's End. The city block was divided up into parcels and housed an auto repair shop, a French restaurant, and for a time, a porn studio within a black fortress. I can still remember the distinct smell of bleach as I passed the old brick building. The entire block always smelled like it was trying to wash itself clean.

The new Bear Flag, the one now draped like a curtain behind the governor's televised press events and present in every California school classroom, is a cipher for the cyclical nature of history. (And the parts of history we don't truly want to remember because they are too painful or shameful.)

* * *

Somewhere deep within Golden Gate Park, a discarded pile of twelfth-century Spanish monastic stones from Heart Jr.'s scrapped vanity project mark the place where Monarch spent so many decades dreaming of his old kingdom—manzanita trees twisting into limestone and the bruised silhouette of the San Gabriel Mountains, the Pacific Ocean westward. These stones have been arranged by unseen hands, one on top of the other. A local community of nature-worshipping Druids has claimed this ritual.

* * *

There are some moments between 3:00 p.m. and 5:00 p.m. when the fog starts to roll in from the sea, and the membrane between the truth and dreams becomes transparent.

* * *

I haven't lived in San Francisco for a long time now. When I walk the same path as before, I know I walk only with my memories. The names of the streets are unchanged, but they are paved with intimate experiences that are only meaningful to me: the smell of eucalyptus and wet ferns, the milky belly of a seagull flying overhead, an unexpected explosion of pink jasmine, the way fog dews on your eyelashes. I remember walking so hard, for so long, that the rush of blood in my ears was louder than the ocean. There is a clearing in the wind-worn cypress at Land's End where you can watch the sun winking on waves like foil, and there is a place on the golf course where someone will tap your shoulder and, when you turn around, there is no one there.

* * *

It's been three years since I've walked this path. I know there is no returning to the beginning. When we have finished walking full circle, the world will have already rearranged itself anew. We can try to seek communion with the world. We can try to rewild ourselves, but can you have a conversation with the disappeared? When we say that we are seeking natural habitats, seeking nature, are we merely seeking dreamed utopias? We don't even truly understand what a natural habitat means anymore.

* * *

I remember reading once that when the first Spanish conquistadors initially arrived near Monterey, they saw California grizzly bears eating the carcasses of beached whales. It was on the golden lip of this state where the Europeans discovered that either their maps were wrong, or California was a savage island of monsters and beasts.

* * *

Just when I think that I'm about to lose my balance, my body knows how to right itself again without my instructions.

* * *

What do I know about what a bear thinks? All I can do is take off my mask of humanity and put it on something else for a time. Perhaps that is why we long to escape: we are so tired of ourselves, we would like to be anything else even for a day. And yet, amid the great wilderness, we seek our own faces again, like Rumi's Beloved, in the hopes of being absolutely certain that we are still here.

What I know about a bear is that it doesn't need our regard to exist. What I know about myself is that sometimes I can be monstrous, with an untamed mind and a body that refuses to conform. And perhaps that is simply the nature of everything that fights for its freedom to live in this world.

Stories without End: Communing with Indigenous Cultures along El Camino Real de los Tejas

It's best to begin both journeys and stories in places without roads, preferably with at least one knee and one hand touching the earth. Walk away from the car, away from asphalt, away from campsites and picnicking families, away from signs and even trails. Go where the air is sweet and smells only of green, where the trees are swaying and you can hear the wind moving through the leaves, where you can see water rushing and falling and pooling, where if you're still enough, you'll see small animals wandering through. Oak trees and bald cypress trees abound. The best journeys and stories span not only distances but also time. The difficult thing is that we've been taught that the past is done and gone, that history is dead, that it no longer lives and breathes around us, and not that what was still is and will go on.

McKinney Falls State Park, about ten miles outside of Austin, where Onion Creek meets Williamson Creek, was where I decided to begin my journey and this story. I knew that I wouldn't only be learning about the history of El Camino Real and seeing related historical sites; I would be *feeling* the history. History is neither distant nor objective; history lives in us. My identity and the history of my ancestors are layered and complicated things, but to me, that only emphasizes the need to honor their struggles. And where else to begin my journey but at the point closest to my home?

The stone marker at the entrance of McKinney Falls State Park proudly proclaims it as being part of El Camino Real de los Tejas, now a designated national trail. The 2,500-mile route, used most heavily by the

"Stories without End" by ire'ne lara silva first appeared in *Texas Highways Magazine*, December 2021, https://texashighways.com/culture/people/follow-texas-indigenous-roots-along-el-camino-real-de-los-tejas/, accessed 20 May 2023.

Spanish from the 1600s through the 1800s, leads from Mexico City, Mexico, to Natchitoches, Louisiana, the earliest non-Indigenous settlement in Louisiana. The best way to traverse the Camino Real in Texas on current roads is to start in Laredo. There, you can forge your own journey by experiencing Los Matachines de la Santa Cruz de la Ladrillera perform every December and dance a variation of the traditional matachín, a ritual brought by the Spanish that over time incorporated Mexican, Indigenous, and American symbols. From Laredo, drive Interstate 35 to San Antonio and Austin, and then continue on State Highway 71 and State Highway 21 to Nacogdoches. Along the way, enjoy Texas' different climates: arid desert, tumbleweed and ocotillo country, hills and canyons, green forests, wide rivers, farmland, ranchland, swamps, and as always, the open sky.

"Although not as well known as trails such as the Lewis and Clark Trail or the Oregon Trail, El Camino Real de los Tejas is the second oldest route of European travel in the country," says Steven Gonzales, executive director of El Camino Real de los Tejas National Historic Trail Association, a nonprofit that preserves, promotes, and interprets the US portion of the trail. "It's second only to its sister trail, El Camino Real de Tierra Adentro," a former trade route between Mexico City, Mexico, and San Juan Pueblo, New Mexico.

Artifacts found in McKinney Falls State Park show Indigenous peoples inhabited the area starting nine thousand years ago. The names of the early groups are unknown, but it is believed the Tonkawa, among others, descended from them. Although very few Native Americans in Texas live on reservations, the total population of Native Americans living in the state is close to 350,000. But this does not include millions of Texans of Indigenous descent.

I count myself among them. When I'm asked for a label, I say I'm an Indigenous-identified Mexican American even though I only have one grandparent who came from Mexico and even though I can't tell you which tribal nations I'm descended from. But it would be as much of a lie for me to say I wasn't Mexican as it would be for me to say I wasn't Indigenous. Beyond blood, it is culture and food and language and storytelling and history and spirituality and worldview. I know who I am—the convergence of the history of my family and the history of this land, of Texas. My whole life, I've been fascinated by how Indigenous beliefs embedded themselves in Catholicism in the Americas, how Indigenous language and culture shaped Mexican and Texan language and culture.

"The Camino Real connects people, places, and cultures," Gonzales says. "Without it, we would not be calling Texas *Texas* today."

Most accounts of the Camino Real span the history between its establishment by the Spanish and its use by US immigrant settlers to enter Texas-which-was-then-New-Spain or Texas-which-was-then-Mexico and converting it into Texas-as-its-own-nation. What is true, however, is that the Camino Real was built upon Indigenous trails and trade routes, and Indigenous culture is still alive and present in Texas.

"The sense is that Indigenous people are people of the past," says Liliana Patricia Saldaña, who holds a doctorate in human development and family studies from the University of Wisconsin and is a Chicana activist and scholar at the University of Texas at San Antonio. "This is not the case. It's important for all people in this state to acknowledge that we are working, teaching, and learning in occupied territory, and that we are living and breathing on the ancestral lands of Indigenous people."

Whenever I'm driving, I always think about the names of things: ranches, towns, creeks, rivers, counties, bridges, and parks. I wonder sometimes what visitors to Texas make of the jumble of languages these are made of—mostly Spanish, English, and different Indigenous languages. I think of curious things like how the names of certain places are a combination of languages and time—like the town of Buda, which is an English adaptation of the Spanish word *viuda*, the town's original name. The number of place names in Spanish are beyond counting, but there are also many places that are still known by their original Indigenous names—like Waco, Anahuac, Nacogdoches, Caddo, Tahoka, and Tehuacana, among others. And of course, "Texas" is derived from the Caddo word *Tayshas*, which the Spanish interpreted as *Tejas*. I often wonder if visitors and residents register how the names capture something essential about the history of this state, the history of this land.

Indigenous people who made Texas their home included the Alabamas, Apaches, Aranamas, Atakapans, Bidais, Caddos, Comanches, Choctaws, Coushattas, Hasinais, Jumanos, Karankawas, Kickapoos, Kiowas, Tonkawas, and Wichitas, among others. Texas' second president, Mirabeau B. Lamar, believed there could be "no compromise" between white settlers and Indigenous people "except in their total extinction or total expulsion," he wrote in a letter to the Texas Congress dated December 20, 1838. While the remains of 6,509 children have been located at residential schools across Canada and the United States, Texas never had residential schools—schools established by the respective governments to both educate and indoctrinate native children. Instead, in Texas, Indigenous peoples were killed or removed to Oklahoma. In my research, I came across many references to "hostiles" as well as many mentions of "Indian raids and attacks," but the history books largely fail to acknowledge that Spanish, French, Mexican, and immigrant US settlers were claiming lands that were already inhabited.

As a consequence of centuries of religious conversion, cultural assimilation, and violence, only three Native American reservations exist in Texas today: the Alabama-Coushatta Indian Reservation in Livingston, between Houston and Nacogdoches; the Kickapoo Traditional Tribe of Texas in Eagle Pass, south of Del Río; and the Ysleta de Sur Pueblo in El Paso. While all three offer gaming facilities that are open to the public, the Kickapoo do not grant any further access to nonnatives. The Ysleta de Sur Pueblo, however, have a cultural center, a smoke shop, and other offerings that are open to the public. And the Alabama-Coushatta Reservation, the only one of the three located directly on the Camino Real, hosts a powwow every June and offers camping and dining facilities to visitors.

"It's important to preserve and revitalize our culture and traditions to ensure that future generations can learn and engage in these types of events, and to teach how our people relied on natural resources as provided by the Creator," says Bryant Celestine, tribal archivist for the Alabama-Coushatta. To combat the way "Native Americans have been erased from the textbooks," according to Celestine, the Alabama-Coushatta organize school programs and presentations to educate kids.

Centuries of violence and shame have not erased the Indigenous identification or cultural reclamation efforts of many Mexican Americans, Tejanos, or Mexican-Texans. "Our mission is to reeducate people who identify as Hispanic or Latino to reclaim their Indigeneity," says Mario Garza of the Indigenous Cultures Institute, an organization in San Marcos that hosts an annual powwow and has a summer program that uses the arts to teach children about Indigenous culture and the Coahuiltecan language. "Ashamed of being considered a second-class citizen, many Indigenous people claimed Tejano/Mexican as their only identity."

Between 1632 and 1793, Spanish settlers built missions, presidios, and settlements along much of the Camino Real. In addition to their attempts to displace Indigenous people and convert them to Catholicism, the Spanish also used the Camino Real to investigate rumors of French colonization attempts in Texas. In 1996, the French fort La Salle, established in 1685, was rediscovered by historians and declared an archaeological site. Their findings are viewable at the Bullock Texas State History Museum in Austin.

Most of the multiple roads that formed the Camino Real ran through Yanaguana, the name of the Payaya tribe's village that became San Antonio. Five of the twenty-six missions that were built in Texas still stand in San Antonio—Mission Concepción, Mission San Juan, Mission San José, Mission Espada, and Mission San Antonio de Valero (otherwise known as the Alamo). The 475-acre San Antonio Missions National Historical Park includes the first four missions as well as various irrigation resources, agricultural fields, and pre- and postcolonial historical sites. You can learn more about the missions through programming and events offered by American Indians in Texas at the Spanish Colonial Missions, a nonprofit formed by the Tap Pilam Coahuiltecan Nation.

In San Antonio, I spent some time at Mission Concepción before making my way to the other missions. My maternal grandmother's name was Concepción, and so I thought of my mother while I was there. She never had any doubts about our identity. We were *Indios*, of Indigenous descent from both sides of the border. My father was much more conflicted: in one breath, he would bring up his pure-blooded Native great-grandmother, and in the next, he would point to his own pale skin and his blond-haired, blue-eyed sister as proof that he was wholly Spanish. While my parents were Catholic and regular attendees at Sunday mass, I never felt any sense of spirituality there. When my mother really needed to pray, she never went inside a church. Her favorite place was the grotto and garden at San Juditas Tadeo (St. Jude Thaddeus) in Pharr. Neither rain nor one-hundred-degree heat would keep her from praying in a space open to the sky, surrounded by green, leafing things.

I wondered what she would make of the missions, where the buildings and stone walls bear a sense of immense age. What she would say if I told her about the remains of Indigenous bodies there, that mission records from 1762 show that in the same year, 792 Native Americans were baptized while 596 were buried?

My heart heavy, I made my way to Mission San Juan, with its imposing walls, and then the much more welcoming Mission San José. I spent the most time at Mission Espada, as it was so incredibly peaceful, and the creek and aqueduct drew my eye. I couldn't resist stopping in the middle of the small bridge on the way to Mission Espada. On one side, the water was a calm and luscious green. On the other, a melodic white froth falling downward. Everywhere: wide-branched mesquites, cottonwoods, retamas, and more. The bridge was small and unprepossessing, but I felt a palpable sense of crossing between one world and another. I don't know if I'll ever be able to be in San Antonio again without wanting to visit that bridge.

In the few miles between the Alamo and Mission Espada, it seems like you see all of San Antonio—the Riverwalk and downtown office buildings, residential neighborhoods and schools, condos and golf courses, strip malls, fast-food chains, taquerias, and houses with abundantly flowery gardens with forests and farmland in the distance. Roadside banners mark the way from one mission to another, so it's impossible to get lost. It's not many miles long, but you can't help but think about how long it would have taken someone on foot or horseback to travel that distance three hundred years ago.

Before my El Camino Real journey, I'd never heard of Caddo Mounds State Historic Site. More than 1,200 years ago near present-day Nacogdoches, close to the eastern end of the Camino Real, the Hasinai built a village that became the southwesternmost ceremonial center of the Mound Builder culture. Mound Builders were Indigenous people located in the regions around the Great Lakes, Ohio River Valley, and Mississippi River and its tributaries. Over a period of five thousand years, they built earthworks, also known as mounds, many of which can still be seen today. Mounds were dedicated to purposes ranging from ceremonial to religious. Three earthen mounds can still be visited at the Caddo Historic Site: the Temple Mound, the Low Platform Mound, and the Burial Mound. A 2019 tornado tore down the Grass House and the visitor center, but rebuilding plans are underway. "We are on the highest plateau—a perfect place for the Caddo Indians to build a village and ceremonial center—away from the flood plain," says Anthony Souther, site manager at Caddo Mounds State Historic Site. Abundant sunshine blankets the forests on the 375-acre site that includes markers for the sections of the Camino Real that runs through it.

While the Camino Real facilitated travel for the Spanish northward, it also facilitated travel southward and westward for immigrant US settlers. In Nacogdoches, you can visit the Gaines-Oliphant House and the Durst-Taylor Historic House and Gardens, two of the earliest pre-Republic white settler structures built in Texas. The Austin area, originally named Waterloo, saw white settlers in the early 1830s.

Researching the Camino Real induced weeks and weeks of deep grieving. As a poet and fiction writer, I write grief. I write Texas. I also write love and nature and transformation and creation, but all of that is always rooted in both grief and Texas. I'm Texan to the very tips of my fingers—hasta las puntitas de mis dedos. I was born here, I've lived almost all my life here, and I plan to die and be buried here. There is no sky I love as much as this sky, no earth I love as much as this earth. I swear even the sun shines differently here.

But that doesn't mean I'm blind to the truth of Texas' past and present. Obscuring history does nothing to help us understand the Texas we are, the Texas we've been, or the Texas we'll someday be.

I traveled no further on the Camino Real than the Caddo Mounds. It felt like a fitting bookend to my journey as I took in the sunshine, the wind; watched the tall grass sway; touched the earth that in some ways was inviolate—to be able to touch that which was inviolate within me. I sat under the blue sky and felt in my body and on my skin how time had and had not passed. I wanted to sit there and think about history and the Camino Real. Traveling it from one end to the other, or sampling it in parts, exposes you to centuries worth of layered stories and events. There is always a *before*. The story of Texas is a story of layers, of people and cultures through time, of what endures or doesn't from earlier layers.

Driving back to Austin from the Caddo Mounds, I thought about how the best stories and journeys have no endings. We're taught to think all stories must end, either tragically or with "happily ever after." But then there are the stories that even after the last page, or the last spoken word, leave you knowing that the story has not ended, that the characters are still living their lives, and you might hear more about what else happened.

I kept hearing the words of my fellow Indigenous-identified Mexican American, the writer Gloria Anzaldúa, born and buried in Hargill: "This land was Mexican once, was Indian always and is. And will be again."

Sara L. Spurgeon

My Father Once Showed Me an Arrowhead

The summer I was nine, before my father's brain abruptly met his windshield on a lonely highway outside Salina, Kansas, he used to stand with me in our backyard in Topeka. In my memory, it is always summer, hot but not scorching, a little humid. Not unlike that terrible day in May, after which I would have only memories of him. The lawn he carefully tended is always lush, a deep, perfect emerald falling from the back of our white, two-story house down a gentle, rolling slope to my mother's careful plantings of daylilies and tiger lilies, gladiolas, and peonies. Cicadas drone their endless hypnotic chant in the dark reaches of the elms shading the house. Like my father, the trees and their fierce tiny singers are unaware of their own fast-approaching doom in the form of Dutch elm disease.

"See there," my father always says, pointing somewhere beyond the perfectly trimmed lawn. In my memory, he's just finished mowing and the scent of fresh-cut grass is heavy and gorgeous, like the perpetual sunshine yellow as pollen on my bare arms. He gestures beyond my mother's flowers, past our back fence. "That's where covered wagons would roll through a hundred years ago," he says.

Was he pointing to an actual place? Some lacunae between our neighbor's backyard and ours? Or to something even more ephemeral, an invisible flood of history rushing away from us in the opposite direction from the approaching Dutch elm disease and his Buick's windshield?

"There used to be massive herds of buffalo right here," he says. "The pioneers could look out of their covered wagons and see them, some of them probably walking right through our backyard."

In illustrations I'd seen in books at school, the velvety brown humps of buffalo on their absurdly dainty legs always plodded across tall, yellow prairie grass, not the short Kentucky bluegrass or zoysia on which my father and I stood. Like the elms and cicadas and my father, the big bluestem and switchgrass probably couldn't see the zoysia coming for them. Probably, the buffalo were no more able to understand what the pioneers in their covered wagons portended than my father could on that May afternoon when he would gaze through the windshield of his Buick for the last time.

Do all things believe in their own perpetuity?

Maybe not all things. Once, my father showed me an arrowhead he kept in the top drawer of the antique oak desk in his office. He reached into a little square box built into the front corner of the drawer, lined with dark green velvet the same shade as the zoysia in our backyard, and gently lifted the arrowhead out of its bed. It rested in the center of his palm, faceted and notched, gray and blue and cloudy and shiny all at the same time. It was made from chert, he said. A kind of flint commonly found in the Flint Hills of Kansas and Oklahoma.

He had exhumed the arrowhead as he shoveled out a square hole in a corner of our backyard, first slicing through the zoysia before peeling back the turf like skin to remove several square yards of rich, black loam squirming with earthworms. He framed out the hole in the earth with wooden planks, then filled it with sand. My younger brothers and I would spend hours sifting through that sandbox, first under the cool, dark shade of the elms, then later not, searching futilely for an arrowhead like the one cradled in my father's hand, dug from our own backyard after being dropped there a hundred, maybe five hundred, maybe a thousand years ago.

"Dropped by who?" I asked.

Of course, I knew about Indians. Our state, I had learned in school, was named for the Kansa tribe. Kansa, our teacher said, meant "People of the South Wind." Those had been good Indians, with a name like poetry. I also knew there were bad Indians who attacked brave pioneers in covered wagons, shooting at them with arrows, presumably tipped with arrowheads like this one. It had not occurred to me until that moment they might be the same Indians.

"Did an Indian shoot that arrowhead at a buffalo?" I asked, "Or at a pioneer?"

I couldn't, at the time, formulate the *real* question I wanted to ask, but its shape hung in the air between my father and me. I touched the cool flint still cupped in his palm and found no blood on its sharp, perfect tip. And yet I sensed for the first time that our backyard might be full of invisible blood, as it was full of buffalo and Indians and pioneers in covered wagons moving in their river of history beyond my mother's daylilies and peonies, swirling like dark water around the soon-to-be ghosts of the elms.

Memory fails when I try to recall his answer, but I remember watching him put the arrowhead back, pushing the drawer gently shut with his thumb. Did he dismiss my question? Refuse to speculate? Mumble something before turning away? Whatever answer he offered was, I understood even then, unsatisfactory. The Indians were not like the big bluestem or the buffalo or my father. They knew exactly what was coming for them.

* * *

Like my father, my mother grew up in the Great Plains, in a small wooden house built by my grandfather outside Rolette, North Dakota, a hardscrabble rural town jammed up against the Turtle Mountain Chippewa Reservation (Mikinaakwajiwing in Ojibway) and the Canadian border. The oldest picture I have of my mother is a black-and-white square photo from the early 1940s edged with a white border. She is probably five years old, wearing a short dress, bobbed hair, and a skeptical expression. Her younger sister, maybe three, stands solemnly next to her in a matching dress, one pudgy finger in her mouth. Between them, invisible, is a tiny ghost—their brother, who died as a baby and about whom neither my grandmother nor grandfather could ever bear to speak.

Behind my mother and her sister and the ghost of their dead baby brother looms a line of my grandmother's hollyhocks. The upright stems of the hollyhocks are like spears thrust straight into the earth, incongruously festooned top to bottom with open-faced blossoms so intensely colored that they seem to radiate brightness straight from their tiny, dark centers like fierce little suns.

Behind the house, not visible in the photo but there nonetheless, is the open prairie. In those days, it was still blanketed with yellow prairie grass, although patchworked as well with soybeans and wheat and pasture for livestock, mostly dairy and beef cattle the pioneers brought to replace the buffalo they had slaughtered. They killed the buffalo, I would later learn, to keep them from eating grass the settlers wanted for their cows, and to keep the Indians from eating the buffalo they wanted to keep themselves and their families from starving.

My grandfather was not a farmer or rancher, however. His mother immigrated from Norway to a small town in Minnesota with my grandfather when he was a baby. The story was that her husband in Norway had died, but that story was always accompanied by a series of wordless glances exchanged by the adults. In Minnesota, a place also newly emptied of as many buffalo and Indians as early settlers could manage to kill, she married another Norwegian immigrant, and they had seven children. My grandfather's new stepfather was a quietly vicious man who drank steadily before backhanding his wife and her son. When my grandfather was thirteen, he shoved his stepfather in the chest, interrupting the beating being administered to his mother, and as a result left home—either thrown out or run away, depending on which of my grandfather's younger half-siblings was telling this story.

At fourteen, my grandfather found a position as an apprentice to a pair of Norwegian brothers who, as master carpenters under the old guild system brought over from Norway, were qualified to take an apprentice. When he turned twenty-one and became a journeyman, they gifted him a set of carpenter's tools, their wooden handles decorated after the Os style of rosemaling, carved instead of painted, with twining, five-petaled wild roses, stylized tulips, ivy, berries, and a tiny, cheeky squirrel holding an acorn on the handle of one of the awls. By the time I touched those tools as a child, the carvings were worn nearly smooth from the forceful caress of my grandfather's hands.

When he graduated from apprentice to journeyman carpenter, he took his toolbox and his flowered tools and headed west, stopping to work and earn a few dollars in each of the towns he passed through. He would later tell me his intention was to reach the Pacific coast. Washington or Oregon. Maybe Northern California. Places palisaded with the biggest trees in the world, lunging toward a sky as blue as the Pacific Ocean he would never see.

My favorite picture of my grandfather was taken on the patio of our backyard in Topeka. The photo is in color and quite nicely composed, shot by my father with one of his heavy, expensive cameras my brothers and I were forbidden to touch. In the photo, my grandfather sits on one of our heavy redwood patio chairs, its fat 1970s cushions patterned with a splashy, abstract flower print flush with harvest gold petals and avocado green leaves. It is late August, so the cicadas are buzzing hypnotically from the dim, green tops of the elms. The daylilies and peonies are past their prime, but beside the chair is a massive cast-iron pot, pitted and dull black, standing on three stumpy legs. My father told me it might have sat in a campfire on a cattle drive and held stew for a dozen hungry cowboys. My mother filled it with potting soil and geraniums, their scarlet blossoms exploding in the photo against the dark green of their ruffled leaves and the flat blackness of the pot.

Beside the geraniums, my grandfather tenderly holds my youngest brother, born just a few weeks before the photo was taken. He is the youngest grandchild, the one everybody says looks just like my grandfather, with white-blond hair and blue eyes and the classic Norwegian ski-jump nose. My grandfather's head is bent, his forehead nearly touching his grandson's forehead, their profiles uncannily similar. Both have closed their eyes. At first glance this is a sweet photograph, peaceful, joyous. But the expression on my grandfather's face is more complicated than peace. Only many years later would I realize my new baby brother was not just the grandchild that looked most like my grandfather; he was also the grandchild that looked most like the baby boy who was born and then died between the births of my mother and my aunt, a tiny ghost cradled along with my brother in my grandfather's arms.

Instead of finding redwoods above the crashing waves of the Pacific when he headed west, my grandfather found my grandmother in the nearly treeless prairies of North Dakota. She was born on a farm outside Rolette, not far from where my grandfather would build a little wooden house and bury their only son in a heartbreakingly small pine box in the backyard.

My grandmother was the third oldest child of thirteen, or the fourth oldest of fourteen, depending on how one counts dead children. She had two older sisters and an identical twin born moments before her who perished beside her at the age of five in the little cot in which they both lay, struck down together with smallpox. Although she survived the smallpox that killed her twin sister, every summer when my grandmother's arms and neck grew tanned from working in her garden, the pale, untanned smallpox scars emerged like cloudy white drops of milk on her skin.

My grandmother told me once that she had almost no memory of her mother in which her mother was not pregnant. She said she and her two sisters would lie together in their shared bed at night listening to their mother in the next room beg their father to leave her alone, she couldn't stand another birth, the next baby would kill her, please. Please. When she was fourteen, she and her sisters lay in bed listening to their mother beg their father to hitch up the wagon and take her to town so she could have this baby in the hospital—something wasn't right. Please. Instead, her father roused the girls and told them to help their mother deliver their sibling. My grandmother called this baby, whom she adored and helped raise, unlucky number thirteen, despite the numerical ambiguity of his placement. He was the thirteenth child in her counting, he weighed a brutal thirteen pounds when she and her sisters pulled him from their mother, and he even had thirteen letters in his name. Her mother never got out of bed again, succumbing to what was still called, in those days, "childbed fever." Her father told the girls to be sure to get the bloodstains out of the sheets next time they did the laundry.

Several years later, my grandmother and her favorite sister would regularly sneak away from their father's farmhouse by climbing out of their second-story bedroom window. They would shinny onto the broad branches of the only tree in their yard, an ancient, gnarled cottonwood that grew gratifyingly close to the house and that, like thousands of female cottonwood trees on the Great Plains, would later be cut down by the descendants of the pioneers because their annual release of cottony, seed-bearing fluff was deemed messy. The settlers were unaware cottonwoods helped stabilize the soil of the land they had taken, anchoring the banks of creeks and rivers and filtering much of the water that would eventually end up beneath the trees' sturdy root systems in the Ogallala Aquifer. The mass removal of cottonwoods would immeasurably worsen the effects of the oncoming drought that would take up the weakened soil of the prairies and use it to choke the land so thoroughly the entire region would be labeled a dustbowl.

Delivered safely on the ground by the old cottonwood, the girls would walk three miles on a rutted dirt track with the star-speckled prairie sky arching black and glittering above them to attend Friday night dances. The oldest photo I have of my grandmother was taken by a traveling photographer sometime in the late 1920s. She and her sister used money saved from selling eggs in town to buy fabric, buttons, thread, and thin strips of raccoon fur to use as trim to secretly sew themselves fancy, flapper-style dresses for dancing. One day, they stuffed the secret dresses in a basket, told their father they were going to walk to town to buy flour and lard, and then changed into the dresses to have their picture taken by the traveling photographer. In the photo, they stand side by side, my grandmother in a coffee-colored dress of cheap imitation satin cunningly edged at its daring knee-length hem with raccoon fur, her sister in a nearly identical dress in pale ivory. Both girls have their hair bobbed, finger waves carefully rippling down to point at their cheekbones. They stare at the camera with solemn expressions behind which lurk laughter, a crinkled eye, a quirked lip.

No town of fewer than five hundred people could support more than one dance hall, although Rolette's lone establishment also drew patrons—like my grandmother and her sister—from the surrounding countryside and much of Rolette County. It did not draw dancers from the Turtle Mountain Indian Reservation, although the reservation today has over six thousand citizens and Native Americans make up 70 percent of the county's residents. Instead, in those days, the reservation had its own dance hall and held competing Friday night dances. While my grandmother and her sister sometimes danced in Rolette with other descendants of brave pioneers, generally they went to the dance hall on the reservation where the Indians happily took their ten-cent entrance fee and treated their colonizers far better than their colonizers treated them. The Indians, my grandmother told me, were generally superior dancers and favored a "sexy French-style polka" rather than the non-French, nonsexy polka danced in town. Yes, she said, sometimes she danced with Indian boys, whom she found both polite and excellent dance partners.

Then one Friday night when she was nineteen, a handsome blond boy no one had seen before showed up at the dance hall on the reservation and began to enthusiastically learn the sexy French polka. A carpenter from Minnesota, he danced beautifully. And he fully supported both my grandmother's love of dancing and her vow to have only three children, no more. In the end, they would have either three or two, depending on how one counts dead children.

Their oldest child, my mother, left North Dakota as soon as she was able. She inherited her father's round face and ski-jump nose, along with her mother's shapely mouth, long, graceful hands, and her green thumb. My grandmother grew tomatoes and cucumbers, corn and squash, string beans, carrots, potatoes, and beets. She canned and preserved much of it to feed them all through the long northern winters, especially during the 1930s when my grandfather's customers could no longer pay cash and instead traded for his carpentry services with cow's milk, a butchered pig, eggs from their hens. While her vegetable garden was nearly an eighth of an acre, my grandmother could afford only a tiny flower garden; her daughter had the opposite.

Although my mother reserved a small section in the far corner for vegetables, her flowerbeds took up the entire lower third of our large backyard in Topeka. She had inherited her eye for color and design so prominent in the secret dresses. Her flowerbeds were arranged for dramatic impact; tall, elegant stands of iris and gladiolas behind riotously rainbowed zinnias bordered with ox-eye daisies shockingly white beside them. My mother even managed to grow fussy, shade-loving hostas and sweet violets under the doomed elms where a coolly shadowed microclimate offered a seductive, though ultimately transitory, protection.

In our living room in Topeka, my mother had a large brass pot with a golden pothos that climbed a thick, square, four-foot-tall sphagnum moss post. The stems of the pothos vines were as big around as my little finger and enveloped the moss post entirely, their green- and gold-splashed leaves covering it like a glossy cloak. My grandmother had given my mother a cutting from the golden pothos in her own living room in the little wooden house in North Dakota in 1954, on the day my mother moved to Grand Forks to go to nursing school.

* * *

My grandfather left school at age thirteen when he ran away / was thrown out of his stepfather's house and, when prompted by us children, would give my grandmother a wink and declare he never missed it. My grandmother, however, had loved going to school, even in a one-room schoolhouse so frigid in the North Dakota winter children would walk to school across the frozen prairie carrying both their schoolbooks and a hot potato, hastily excavated each morning from where it had been buried the night before in the banked coals of their family's wood-burning stove. They would shove the hot potato in their coat pocket and use it to warm their hands as they sat at their desks in the morning, breath smoking in the small, icy room until the school's wood-burning stove and the close-packed young bodies raised the temperature to something resembling comfort. Each child then ate their potato for lunch.

Like her two older sisters, my grandmother had been forbidden by her father from returning to school after her mother died. My mother, on the other hand, not only graduated from high school but finished her four-year nursing degree in three years. She was valedictorian of her high school graduating class (which she always laughingly pointed out consisted of only nine students), but she was also valedictorian of her graduating class at the Deaconess School of Nursing. This honor helped her get a rather prestigious job for a brand-new graduate, at the world-renowned Menninger Clinic's pediatric hospital in Topeka, Kansas. The Menninger Foundation provided small apartments for its unmarried female nurses, and my mother moved in with her nursing books, two small cardboard suitcases, and the cutting from her mother's precious and exotic golden pothos.

She met my father in the clinic's hallway. He was working his way through college as an orderly, mopping floors and emptying trash cans. Once he graduated and they married, she would use her salary as a pediatric nurse to support him through law school, after which he would be hired as an attorney at a well-respected law firm in Topeka and they would buy a white, two-story house with a spacious lawn, mature elm trees, and an antique oak desk for his office.

* * *

Two days after the police knocked on our front door to tell my mother my father had crushed his brain against his windshield, my grandmother arrived. My grandfather had been away from Rolette when the news came, necessitating that he catch a later flight. The day my grandmother arrived, my youngest brother—the one who looked the most like my grandfather—was two years old and napping upstairs along with my mother, who was so stricken with shock she could barely speak. My grandmother bustled around the kitchen, washing dishes and wiping countertops before telling me to take my other brother outside to play. He and I were nearly as stunned and confused as the adults, too young to fully understand what had happened but too old to sink into the untroubled, flush-cheeked slumber of our youngest brother.

It was May, a week or two early for the cicadas, but the sulfur-yellow butterflies had already begun hovering over my mother's tulips, purple petunias, and daisies, occasionally making erratic crossings of the velvety green lawn to investigate the sweet violets under the elms. I stood for a while, picking restlessly at the bark on one of the elms while my brother halfheartedly shoved his Tonka trucks around the sandbox. I could not settle myself, could not fully name the anguish rushing through me like the invisible river of buffalo and blood, as though the vast lacunae my father had so often pointed at had somehow moved from our backyard into my small body. The notion that I could stand in my backyard forever but my father would never again join me seemed unthinkable. Unbearable. Every time my brain came near the thought it skittered away, and I had to concentrate on drawing in a breath, pushing out a breath, drawing in a breath, pushing out a breath.

Eventually, I let myself back in the house and slipped quietly into the living room where our dachshund, Penny, luxuriated in a slanted rectangle of sunlight. The top half of her sinewy body, russet as autumn leaves and sleek as a seal, stretched under our round, stone-topped coffee table. I wiggled under the coffee table and curled myself against her, stroking her velvety hound dog ears and staring absently up at the bottom of the table, poised above us.

The coffee table had been in the house when my parents bought it, along with other pieces of old furniture my father restored. Four slender, gently curved oak legs supported a round bentwood hoop. Like a wagon wheel, I imagined, on top of which rested a circular slab of polished limestone. The limestone, which my father told me had been quarried in eastern Kansas, was a hundred different shades of cream and ivory, but more beautiful in my opinion were the multitude of tiny fossils embedded in it—little sea creatures with intricately folded shells like clams or the spiraling shells of snails, some round, some long and pointed, a special few sparkling with quartz crystal that my father explained had filled in their vanished bodies, turning them to stone millions of years ago when all of Kansas, even our backyard, was just the muddy bottom of a prehistoric sea alive with creatures from species already ancient when dinosaurs first abandoned the oceans for dry land.

From under the coffee table, I could hear my grandmother talking to my grandfather on the phone in the kitchen. Her voice, a soothing contralto tattered around the edges like old velvet, was the only sound in our now strangely quiet house. At one point, she stuck her head out the kitchen doorway to scan the living room, but I was drowsy and still, half in the square of sunlight, half cuddled under the coffee table with Penny, and so she didn't see me. Her side of the phone conversation with my grandfather was a comforting murmur that I heard—as children often do with adult conversations—without really listening to it. What time was my grandfather's flight exactly? Oh, in all the rush she had forgotten to pack her shower cap and bedroom slippers; could my grandfather bring them?

Then: "He was drunk. Again. After six months sober. Six months!" For a moment, I couldn't understand her words. They seemed to belong to an unknown language I didn't speak. She said, "The deputy told her when he got the car door open, empty whiskey bottles rolled right out at his feet." I froze with my hand on Penny's warm red flank, my brain gone equally motionless, soundless as the blank space of my grandmother pausing to listen to whatever my grandfather said to her across the telephone wire from the little wooden house in North Dakota. And then, "He swerved across into oncoming traffic and hit a semi head-on. Thank God the truck-driver is alright, or this could've been even more awful." Then another black, suffocating pause in which I felt the vanished waters of the ancient sea rushing back and drowning me in my living room.

"His head hit the windshield." Her voice wobbled. "He's in a coma now and they don't expect him to wake up. Even if he does, they said his brain is too badly damaged and he'll probably . . . he'll never . . ." My grandmother made a noise somewhere between a moan and a gasp. I imagined the vanished sea choking her as well.

I don't recall the rest of the conversation, although I must have heard it. I remember instinctively pressing my hand hard against the limestone slab above me, its unpolished underneath surface rough and cool against my palm. As though my hand alone could stop whatever had just fallen, or was about to fall, or would fall for the next hundred years on me and my mother and my brothers—the youngest of whom looked just like my grandfather and was sleeping upstairs with my mother's grief-wracked body curled around him much like I was curled around Penny. As though my nine-year-old hand could hold back the rush of ancient seas and my father's windshield, dead buffalo and elm trees, pioneers and Indians shooting exquisite blue-gray arrowheads at wagonloads of killers right in my own backyard. Knowing exactly what was coming for them. Unable to stop it, but somehow bound to try.

Part III

Practices

> Hands joined by grass, can we bend our heads together and make a braid to honor the earth? And then I'll hold it for you, while you braid too.
>
> Robin Wall Kimmerer, *Braiding Sweetgrass*

The Windmill

For Sapphire Skye who walks softly on the earth

We stuffed pillowcases with dirty laundry,
filled recycled empty lard pails with soap flakes,
brought the washboard too and
walked the three miles to the windmill,
because Nálí said we should go early
before the men came to fill their
water barrels.

Late summer rains had poured from female clouds
that left puddles and ponds on the thirsty earth
and curls of delicate and dried mud, like a jigsaw puzzle
that crumbled in our hands whenever we tried to move a piece
no matter how carefully we lifted them,
like they were only meant for admiration,
not meant to be disturbed,
not to be touched
by hand or foot,
these mud cracks that splintered the desert floor.

We followed the path into and out of the sandy wash
toward the windmill past the place where
rabbitbrush and the ubiquitous tumbleweeds grew wild and,
still fiercely seaweed green,
grew their yearly bundle of sharp points
that stabbed at our bare legs
whenever we got close.

They spread themselves thickly over Halgai,[1]
until the seasons part and they begin to pull away
leaving their legs buried,
no longer rooted to the earth,
surrender themselves to the autumn winds
to blow them aimlessly like a vagabond
across the dry flatlands until caught
on the jagged points of barbed wire fence
surrounding my aunt's land,
no longer a traveler
in this place called "whiteness all around,"
a place that grows few colors
and allows trees to give only
skinny shade.

To the north the windmill stood—a beacon, an oasis—
that spun a dissonant tune with percussionist metal blades
smeared against the empty sky
bringing the scent of water to the surface that
beckoned the four-leggeds and us,
to embrace the wetness that created the Bitter Water People,
to drink the precious water brought home in barrels
not to waste, not to play with because,
only the clouds have the freedom to scatter water
willy-nilly.

Our pilgrimage complete, we opened
our bags of laundry, like an offering,
because no water flows
in Nálí, her house,
so, we perform our ablutions in public
at the windmill
as modestly as possible.

1 Prairie.

Old Man Plummer, the self-appointed marshal of the community water,
watched from his windows—house and pickup truck—and
kept a pointed eye out for anything fishy,
for any violators who dared to play with the water,
interlopers who would let the water run
through their fingers without destination,
any water flowing in the direction of anarchy
                                        must be stopped in its tracks.

From the dirt road came a rumbling
bringing Old Man Plummer.
He reined in his battered truck
and rolled down the window;
it flashed silver in the morning light,
poked out his head and shouted
hey'! díító doo daanéé át'éeda!
                    hey'! this water is not to play in!

We stopped our washing, turned to his voice;
my cousin and I had let the water run freely
through our hair, washed our laundry,
had rubbed a rebel tune against the metal washboard
that created streams of water conspiring with soap to make bubbles
that flowed in every direction beneath our bare feet.
We were insurgents of the water which
                                        went against his grain.

Nálí, our protector, our grandma shield,
not one to acquiesce so easily,
let him go on before she rebuked him,
díí doo nitó at'ée da,
        this water doesn't belong to you,

then paused before adding,
nihi éé' táá dadiigisgo biniinaa niikai,
        we came to do our laundry,

part declaration, part appeasement because he is her clan brother,
as such, must be given respect.

He scanned our clothing fluttering
in the breeze on the sagging fence line,
a composition of laundry—
Nálí, her three-tiered skirts and her flowered-print blouses
danced partnerless in the wind;
her boxer shorts fluttered freely with the breeze;
our panties and bras waved "hello,"
which he took all in.
He may have been the self-appointed officer of water,
but Nálí was not to be challenged either,
because women's words can be stones or clouds.

He kicked his truck into gear, turned around,
and left a cloud of dust billowing behind him
leaving us to our rebel work at the windmill
where water is God,
where God is water.

Feeding You

I have slipped *chile* under your skin
secretly wrapped in each enchilada
hot and soothing
carefully cut into bitefuls for you as a toddler
increasing in power and intensity as you grew
until it could burn
forever

silently spiced into the rice
soaked into the bean *caldo*
smoothed into the avocado

I have slipped *chile* under your skin
drop by fiery drop
until it ignited
the sunaltar fire
in your blood

I have squeezed *cilantro* into the breast milk
made sure you were nurtured with
the clean taste of corn stalks
with the wildness of thick leaves
of untamed *monte*
of unscheduled growth

I have ground the earth of these *Américas* in my *molcajete*
until it became a fine and piquant spice
sprinkled it surely into each spoonful of food
that would have to expand to fit your soul

Dear *Mijo*, Dear *Mija*,
Dear Corn *Chile Cilantro Mijitos*
This
is your *herencia*
This
is what is yours
This
is what your mother fed you
to keep you
alive

I Should Like to Fall in Love with a Burro Named Saturnino

I should like to fall in love
with a burro named Saturnino
and sleep murmuring
that name as lullaby.

Warm my bed
with a *xoloitzcuintli*
the color of blue corn,
and will myself to be reborn
sunflower, ever
faithful to the sun.

I should like to learn to love
with the monogamous
passion of the parrot
and the foolish
valor of the *chihuahua*.

I should love to dedicate
my morning glory years
to the inspirational ants, who
peacefully and, without remorse
or humor, successfully evict me
from my shower every winter,
lessons in nonviolent persuasion.

"I Should Like to Fall in Love with a Burro Named Saturnino" by Sandra Cisneros first appeared in *Woman without Shame: Poems*, Vintage, 2023.

I have much to learn from
the sentinel *maguey* about
fortitude, resilience, patience
in this season of *los santos*
inocentes de la política.

And day by day I am a student
of the morning sky.
And night by night I memorize
The sermon of the guru moon.

Next to my door
there is an *ixtle* rope
attached to a bronze bell
announcing visitors.

It does not ring when dawn arrives
with her furious scent of *bolillos,*
orange peels, and doorways
flushing buckets of Fabuloso
across wet stone.

Every day the same as the one before.
And never as the one before. Each moment
wrapped in newsprint and twine
and delivered always on time.

Kimberly Blaeser

I was built by inherited hungers. This is not a poem that names them.

i.

As a body politic we take up space in their ledgers.
Yes, my relatives are the salvage bodies of history.[1]

We have ways they do not approve of.
How we feed ourselves for one:

I have been taught where to find the winter cache of squirrels—
and how to walk away.

We learn from makwa, from maa'ingan—sometimes, even from
Nanaboozhoo.

My Aunties caution you cannot tell stories
until you visit the places where they make their homes. So we walk.

Spring comes overnight, but we plant slow.
Old ones swear garden songs call the pollinators—
and we must sing in tune.

1 As a verb, *salvage* means to collect or rescue . . . or more generally to save something from harm or ruin. Salvage ethnography is the recording of the practices and folklore of cultures threatened with extinction, including as a result of modernization. It is generally associated with the American anthropologist Franz Boas; he and his students aimed to record vanishing Native American cultures.

Nimaamaa said leave some for the spirits and the little people
(and what she meant was we are small in the green frayed body of belonging).

By this I mean not everything tattered is ruined.

ii.

They believe I was built of equations for gain.[2]
(This poem is not an anthem for the fatted calf.)

We still follow picto-spirits,
animal tracks, and seed paths:

Not all of our tools have price tags.

Not all of our safeguards are weapons.

You will not find *wild game* in our lexicon.

Ask yourself— are we the meat they covet?

2 How is a fatted calf different from a regular calf? A fattened calf (Samuel 28:24) was one that had been set aside for a special occasion. While most cattle simply grazed in fields, these select animals were fed in a stall. The extra food and the inability to roam freely meant that they would gain more weight.

||||Walled in Her Dreaming. Subject |||| Position||||

I've been measuring it. The wall.
I spent nights woken up
immersed in the wall's forensic characteristics. Nobody
officially knows how many pillars make
the wall. Like the detribalized and nonrecognized
Indigenous,
nobody keeps track of numbers.

||||Blurrrrrrrrr. Fogggggggg.||||

Each time I go counting, I'm surrounded.
Armed CBP. Drones. Twenty-four-hour cameras spin 360 degrees
remotely controlled. White blimps, salvaged
from a Pentagon repurposing pile surveils me at
ten thousand feet above collecting aerostats. A net
of underground magnetic
seismic and infrared sensors detecting
movement along the riverbank.

Fiber optics eyeing,
I wonder how many pillars make up the wall. I want
to know. I spend months obsessing.
Years walled, forgotten, damned,
revealing numbers, in genocide, is
an emphasized activity.

Michelle Otero

The Shrinking River Age

Conservancy district trucks block the ditch entrance. I cross to the other bank, the one I usually avoid because the fenced-in dogs on that side are louder, more aggressive. They require more work on my part to keep Roxie, our ninety-pound pit bull / Great Dane mix in line. Two men wearing blue conservancy district vests weed whack acequia banks, lowering the blades as Roxie and I traverse fragments of horsetail, sunflower, carrizo, nightshade, and Russian thistle. I think of us as a spring bride and maid crossing a threshold of rose petals to a waiting groom. In reality, I am fifty years old and have been married just over a decade, and Roxie is my contemporary in dog years, each year now revealing itself in her graying snout, the slight tremble in hind legs when she settles onto her cushion for sleep—although she still tears out of our garage ready to fight the rottweilers who live across the street. She settles into a rhythm once we reach the ditch path and slows her pace by the time we round the last corner back to the house. Though she still doesn't play nicely with other dogs, she's not the threat she was when we took our first trip after bringing her home from the pound and the kennel called to say she'd have to stay in an isolated pen until we picked her up. They used the term "bully."

* * *

Summer headline from *New Mexico Political Report*: "As drought continues, river flows dwindle in the Albuquerque area . . . only the Pueblos will be able to draw water from the river."

And: "The Middle Río Grande Conservancy District has now used all of the available San Juan-Chama water it had in storage."

Finally: We are in a state of "perennial crisis management."

* * *

The past few summers, freak rainstorms on the edges of monsoon season replenish some of the river, fill rain barrels, drip through the flat roof onto our dining room table because another season has passed and we've failed to clear fallen leaves from the canales. The storms are not enough to end the drought, not enough to shift our status from severe to moderate to abnormally dry, but just enough to give us hope, to say, this land can still be your home; you haven't yet damaged it beyond repair.

I believe Pueblo people tending, praying, living in long relationship on their ancestral lands are the ones who call down the rains each year. They shouldn't have to save us. We don't deserve it.

I think of us, they, we, them and why I've written the sentences above around those words. The "we" and "them" inside me is 32 percent Spanish and 26 percent Indigenous from the Americas, New Mexico, and southern Colorado, according to Ancestry.com.

Who might claim me?

I grew up thirty miles north of the US/Mexico border, learned Spanish in college, during a summer in Guatemala, and finally spent two years in Oaxaca in my thirties. A percentage is not a story, not a grandmother, not a recipe or a prayer. A number is not a home on a mesa, nor should it be. And yet, how do we find our way to each other? What makes us kin?

I am Chicana, a fronteriza,[1] New Mexican, one of the people of this forty-eighth state, this place older than its statehood, older than the union that took us by force and then adopted us reluctantly, only when we swore we were Spanish rather than Mexican, European rather than Indigenous.

I think of the white friend who moved here, rented a house in the South Valley, and asked three months and eight months and two years in, "When do I get to be a New Mexican?" Six years in he bought a house. He and his wife had two children. He stopped asking.

Do I get to die here? Will I still be here when the water runs dry?

* * *

Our hallway overflows with sávila.[2] I can't repot it fast enough. It turns out I am now allergic to its cooling insides, which I've applied to my stepchildren's sunburns and the part of my wrist that brushed against the oven rack when I pulled out my first batch of homemade granola, a project I took up in the pandemic. My eyes water and itch. I rub, drawing tears. It passes.

1 Border dweller.

2 Aloe vera.

But I feel betrayed by this miracle plant that once soothed a leg burn from the exhaust pipe of a motorcycle in Oaxaca. Sávila, egg white, arnica, and sunlight reduced it to a patch of scar the size of my thumbnail.

I don't want age—mine or the earth's—to be about betrayal, about the herbs and plants, the flora, fauna, and places that were once medicine to me, turning toxic. On Albuquerque's west mesa, ranch houses cordoned by corral fences sit overlooking strip malls, apartment complexes, and one of the city's busiest thoroughfares. I wonder out loud why anyone would situate their ranch so close to traffic. As the words leave my mouth, I recall that Coors Boulevard didn't always extend this far north, that the nodes and corridors housing Albuquerque's middle class were once home to cottontails and coyotes. Some nights the coyotes welp louder than traffic, reminding us whose place this is.

* * *

A house sitter overwaters the jade plant my mother-in-law gifted me. At eighty-three years old, she is still a beautiful woman, still smooth skinned on her cheeks and forehead. She is elegant and timeless in a Sophia Loren kind of way. Her nephews and nieces speak of her beauty in reverential terms.

We don't speak much of beauty in my family. I am one of five siblings, the only daughter. Each of my parents has one sister and three brothers. What is beauty when there is work to do? When everyone in your small town looks like you with their dark hair and brown eyes and skin that only gets darker in the summer? When boys don't have to—or get to?—be beautiful? When beauty *did* visit, it came from somewhere else. The blond woman on my uncle's arm when he visits from the East Coast. The new auntie with her three green-eyed, caramel-skinned daughters.

When I am old, my nephews and nieces won't speak of my beauty. I imagine they'll say I made them laugh, gave strong hugs, and always gave them books for Christmas.

At eighty-three, my mother-in-law clears out a storage room, gives away or donates what no longer serves her. After knee replacement surgery, she no longer scrubs the kitchen floor on hands and knees. She takes marijuana gummies for back and joint pain. My father-in-law died in 2015 at age ninety-three. They met when he was thirty-six and she was eighteen. He was the new village priest. She was the girl sent by her mother to clean the rectory. She says doctors don't believe her back pain is as bad as she claims. She says, "I wish I didn't look so good. Maybe then they'd believe me."

Despite my repotting the jade plant, over the course of days, the waterlogged branches sag and then surrender one by one.

* * *

Atmospheric rivers in California. Levees built more than one hundred years ago. Tornadoes in Selma in the days leading up to Martin Luther King weekend. Activists will still march across the Edmund Pettus Bridge.

I visit New York the first week of the new year, walk across Central Park in sixty-degree weather. How thankful I am to walk in sunshine, that the rain forecast for my entire trip has held back and will wait for me to leave.

But it's not supposed to be this warm in New York in January.

Snow in the Sandias, but none on the ground in Albuquerque. My husband moves a cottonwood that sprouted in our courtyard three summers ago. The dirt holding it is black, teeming with organic life, built up over years by his attention and labor. Every cottonwood leaf, every apple core, every zinnia stalk, every end-of-season tomato plant, every wheelbarrow of soil from Barela Landscaping turns to life-giving dirt, the story of us, of this place.

He is working when I return from hot yoga, my main form of exercise. I took it up a few months after turning fifty, when jogging on the ditch left me in too much pain and swimming came with too much overhead (read: shaving). I set up my mat close to the door, in what my yoga friends and I call the middle-age-artist-lady section of the studio. A poet, an actor, an arts administrator, a director—each of us came to hot yoga when our metabolism slowed and our first exercise loves (jogging, kickboxing, rock climbing) got too hard on our joints. We stretch near the door to the lobby, catching a hint of cool air as yogis enter class late or leave early. This morning I held a side plank on my right and left side with no modifications, both knees off the mat.

My period still comes. Once a month I hate the entire world more than I've ever hated anyone. I am weepy and sensitive and can't get myself to answer an email, much less write a poem. I carry myself like a linebacker, wear soft clothes and curse another month of feminine hygiene products.

* * *

This is the disappearing age, the invisible age, the shrinking river age. This is the age when my voice has to be louder, my shoulders more square, when I question, when I clear my throat and say, "Excuse me."

Excuse me, I have been standing at the counter and no one has acknowledged me. I'd like a pot of chamomile tea.

Excuse me, I am holding an A group boarding pass for a Southwest flight. You, who just stood in front of me, what number are you?

Excuse me, I put my yoga mat down first. This is where I want to practice.

I think of porcupines nibbling on mistletoe in the high branches of cottonwoods, how mistletoe is a parasite that damages the host tree by sucking nutrients, how Río Grande cottonwoods need all the nutrients they can get, how maybe I've missed out on decades of porcupines because I never knew to look up.

What are the quills, the protective cover that will get me through the rest of my life? When you are a stepmother, there is no guarantee that the children you raised will care for you in your final years. I suppose this is true even with biological mothers and children. But still, my position feels more precarious than that of mothers who birth, absent the scaffolding of blood and obligation. What is any of us owed?

How, like the porcupine, will I be of service? What parasite will I feast on to spare the beauty and life that make this landscape, this home?

* * *

My grandmothers died in their seventies. One, a lifelong smoker, succumbed to lung cancer a decade and a half after snuffing out her last cigarette. The other suffered a ruptured intestine. Ruptures: a vessel in grandfather's brain, the valve of my other grandfather's heart. Levees in New Orleans. Mudslides down the burn scars of northern New Mexico fires. What is destroyed in the burst, the overflow?

My fifty-year-old body is broader than my forty-year-old body, that body I shamed when a woman standing in the Trader Joe's bathroom line said I could go first, since I was "expecting." I was not expecting. I've never expected anything other than this body to give back what I put into it. I run or swim or walk or go to yoga. I eat what I've always eaten, and my body is supposed to retain its shape and size. This expectation gets me nothing in the bathroom line, nothing but frustration, shame, and estrangement toward this vessel that feels different every day. Which body will show up for me today? How will I relate to it/her/them?

Elsewhere, dams come down. The Snake River returns to its natural flows. Will it find its way again? We moved less than a mile from our old house and no longer need flood insurance. The Río Grande has not flooded in my lifetime. As a child watching the news with my parents, I wondered why we couldn't take water from flooded places and use it to douse flames in the dry forests of my home state.

The largest fire in New Mexico's recorded history started as a controlled burn. The second-largest fire in New Mexico's recorded history also started as a controlled burn. We can't control the elements. I can't control all ninety pounds of Roxie when a cat crosses the path, can't control my belly pressed against the unforgiving waistband of my favorite jeans.

* * *

We fear fire. In 2009 I lost my apartment and everything in it to a conflagration caused by old, faulty wiring in the opposite corner of my U-shaped building with high ceilings, crown molding, wooden floors, and a gorgeous courtyard I never visited.

The following summer, red itchy bumps surfaced on my upper arms, then my shins, then on my torso, side body, and lower back. The acupuncturist said I have too much heat in my body. She admonished: no chile, no coffee, no ginger, no cream sauces, no shellfish, no spicy foods. Eat watermelon, cucumber, mint. The bumps return every few years, and I must strip my diet down to cooling foods. I try to grow this medicine in my garden. The mint is contained in a terra cotta pot. It gives and gives.

Watermelon and cucumber spread leaves and tendrils across the backyard, a yellow flower here, another there. A fuzzy bulb develops into a softball-sized orb. A tiny finger of fruit straightens and swells. But always before ripening, the fruit hardens, the vine shrivels. Our land has given all it can. I pull the vines up by the roots, carry it all to the compost pile, and start again.

* * *

COVID finally struck me in early November. The cough lingered through mid-December, until a friend gifted me syrup and honey with oshá root. I tracked down an oshá tincture at a local acupuncture clinic, its lobby adorned with floor-to-ceiling shelves of roots and leaves and bark in clear jars. Even the lobby is a healing place. Even if I'd left without the tincture, I would have been held by the contents of those jars, their medicine every bit as powerful as sunlight, fresh air, and a walk along the acequia.

When my mom catches a respiratory virus, she asks for that herb I talked about. She won't find it in Deming. The woman at the herb store says, "I'm telling everyone who buys oshá about Lomatium. It has all the benefits of oshá, but it's not endangered."

I didn't know oshá was endangered. But of course it is. What does it mean to love something well? To be in relationship with it? To take only what we need? Gone are the days of Rudolfo Anaya's old curandera,[3] Última walking the riverbanks with a young Antonio, asking the herb for permission to cultivate, to uproot.

"It's not being ethically harvested. And it can't be propagated."

How can we not grow something? How have we humans wandered so far from our roots?

She says something about Lomatium being from the Pacific Northwest. I don't want another geography to heal me. I want the things from this land, this place to heal me.

* * *

Maybe fifty years old is not about drying up, not about oiling the joints, shrinking and shriveling. Maybe it's about hot yoga at sunrise, still being able to touch my toes. Maybe it's about the orchid my mother-in-law gifted me when I turned forty-eight. It was one month before COVID shut everything down, and I remember feeling fortunate in those naive early weeks and months of the pandemic, as friends posted altered plans and virtual celebrations on social media, that I would not have to mark a birthday in isolation. The flowers are a deep pink, color de rosa mexicano. The first time they shriveled and dropped I thought I had killed the plant. It lies dormant, perhaps a new leaf growing, waxy and thick, for months at a time. And then a bud. And another. An opening. Color. Life.

3 A traditional folk healer who practices Indigenous medicine and healing.

Shelley Armitage

Place Matters: Writing the Llano

In *Walking the Llano: A Texas Memoir of Place*, I write at one point that I need to be adopted by Mother Earth and Father Sky. I had been hiking an intermittent creek that headed on our farm, awash in discoveries of Comanche and Antelope Creek people sites, Folsom and Clovis artifacts, records of Spanish entradas, and the faint wagon wheel ruts of nineteenth-century expeditionary explorers—all surprises. My comment may sound romantic, even unlikely, but then writing, particularly memoir, reveals certain emotional truths. "Felt thought," I like to call it. When I began my hikes, I had already lost my father some years before, and during the overall series of hikes, I further lost my mother and my brother. An adopted child myself, perhaps it was only natural that at that moment I wanted most to be a child of nature—someone desperate to belong, find balance, a personal ecology.

Ecology—a big word, yes, especially when we think about all it encompasses. By definition it is "the science of relationships between organisms and their environments." But what about "personal ecology"? How can something so large be so small, so intimately felt?

For some, ecology, like the common Western view of landscape, suggests something out there, separate, other. The Laguna writer Leslie Silko reminds us of the short-sightedness of this perspective when she implies a personal ecology in her redefinition of landscape:

> The term landscape, as it has entered the English language, is misleading, "A portion of territory the eye can comprehend in a single view" does not correctly describe the relationship between the human being and his or her surroundings. This assumes the

Portions of "Place Matters: Writing the Llano" by Shelley Armitage first appeared in Proceedings of the Southern Plains Conference, "Shaping a Sense of Place," 23 February 2018, Center for the Study of the American West, West Texas A&M University, Opening Plenary.

> viewer is somehow outside or separate from the territory he or she surveys. Viewers are as much a part of the landscape as the boulders they stand on.

Her understanding echoes the etymological origin of the word *ecology*, which in the Greek means *oikos*, or house. The question, then, of experiencing an ecological relationship to place might be thought of as how we make a house our home. Personal. Personal ecology. And perhaps this process is what we mean when we talk of shaping a sense of place.

Place studies have been around for quite some time. Analyses range from the philosopher Edward Casey's question of which comes first, place or space, to the observations of cultural geographer Yi-Fu Tuan, who says, "A great city may be seen as the construction of words as well as stone." Sense of place refers to our subjective human reactions to place(s). The concept appears in works concerned with expanding an understanding of human experience, memory, imagination, emotion, and meaning. It is a core value in many endeavors, including theories that place humans into Earth's time-space continuum. And in practice, too, for example, building "green" or selling places as commodities. But the key to all these considerations is that sense of place contributes depth and understanding to what it means to be human.

Other writers have said so. Historian Elliot Porter notes that our plains are a place where the energy of grass flows outward due to the economic use of a chain of resources. We might add to this wind and water as energy extractions and energy relationships. The poet Peggy Church also used a similar image to describe connections between the human and natural world. She wrote of "the grass becoming man" and of the manure of our shaggy friends serving as energy for light as created by late nineteenth-century lamps. In her poem "Stones on an Arid Hillside," she likens the markings on stones to grooves of music. "Would their colors be audible?" she asks. "If I could listen, would I someday hear the stone's voice / that goes on and on putting God into its own voice?"

The memoirist Patricia Hampl remarked that perhaps we only really begin to live when we see our lives as a story. But as I discovered in the series of llano walks, perhaps we only begin to live when we can see our lives in another's story, as part of the landscape. Adopted indeed.

A few summers ago—well, several, beginning in 2005—I sought the inclusive stones and boulders referenced by Church and Silko in a creek bed in my own backyard, you might say. I grew up in the small agricultural and ranching community of Vega, Texas, on the tip of the llano. Initially, I was just curious about the two draws on our land. Growing up, I had spent hours along them, checking the farm and grasslands with my dad and later jogging and walking them. But I asked myself, what if I climbed over my neighbor's fence and followed the draws north? What if there were no man-made barriers, just the land before me, uncharted, unknown? Investigating this prospect, I later discovered on a topo map that the creek bottom formed by the two draws had a name—the Middle Alamosa—a snaking tributary to the Canadian River some thirty miles north. I still remember the day I asked to see the old 1930s aerial photographs at the Farm Services Administration (FSA) office. I laid the 2′ by 2′ photographs out like blocks on the floor as I followed the creek on my hands and knees, only stopping when I discovered I was headed out the backdoor toward the Methodist Church parking lot. This creek and its drainage are tiny features of one of the largest plateaus in North America, the Llano Estacado, its thirty-two thousand acres covering parts of eastern New Mexico and western Texas, rising to about four thousand feet on Armitage Farms. This was a country tagged by early Spanish and American explorers as a "sea of grass," what they viewed as part of the Great American Desert. Despite the praises sung by the Spanish explorers for the excellent qualities of the local grapes there for wine making, the land was considered utterly uninhabitable. Tourists today still speed across this landscape they find mostly boring, empty, and unworthy of love. But I know better. The subtle draws are old waterways, highways to the canyons of Canadian Breaks, home to ancient and historic peoples, a fuchsia land of surprise and natural wonders. Chavez Springs still runs, first recorded in 1504 by Spanish explorer Juan Onate. The Antelope Creek people's high settlement on Landergin Mesa persists, evident in its crumbled walls, continuously occupied for three hundred years.

But more: To my surprise, when the bemused FSA employee made a modern colorized topo map, I realized that the mostly dry creek bed headed on Armitage Farms. And I also discovered the creek emptied into the Canadian River near Ysabel's camp—a cow camp built near sheepman Ysabel Gurule's original 1870s dugout. Despite the farms, fences, ranches, oil rigs, microwave towers, and sand and gravel pits fragmenting portions of the breaks and landscape, here was a wholeness—360 degrees of earth and sky in a meandering but contiguous relation.

My dad told Ysabel stories. Ysabel was known for wearing his beloved Stetson for thirty years until the brim flopped so that he could no longer see the horse he was riding. One of the earliest settlers in the Canadian River Valley, Ysabel was among the early sheepherders from Anton Chico, New Mexico, who had built a dugout on the Canadian riverbanks. Dad knew Ysabel when he was an old man in his eighties, Dad only sixteen. The two men shared a love of the open spaces, its challenges and adventures. Ysabel had witnessed one of the last Comanche raids as well as the earliest pastores settlements in the Canadian River Valley. Dad's generation was the last glue to that Old West. Over those thirty miles was the arc of the two men's stories linked by the narrative of the land itself, written in wind and water. Walking it would allow for not only their stories or mine but the land's—all bound up together. I remembered as a girl helping my dad take down an old, sagging XIT ranch fence on our place. Now I realized that the land was bounded not by fences but by our stories. As Nora Tilden has said, "Places pretend to be blank, though beneath every place is everything that has ever happened there."

Later, when I decided to try to write a memoir of that place, to tell its stories—the interrelationship of the natural world with the recovered voices of Hispano, Native, and ancient peoples—I remembered Tilden's own definition of landscape, of writing llano: "To write a place is not simply to inscribe the place onto a page. . . . To write a place is to lay across it a skin, a membrane of text and experience. The skin is there to hold the stories of place in place, transforming the illegible land into a storied landscape. Land becomes landscape once humans have touched it—once it contains and embodies our stories."

Memoir as story is different from autobiography. It reveals not only an interior "I" but an "I" that engages the exterior environment. Its subjectivity is externalized and dialogical. It promotes conversation, a relationship. As I walked, I found the land did most of the talking, if I would only listen. I learned that the land was lyric, the rhythm of its shape coming into my legs, up into my chest and heart, and out my mouth as breath. Later it came out as writing:

I've ridden this road with my dad since I was a baby, later jogging it, giving the gloved wave back to his one-finger greeting as we passed each other when he drove south back into town. Lately, the resident Swainson's hawk, territorial on his cedar post, eyes my walk. Running days over, I am slowed to a pace fit for my desire to write the llano, for pointed north and alone, I understand the act of walking to be writing, the act of writing listening—inside and out.

What does the land say to us? I have wondered for years. True there's been no famous poet of these plains. Plains history is often a history of migration, movement, and change—conditions that make people look ahead, look past. But there is a poetry of the plains. This part of the llano, both rolling plains and flatlands, exists as a shape of time, requiring the rhythm of a habit of landscape, of the repetition of experiencing... I think: if we could read the land as a poem, we might more intimately learn from it, understand what it says of natural and human cycles—and that sometimes uneasy relationship between them.

Some Native people describe this relationship as the wisdom of place. Likewise, environmentalists have advocated "thinking like a river" to gain knowledge of natural cycles and inform our own actions and decision-making about their resources. Keith Basso relates in his book of the same name that the White Mountain Apache say, "Wisdom sits in places." Stories told by the people he interviewed were not "set" in a place but emanated from the energy and history of what had happened there, available through memory and storytelling.

I remembered this admonishment when, nearing Ysabel's camp, I realized again how calming the land was. During the decline and then death of my mother and the unexpected passing of my brother, I had touched ground like a worry stone. I had had to sell the old home place, caregive when I felt doubtful and ineffectual, and work at my profession while managing a farm and my mother's needs alone, some four hundred miles away.

It's quiet, getting late. I made a late start. It's not quite the crepuscular time of skunk, badger, bobcat, and cougar, but the wind has died down and the light lingers yellow in the west. It's as if the land holds its breath before exhaling into the night. I linger when I should drive. The silence is such that a buzz sets in my ears—a ringing from within held by the lassitude without. Time doesn't stand still. But I do, for the first time in weeks, permeated with nature, the calm settling in for the night.

This must be what Keith Basso means in his reports of the White Mountain Apache. His informant tells him not only that "wisdom sits in places" but, if one heeds this wisdom, he will have "a smooth mind" like water—that is, calm, without worry. The wisdom of place, like the thinking river, is about emplacement, something the Navajo describe as being "in place." It's not simply a physical state of being but a state of being conscious of the storied place, of all that has gone on before it, of the natural layers and the membranes laid down through time. The old South Draw, where I began my hikes, is one of these places. Here, at age seven, I first learned how to drive.

We were in the 1947 International pickup. I liked it because that was the year I was born. I thought of it as a friend until I tried to drive it. The excuse was feeding cattle cake, the elongated pellets of molasses and pressed grains, to the winter herd. I was helping my daddy at the farm; out of his good graces he said so. I can still see myself in the dark green pickup, head barely level with the black steering wheel, seat cushions stacked so I could see over it. The long-necked shift fronted the bench seat. I like the feeling of the soft plastic knob, malleable, a guide, a tool, to be cupped in my sweaty hands.

My dad chose to teach me to drive on the smooth cusp of the South Draw. I might as well have been looking out of a space shuttle; a whole unknown world seemed poised in the air below. The pickup pointed slightly down the slope, ready to buck and pitch at any slip of the clutch.

"Now put your foot on the brake," he instructed matter-of-factly, in what I thought was a life-and-death situation. "Keep the clutch down, and ease off the brake. Here. I'll put it in neutral

first and you can just ease it down the hill. I'll be in the back tossing out cake."

What kind of a crazy daddy was this? In the back. Tossing out cake. Me in the cab. Alone. The cattle bunched around the truck, slobbering on my window, bawling so loud I could barely hear. We both knew I would have to master the clutch. I sweated beneath my Peter Pan bangs. I heard a suction sound from my wet armpits.

"You just ease off the brake and steer straight downhill until I yell stop."

By now the cattle had completely surrounded the truck. They bellowed and begged and blocked my way.

"But won't I run over the cattle? ..."

Dad persisted in his instructions. There were too many of them. And all at once, my stomach clutched like it does at night when you think you hear something scratching at the window and, even if you know there's only a bush out there, you gulp at the shadow.

I tried several times. I eased the clutch out. The pickup lurched forward. Then died. My dad was a tall man with long arms and legs, a kind of Hollywood hero in my mind. He seemed larger than life, like a western movie star. When he reached over the wheel to correct me or straddled the gearshift knob to hit the brakes when I popped the clutch, he made me nervous. I didn't want to make mistakes or disappoint. I wanted to help my daddy. I wanted to keep coming to the farm with him.

Finally, we got to the point where he left me alone, the truck in gear, the toes of one foot pointed like an earnest dancer.... He climbed back into the truck bed where the feed sacks were—oh trust, oh terror, oh dangerously living daddy. He said he would yell when it was time for me to stop. I managed to look up from the dizzying mantra of "how-to's" and glimpse him saying something back. But I couldn't hear him. How would I know how to stop?

Memory is a strange thing. How much is the lingering sense of place? There was a piercing whistle at one point. I stopped. I was right on the edge where the draw pitched to its more rugged bottom. To this day, if anyone whistles, I snap my head. I brake. I stop.

Being in place also means recognizing nature's Being. Eckhart Tolle writes that nature exists in innocent stillness that is prior to thought. "When you perceive nature only through mind, through thinking, you cannot sense its aliveness. Thought reduces nature to a commodity. The ancient forest becomes timber, the bird a research project, the mountain something to be mined or conquered." If we become still, he posits, recognizing our interconnectedness with nature, there is an added dimension of knowing, of awareness, in the stillness beyond thought. "The moment you become aware of the plant's emanation of stillness and peace, that plant becomes your teacher," Tolle says. "A sacred harmony."

Out on the llano, the Comanche revealed this harmony linguistically, in their linking of seemingly disparate aspects of the natural world in a language of kinship. Echoing Tolle's notion, one linguist calls these cultural connections a "sacred motion." The Comanche used the same word to designate both flowers as a category and foam on water. Likewise, whirlwinds and butterflies carry the same prefix. Similarly, the many seemingly varied stories I discovered looped round in animated interconnections. In this way, writing may double as experience and memory.

Back in my Vega house, I packed to go and remembered something I had written in my journal in an earlier August. Shored up in my notebook.

Thinking about the circles, the tipi rings of the Comanche, the sacred motions. And then out in the yard, for the last watering, I see the monarch butterflies that migrate through here to Mexico. They come each year, in the time of sunflowers, just before school begins. Their larvae feed on the milkweeds in the pastures; they are attracted to smells, the fruit rotting on my apple trees. They like the sound of running water. I walk among the trees, the butterflies' orange delight crowning me in elliptical joy.

Told through experiencing its landforms—the draws, springs, the suspended pool—one of the main tropes in *Walking the Llano* is water and its markers. Walking the cobbled dry creek bed, a rubboard of ridges, a physical memory of the force of water, I was reminded of the MRI images of my mother's brain, revealing her hydrocephalic condition, what contributed to her death. What we used to call water on the brain. As I climbed out of the creek bed, I could see myself in its story. I wrote of both: "Water will have its way."

Basso's informant also made clear that a smooth mind, a mind open to the realization of kinship, only comes from time spent deeply inhabiting a place. The words *habit* and *habitat* share a root word meaning "to dwell." Dwelling and kinship are perpetuated through memory and story. As an example, I remember reading that in 1999, a Comanche elder, Carney Saupitty, recounted cultural memories of fighting the Spanish, fleeing Mackenzie's troops, and other earlier historical events *as if he had been there*, though they transpired at earlier and different times. But these storied places were relived and passed forward in his telling. I reflected on this notion when sitting high on a tractor out at the farm one day.

> *The plowing made me see time differently, looking back while moving forward. I checked over my shoulder to see if the rows were coming out straight while at the same time I moved ahead through the unplowed ground, creating them. These comings and goings connect like the wishbone of draws joined out north. Memory isn't about the past; it's about the process of shaping a continuity.*

At the end of the walks, when I arrived at Ysabel's camp, I found a mostly collapsed adobe slowly dissolving into the earth. Dusty whiskey bottles lined the warped mantle inside, perhaps the leftovers from some last lonely night cowboy parties. But in the research and writing that followed each hike, I uncovered some Ysabel stories. I had hoped at one point to establish verbal or site-specific links from my dad's generation back through Ysabel, the pastores, the Comanches, the Antelope Creek people, and beyond because each had shared a story remnant, a connection. What I had instead was a report from the birth records of the county where Ysabel was born that helped explain the illusiveness of his story. Ysabel initially had been christened a girl. When I quizzed the resident historian from Anton Chico, New Mexico, about this fact, she quipped, "Oh, you know, the priests liked their wine and sometimes got tipsy." But from Works Progress Administration interviews, I did uncover some details of Ysabel's life through the record of another Mexican sheepherder, thus establishing a kind of continuity. Recounting his exchange with a Comanche atop Landergin Mesa—part of the Middle Alamosa drainage—the sheepherder reported they stood among the Antelope Creek ruins. Here was a connection linking the 1930s (the time of the interview) to the 1700s (the Comanche period), to the 1200s and even to earlier Woodland people who migrated into this area prior to Landergin Mesa dwellers.

As I headed back to Armitage Farms, I savored the notion of how I had decided to restore the farm to grass, hoping to contribute to habitat preservation and wildlife corridors—another continuity. But there I saw a different narrative developing. On the escarpment near Armitage Farms where I had begun my walk was the march of 260 wind turbines being built, awaiting my return. I couldn't help but think of what the Antelope Creek people discovered too late. In order to build new dwellings atop Landergin Mesa, they stripped the rock from the mesa top underneath them, thus undermining their very foundation. Of course, I support green energy initiatives, but could they also threaten the environment? I resisted the turbines, raising environmental issues at meetings as hazards to birds and bats and migrating animals. Personally, though, I had to admit that what mattered most is that they would also forever change my habit of landscape. Roads cutting through the native prairie, the constant maintenance of the turbines, strangers on the land, and the blades shadowing the earth and tearing at the sky all obliterated that immeasurable value—beauty. Even though no turbines were on my place, I was surrounded. As environmentalists continued to warn of the turbines' threat to bird life, to bats, to migrations, it was the fragmented landscapes, the fragmented stories I also mourned. I had to admit that kinship and memory were forever fragile and forever changing. One of my hiking buddies, Genneil, and I experienced this realization on an earlier Middle Alamosa exploration.

> *I kept holding a vision before me, memory a kind of mirage. In it, Genneil Curphey and I were walking the old creek bed north of Tom's camp. She specialized in wildflower identification, and I kept close behind, listening to her musings over one plant or another.*

We came upon a webbing of sorts, a translucent wall, and stopped suddenly to avoid entanglement. It was about three feet across and suspended between rank weed stalks. At first we thought it was a spider web, all building up and creation. Then we sensed it was something in its last stages, delicate, decomposing.

"What's this?" Genneil asked, tipping her straw hat back, bending more closely.

The filaments danced in the wind, buoyed this way and that, catching the afternoon light, billowing shadows.

"I think this may be the skin of something, no, I mean—look—just the hair. What's left," I said, reaching out but not touching.

"Maybe the last stages of some animal—a coyote?"

Shape-shifter. Trickster. Death is like that.

I was filled with wonder, fear, and the desire to care for.

It was the same feeling I had trying to take care of Mother. The fragility, the threads that barely hung on. One misstep and.... And now that feeling about the land, and the turbines too.

"Whatever it is, it will go to the loving embrace of Mother Earth," Genneil said.

We hovered there, perhaps a moment just before the skein's vacancy filled the air.

"We'll buy your wind," the Cielo wind turbine representative had said.

But the breath of the story is not for sale.

Leslie Silko famously has said, "We are nothing without the stories." I think she meant something like what an earlier Lakota chief said to his tribesmen before their lands were taken away. "Look upon these lands with care," he admonished. "Memorize them, hold them dear. Your memory will keep them close—only this will last because the land itself will be taken away." Memory as story is not about facts but about how we shape them.

And so I continue to learn from these experiences of place. The pronghorns had seemingly disappeared with the coming of the trucks, the giant cranes, the teeming men upon the land. Research was already underway in Wyoming, suggesting turbines threatened historic pronghorn migration patterns. But even if I could no longer walk the old farm road without disturbance, the pronghorns *did* return. Perhaps they picked their way around the turbine lines coming up the swale of the Middle Alamosa creek bed. Now when I chance to see one, I am heartened by the idea of deep time, as these fellow mammals' DNA stretches back to the Pleistocene period, some twenty million years ago. A living continuity.

Our propensity is to shape, to hold, even to control the natural energies of these plains.

But I think: *We* are held by *them*. In place.

Works Cited

Armitage, Shelley. *Walking the Llano: A Texas Memoir of Place*. University of Oklahoma Press, 2016.

Basso, Kenneth H. *Wisdom Sits in Places: Landscape and Language among the Western Apache*. University of New Mexico Press, 1996.

Church, Peggy Pond. "Stones on an Arid Hillside." *This Dancing Ground of Sky*. Red Crane Books, 1993, p. 173.

Lane, Belden C. *Landscapes of the Sacred: Geography and Narration in American Spirituality*. Paulist, 1988.

Silko, Leslie Marmon. *Yellow Woman and a Beauty of the Spirit: Essays on Native American Life Today*. Touchstone, 1996.

Tilden, Norma. "Stratigraphies: Writing a Suspect Terrain." *Biography*, vol. 25, no. 1, Winter 2002, pp. 25–45.

Tolle, Eckhart. *Stillness Speaks*. Namaste, 2003.

María Eugenia Guerra

I Am in No Rush for the Ineluctable Departure from the Earthly Plane, but I Have Questions

Like the baby calf dropped at the edge of the wilderness,
I move in small, tentative lurches toward a place yet known to me

As we worked to extend the life of the shed roofs over the chutes and troughs of our corrals, a mama cow nearby effortlessly dropped her new calf onto the grass.

Lucky were we to witness the tender miracle. She licked the newborn a bit, and when it stood on shaky legs, they walked into the brush, she far more sure-footed than the calf that followed in small, tentative lurches.

Her job took less than half an hour, and ours continued well into the afternoon as Sergio and Beto repaired all three roofs and painted them, adding perhaps another two decades to their utility.

I took a shot at calculating how long the screws might remain fastened to the wood, how long before the corrugated roof panels would rust through. Those calculations mattered little, however, because at my age and as one on the inevitably charted march to el olvido,[1] it's likely I won't be here for the next round of corral maintenance.

At seventy-four I am in no rush for that ineluctable departure, but like the baby calf dropped at the edge of the wilderness, I move in awkward lurches toward a place yet known to me, each step on the soft sand of this ranch leaving questions in its dusty wake.

Who will care for what has had value to this writer's life—my books, my stories, the old tools and saddles of my workshop, the ranch itself?

The question, freighted with more footnotes than a dissertation, serves up memories of important relationships, love lost, time squandered, my life in words, but also por siempre the immutable joy I have shared here with my granddaughters, Emily and Amandita.

1 Being no longer remembered.

This peer into the natural order for how the life clock winds down is daunting—a reckoning embroidered with the rich recall of life on this landscape.

Our work this day was well executed and included collecting fallen mesquite branches in the barnyard pasture and replacing the outdoor sink where we wash up after working cattle.

Day's end found me alone on this beautiful piece of earth that had been the touchstone of my childhood, a place of raw energy and a beating heart. This has been my home for the best years of my adult life. I've known it as a writer's paradise—a fortress of idyllic privacy and something beautiful to contemplate at every turn of the head.

I've known it, too, as the cradle of family history, which has presented me with two certainties—the first about ownership.

Deeds and abstracts provide the narrative for dates and names of all the Uribe-Benavides-Treviño-Gutierrezes before it was my turn here.

Before the word *copier* came into the lexicon of duplicating documents, these old abstractos were reproduced on a typewriter with carbon paper between sheets of onionskin paper. Bound by a thick and faded yellow folder, those recorded documents offer a family archive that supports the oral history we had heard as children.

Well before I understood how land moves by attrition through a family, I have known that the ranch has held title to my heart over the many decades I played and worked here and was loved here. I've known, too, that the land will endure beyond my tenure as its steward.

The second certainty is that the ranchland and the work it asks of you are the balm of sorrow and loss.

My Mamagrande,[2] María Dionicia Benavides de Gutierrez, was a child here and later a young widow raising four sons and three daughters during the Great Depression.

I've come to know, as surely she must have known, that this place calls heartbreak by its name and then casts it to the generosity of the brushlands that are swept by the soothing susurrus of the night winds.

Some sorrows, I have learned, are slow to diminish and they rest here for contemplation and prayer, such as the loss of my brother, Eduardo,

2 Grandmother.

over which I do not quietly weep but instead still wail inconsolably all these years later.

Mamagrande had a few simple rules. One of them was to not invite strangers here, and I've held to the same custom, preferring the company of close friends, cousins, and especially that of my granddaughters, who are now eighteen and fifteen.

The quietude of this place at sunrise, the fierce amber and orange blazes of sunsets, the star-pricked indigo canvas of the night sky—these hold me here, as does the history of this place and stories about Mamagrande—that she christened the ranch Santa María after she had a vision of la virgen María[3] while milking a cow in the corrals; that during the severe drought of the early 1950s she organized a walking rosary, enlisting her children and their young families to walk along the boundary fences to pray for rain. I was too young to remember the walk, but the family memory, true or embellished, has the participants slogging through rain and mud in the return to el pie del rancho[4] where the walk had originated.

Since childhood I have been held rapt by family accounts of aquel entonces[5]—my grandmother and her children traveling to the ranch by ox cart from their home in nearby San Ygnacio, that conveyance giving way to a horse-pulled buckboard and later to gasoline-powered vehicles. In the late 1940s, the vehicle of choice for traversing the ranch was a huge World War II surplus truck made by Chrysler, what must have been a few tons of steel with a hooped canvas cover over its bed. The expressions of my grandmother and my Uncle Oscar in a small crinkly edged photo standing in front of that six-wheeled behemoth imply, I like to believe, the adventure they had just experienced checking on the fences and cattle.

As she began to age and as her sight diminished, Mamagrande had relegated full management of the ranch to her sons, rather than to her daughters, whose work centered on home and family.

3 The Virgen de Guadalupe is associated with a series of Marian apparitions to the Mexican peasant Juan Diego in 1531.

4 The ranch compound of houses, corrals, and bodegas.

5 Back then; once upon a time.

The chores of female cousins were to feed the chickens and goats. We weren't allowed to work in the pens as our male cousins did, for the boys were in training for one day running a ranch, this one or another.

Toddlers on the ranch were the objects of the affection of watchful aunts and uncles who kept our collective behavior in check with discipline, but also with the joy of being swooped into their arms, kissing us and calling us by our sobrenombres[6] as they hoisted us onto the leather expanse of an old saddle atop a tame horse, walking the horse a bit ahead as we wrapped our little hands around the saddle horn.

The death of my mother's beloved twin, Oscar, presented my father, José María Guerra, and me with the challenge to continue the sunbaked work that had ensured our family's ownership of the ranch through almost two centuries.

When I moved onto the ranch after having lived in Austin and the Hill Country for twenty years, I saw that the wild land had held its beauty and its power, but I was struck, too, by the stark void left by the absence of those who had populated our childhood.

I made my home in the eight hundred-square-foot bunkhouse that had been built in 1938 as a dairy barn. I fell in love with the kitchen hearth and how the early morning sun poured through the windows to fill the small house with golden light.

Paint, my books and music, and found objects transformed the small structure into my home. Among the found objects was a precisely crafted door of narrow machimbre[7] planks, the stain of its utilitarian green color faded over a century. When I trimmed the door an inch in height to fit in a doorway, I was stunned that the cut and sawdust revealed the appearance and fragrance of new pine. So much about the comfort and meaning of this place has hung on that door.

My mother, Amanda Margarita G. Guerra, looked askance at my decisions to take on the work of the ranch and to live in my modest home of aged appliances, a space void of the amenities of a telephone, potable water, and air conditioning. Her true concern, however, was that I would be safe alone in so remote a place.

6 Nicknames.

7 Tongue and groove.

That remoteness, however, attuned my life to the solace of the still silence just before daybreak, a silence followed by the raucous din of birdcalls, and at last light another still pause, this one punctuated with coyote communiqués.

My father drove to the ranch from their home in Laredo so that we could shorten the formidable list of repairs and improvements to water delivery, fences, and buildings.

One of our first chores was to port potable water from San Ygnacio via water wagon, a fixture on neighboring ranches that, like us, had a saltwater well. Another chore was to make sense of a felt pouch of a hundred or so unmarked keys that opened gates and the doors of ranch buildings, vehicles, and my grandmother's sandstone block home in San Ygnacio that had been built in the 1880s.

Though my mother often voiced her opinion that working with my hands was a poor choice, she eventually recognized that fresh paint, mowing, repairs, recently hung gates, new fences, and a massive cleanup of the house pasture grounds and the barnyard had brought much-needed order to the operation.

I can't remember when I stopped filling buckets with what men had thrown to the ground over decades—cigarette butts, soda and beer bottle caps, pull tabs, fence staples, wire, and nails.

Many, many years after my mother stopped offering the consejo, or advice, to let men do the hard work on the ranch, she voiced the observation that I was very much like Mamagrande in the way I had cared for the ranch. She said so in passing, but her words resonated with genuine gratitude.

Working on the ranch alongside my father in the last years of his life opened wider the vast portal of my love and admiration for him, and in a way I cannot fully explain to myself, it prepared me for the eventual loss of him.

He was as precise in pricing the cost of materials for a project as he was in stories about the arrival of his own family, the first Guerra-Cañamars, in the New World in 1602 and their migration northward over a century and a half to Pesqueria Chica and Monterrey, Nuevo Leon, and then to establishing Ciudad Guerrero, Tamaulipas (Guerrero Viejo), eventually crossing the Río Grande to settle Los Ojuelos before the river was an international border.

That I have been able to mine the rich treasures of both my maternal and paternal genealogies has provided me with a compass to navigate our journey from Veracruz to the banks of the Río Grande.

To share the history of this timeless, storied plot of earth northeast of San Ygnacio, Texas, with my granddaughters has been the gift of my lifetime.

When they were younger, and I was to them some kind of guide to the universe—that title retired now and without ceremony to Facebook, Google, Instagram, and YouTube—we had sleepovers here that filled the ranch house with warmth and merriment. When weather kept us indoors, we baked, painted, and watched (again and again) *Old Yeller* and *The Indian in the Cupboard.*

But out there in the brush beyond the house pasture, there was breathless excitement at the sight of a new calf or the true inhabitants of this place—birds, deer, javelina, jackrabbits, coyotes, snakes, and a family of foxes.

We've enjoyed picnics in the brush and shared the excitement of the petrichor-charged atmosphere of weather rolling in as we took la vuelta[8] along the perimeter roads.

There was singing—their voices dulcet and mine an affront to the harmony of the natural world.

A while back when I didn't know what would claim victory—chemo or cancer—the kindness of those little girls changed how I would live the rest of my life.

That they felt at home here as children; that the horses, cattle, goats, dogs, rabbits, ducks, and chickens held their interest, affection, and a sense of responsibility for their care; that they never met a padlock or a gate they couldn't figure out; and in particular, that they have had a part in the work of the ranch and that I was witness to their young lives and their hearts taking root here—these were all gifts.

The memories—theirs and mine—of our time on the ranch are the patchwork of the quilt under which we find the comfort of being bound to one another and to the land.

8 Turn; round trip route.

Along this machista stretch of the borderlands, women ranchers are often considered outliers. Many have earned their spurs and their place in history—especially in their own family history—while others are regarded as anomalies to be humored.

I don't suffer being humored. Long have I known my place, latitude and longitude, on this edge of the Chihuahuan Desert.

Krystal Toney

As I Heal, So Does the Land: A Story about Blackness, Conservation, and Healing in America

My great-grandmother would often carry me to her small backyard garden and sit with me in the dirt. I remember the feeling of fresh soil moving freely between my exposed toes as I forced my feet deeper into the dark earth. I remember my tiny hands clenching a fistful of moist earth, smelling it, examining it . . . wanting to taste it. In front of us, my great-grandmother's garden stretched the length of our backyard. To my tiny self, it seemed to stretch on forever. Collard greens, mustard greens, tomatoes, cilantro, cacti, native vines, grasses, and mushrooms existed in a complex web of life that thrived beneath her fingertips. She would often sing as she collected big leafy greens and sweet baby tomatoes, her voice as deep and rich as the soil that bore her fruit. She would light candles for Oko, the African Orisha of agriculture and fertility. She prayed for her garden in the same way that she prayed for her family.

My great-grandmother never took an ecology class. She did not use terms like *biodiversity*, *ecosystem*, *balance*, *abiotic*, or *biotic*. She never took an entomology course, nor did she understand the details about plant reproduction or soil chemistry. Yet here she stood beside her backyard shabby patio in South Dallas, entangled in it all. This once dusty, desolate land now thrived with life, provided food, and became an outdoor classroom. She went to her garden to learn, to sit, to sing, to pray, and to heal. This was her conservation work, intimately entangled within our Black culture. When we ate, we thanked the land and fed her a portion of our dinner by burying leftovers at the base of trees and near tomato and basil plots. During family gatherings, everyone assisted in harvesting, seeding, and tilling; we ate together. This was our conservation. This was our form of healing that connected us to the land and one another. However, this is not the type of conservation that governs today's conversations. In fact, current conservation initiatives actively work to take land from Black communities in the name of environmental progress, ignoring the ways in which Black communities have already worked for generations to bring life to the land through cultural practices, beliefs, and physical labor.

Through a Western lens, conservation work foregrounds the healing and restoration of land. John Muir, an iconic Sierra Club figure known as John of the Mountains, was considered a great ecological thinker. In his book *Our National Parks*, Muir referred to Indigenous people as "dangerous," writing, "When an excursion into the woods is proposed, all sorts of dangers are imagined,—snakes, bears, Indians."[1] Such "warnings" have regularly been placed upon people of color, as Muir's narratives continue to influence discourse around conservation. Muir reminds me of white Amy Cooper, yelling for help in New York's Central Park in 2020, as she falsely accused Christian Cooper—a Black birder minding his business—of being dangerous and threatening. And although in 2020, the Sierra Club issued a public apology for Muir's harmful racist stereotypes, Muir's narrative and the dangerous beliefs he espoused continue to shape a modern imagination in which nonwhite individuals are seen as dangerous when occupying natural spaces. The conservation movement's central priority was to preserve natural features and regions within the United States at all costs. Muir's ideology, while problematic, fuels conservation research even today and, in conjunction with his conservation stance, continues to omit the voices of marginalized communities, including Black communities.

Researchers currently focus on preserving the biodiversity of birds, insects, fish, and plants but fail to actively preserve Black communities, Black culture, and Black ecological knowledge. Black ecological knowledge is the accumulation of information related to plants, animals, the environment, and environmental issues encapsulated by the Black experience. It is valuable insight and understanding that is passed on from generation to generation. This amassed knowledge is not only critical to the survival of the Black community but imperative to the preservation of the Black experience in relation to the natural world. Black ecological knowledge encompasses Black narratives that intimately describe the ways in which *Black folk* have connected with the land to survive, heal, thrive, or escape. In *The Intersectional Environmentalist: How to Dismantle Systems of Oppression to Protect People + Planet* by Black environmentalist Leah Thomas, she accentuates how concepts such as "conservation" and

1 P. 28.

"sustainable living" were not, and have never been, "theoretical" for Black communities. She describes how her grandmother would reuse plastic bags and glass jars, compost leftover food, and repurpose old clothes and furniture—strategies that supported her Black community alongside the environment. Carlyn Ferrari, in her article "On Black Women's Ecologies," discusses how these long-standing practices within Black communities have been wholeheartedly disregarded, their narratives dismissed.

The current trajectory of Western conservation ideology is fueled by the dualism of human and nature, or human versus nature. This form of scholarship continues to be the dominant environmental strategy largely adopted within the United States and further endorsed by numerous regions around the world. Espoused as a form of "healing" and "restoration" of the land by Muir and Roosevelt in the early 1900s, such binary thinking has largely been at the expense of marginalized communities whose values and relationships with the land continue to be wholly disregarded within academia and conservation conversations. Dominant narratives surrounding "conservation," "healing," and "restoration" have led to the disproportionate displacement of Black communities throughout the nation in the name of conservation, as many of these communities have been destroyed to make way for parks and preserves. Where the threatened life cycle of the monarch butterfly has become a symbol of hope and healing for many conservationists, Black life continues to be strategically targeted and eliminated. Rarely does conservation work aim to acknowledge the ways in which Black communities heal *with* the land and *through* the land. Black narratives about survival, healing, and restoring the spirit through environmental stewardship are all but absent from environmental discourse, but these counternarratives are powerful, resilient, and joyful.

My family's history in America began on a plantation in the Deep South, well before my great-grandmother's garden flourished along the alleyway of a South Dallas neighborhood. My great-grandmother would often tell me stories about our enslaved ancestors and how they were forced to learn the landscape of a foreign country. Despite hardships, my ancestors built deep and intimate relationships with the land, crops, and wildlife. They learned to read the stars, navigate the forests, and predict the weather. They were medicine men and women, plant and animal whisperers, insect lovers, soil experts, and stewards of the land. Through the application of these skills, my ancestors farmed their way to freedom. Most of my ancestors were never allowed to learn to read, but they understood the complex communication of trees, plants, animals, and water. They sang songs about them, prayed with them, sat beside them, and learned from them, early echoes of the practices my great-grandmother cultivated a generation later in her own garden. Ironically, their knowledge and understanding of the land, soil, and plants were sought after by plantation owners with dwindling and dying farms.

Once my ancestors gained their freedom in 1863, they moved to Plano, Texas, where they bought several acres of land. White real estate agents considered the land barren and lifeless, which is why owners didn't mind selling it to a freed Black family. My ancestors worked the soil, transplanted native plants, studied the wildlife, and paid attention to the insects, weather, and wind. Every detail was shared among family members as they worked collectively to anchor themselves to the land. As they danced free of their shackles, the land beneath their feet followed suit. During the annual family gathering—something we still practice today—my ancestors would honor the land with their leftovers. If an animal died, its body was ceremoniously buried in the earth and churned with the soil. If berries were collected, excess portions were tossed out into prepared plots where their sweet flesh disappeared back into the earth, encouraging insects to burrow, dwell, and reproduce beneath its surface once again. Plots were designated areas of land where my great-grandmother would plant crops. My great-grandmother learned that certain plants needed very specific conditions in order to thrive. She obtained this knowledge through decades of stories passed down from one generation to the next. She placed her strawberries in direct sunlight, while elephant ears were planted in partially shaded plots. She vigorously mixed compost into each plot and left it to settle before crops were added. Oxygen and nutrients slowly dispersed through the tightened clay, loosening the particles and crushing the hardened surface. The earth began to open up, and for the first time in forever, the soil took a deep breath and exhaled slowly. It was alive.

As my ancestors worked to heal the wounds enslavement had lashed across their backs, so too did the soil that had suffered beneath the weight of continuous cotton production slowly reanimate between their fingertips. Soils, like ancestors, are alive.

Large-scale cotton production drained the soil of essential nutrients and led to an increase in pesticide use that indiscriminately killed soil-dwelling insects. Although "biodiversity" was not in her vocabulary, my great-grandmother recognized that biodiversity was imperative and so followed principles of companion planting. In tandem with the art of symbiotic gardening, she planted her carrots with her onions and her basil with her tomatoes. In her lush garden, ladybug larvae acted as both warriors and friends, marching along stems and leaves, eating sap-loving aphids. Her methodology relied on connectedness, community, understanding, and a willingness to labor in tandem *with*, not against. It was not her versus nature; she was in nature and nature existed in her.

As more and more freed Black families moved to Plano, Texas, and began to work and connect with the land, food grew in abundance, homes were built, and the community flourished. The land was alive, and the community thrived as farming secrets, techniques, and knowledge were shared among families. Generations later, my great-grandmother was born in the back room of a small farm in Plano, surrounded by medicine women from within the community. She told me stories (many of which were passed down to her) about how she loved to play in the soil, learning, perhaps even memorizing, its textures and scents at an early age. During the mosquito season, my great-grandmother would make a soil-based paste and plaster it on her arms and legs like the hogs that walked the family farm. Digging beneath muddied surfaces, searching for worms and beetles for fishing, eating, or the simple pleasure of pure observation of life, she would follow her parents into the forest, leaving offerings along the way, honoring Oko. Her connection with the land was spiritual, guided by beliefs that were woven intimately into the cultural fabrics that fed her family just as heartily as these fed the earth. This was their conservation—nothing such as Muir or Roosevelt would ever describe. Black conservation does not pit humans against nature; it is not about "taming" nature or enjoying nature. Following Oko, nature is stored knowledge and growth; it is increase that smiles with the innocence of a child. It is living and breathing, and we give to Earth as though she is our neighbor. She is not ours to own, but our sister who is just as battered and bruised as we are.

By the 1950s, the state began to shift its policies, and the dynamics of my ancestors' community began to change. As banks proceeded to seize properties, more people moved into the city, forcing Black families to abandon their farms when they couldn't afford the rise in property taxes. More people began obtaining their produce and meat from convenience stores rather than buying locally, creating barriers for local farmers that relied on that income, my family included. Eventually, my family lost the farm, and they were forced to migrate into the city to find work. My great-grandmother took odd jobs cleaning houses and babysitting for wealthier families in North Dallas. Whenever she talked about those years away from the farm, the spark left her eyes; she felt as though she had abandoned her sister. She had grown up with the soil, the land, and the trees. Now her life was filled with skyscrapers, light posts, burning cement sidewalks, and the noise of city life. She often returned back to her small family farm, cruising by the land when she had a few moments to herself. If no one was around, she'd park her car along the side of the road, remove her shoes, and bury her feet in the soil once more. For a moment, peace washed over her as she felt the moist soil cling to her toes. "Sister," she'd whisper.

My great-grandmother would eventually marry and have nine children. In the 1990s, just after my birth, she'd buy a small house on a large plot of land just south of downtown Dallas. The neighborhood was predominately Black and located next to an illegally operating landfill that once caught fire and burned for months. Ash rained down on the neighborhood and houses quickly went up for sale, as residents feared they'd lose their real estate to the fire. My great-grandmother jumped at the opportunity. "The soil will be rich" is what she supposedly said on the day she and my great-grandfather closed on the property. When the fire was finally subdued, their house remained standing. She spent the next several years reconnecting with the land; relearning her texture, her depth, and her songs. She learned to pray again, to sing, and to honor. She had not forgotten the feeling of churning the soil, plucking the weeds, and laying the seeds. She discovered new insects that lived among the plants and vegetation of her new home, noting the life cycles of the ladybug and butterfly. She buried her leftovers, shared her harvest, and spread her knowledge once again. This was her conservation, and her story is testimony to what remains absent from both present and past conservation movements. Conservation is not merely protecting the land, as Muir's narrative implies, but honoring its life, its bounty, and its people. Conservation is the melody that shakes my great-grandmother's garden once again. It is the coolness of soil between our toes; it is Black history, Black lives, Black knowledge, and Black stories. It is as deep and heavy as the roots of a mighty oak tree, and as gentle as the wind that shakes its leaves. This is our conservation.

Works Cited

Ferrari, Carlyn. "On Black Women's Ecologies." *AAIHS*, 3 July 2020, www.aaihs.org/on-black-womens-ecologies/. Accessed 13 February 2023.

Muir, John. *Our National Parks*. Project Gutenberg, 1901.

Thomas, Leah. *The Intersectional Environmentalist: How to Dismantle Systems of Oppression to Protect People + Planet*. Souvenir, 2023.

U.S. Department of the Interior. "Theodore Roosevelt and Conservation." National Parks Service, https://www.nps.gov/thro/learn/historyculture/theodore-roosevelt-and-conservation.htm. Updated 16 November 2017.

Leeanna T. Torres

Golondrinas: Reflections of Resiliencia in the Río Grande Vallé

They use more mud than sticks. They use the earth—la tierra—to make their nesting place. And I watch their copper underbellies, flashing wildly as they fly in and out, back and forth, busy and intent on constructing their nest in the notch of my front porch, their urgent comings and goings becoming part of my morning ceremony, a pair of golondrinas[1] preparing for spring.

* * *

Here in Nuevo México, there is a certain devotion to San Antonio, to San Isidro, and to agua querida,[2] water that is present in rain, acequia, and río. I think about the origins of our devotions, how they shape us, define us, ground us. I have seen Papa weep over the dozen of his cattle that perished one summer when the Public Electric Company field-site worker accidentally closed the gate behind him, leaving Papa's cattle trapped on the other side of the terreno,[3] without access to the water in the stock tank. His cows died of thirst, and he drove up to his rancho to find their bloated carcasses in the sun.

Conversely, there are songs, tunes, melodies, shades of daylight that remind me of Nina, my great-aunt—that woman so often singing or whistling with a contagious joy, even as she cleaned other women's houses. Dusting their curio cabinets, washing their curtains and windows, ironing their husbands' jeans and dress pants. All her life, Nina worked, and she worked hard, but always her joy was contagious. Wildly contagious. Even

1 A species of barn swallows native to central NM (*Hirundo rustica*).

2 Our beloved water.

3 Field—more specifically, a farm field.

"Golondrinas: Reflections of *Resiliencia* in the Río Grande Vallé" by Leeanna T. Torres first appeared in *Reflections on Resilience in Uncertain Times*, no. 42, 2020, pp. 18–21, https://quiviracoalition.org/.

now, gone for so many years, I remember her singing along with Las Hermanas Huerta,[4] the scratchy record playing in the background. Nina, stirring beans on the stove, singing con such corazón that I wanted to be her.

La resiliencia de mi familia originates in land, water, family, and food. Originates in the traditions throughout the seasons as well as the ordinary ongoings of our daily lives. Land and water, tierra y agua. Famila. Rezos. Cielo. But the undercurrent of our resiliencia also lies in that subtle unspoken of our traditional lives, the deep querencia[5] of our daily living.

* * *

The pair of golondrinas finish their nest in the crux above our front porch. Made of mud and string, it is a structure for survival. The golondrina couple will lay their eggs in this nest, then settle in until their young are born and grow to fly away. For years, my mama used to let the golondrinas make their spring and summer nests in the hiding places of her front porch, until it got too messy, the birds' mud and poop too much to clean. These days she takes her broomstick and breaks down the first signs of their efforts under her portal. Mama is getting older, getting tired.

For years, Mama has cooked every breakfast and dinner, cleaned out the woodstove in winter, done the laundry and ironed the jeans. While my father gets all the glory, the active life of a farmer and rancher, Mama has always remained in the shadows. What does Mama have to show for all these years? Where are the fruits of her labor and love? She will not admit her weariness. She smiles and sits in her silence. And she chases off the golondrinas trying to make a nest on her front portal, shooing them away with a broomstick and afternoon "quítate!"[6]

* * *

4 A popular and prolific Mexican duo (sisters) of the 1930s and '40s. Based in Los Angeles, the Padilla sisters, Margarita and María, set a standard for their style of singing boleros and rancheras, becoming among the first internationally successful recording acts to emerge from the Mexican American music scene in Southern California. They recorded over eight hundred songs over sixty years in show business.

5 A term in New Mexico with deep meaning, referring to a deep love and ties to a place/landscape.

6 Get out of here!

A few days before his last breath, Tío Eppy begged his brother (my father) to take him aya camino,[7] saying he needed to see the corrals, the cattle, the fields. So with the help of his two sons and youngest brother, Tío Eppy was lifted up from his bed and taken out across the road to the place of his querencia. Flanked by the old work shed (crowded with tools and tractor parts), Tío Eppy looked out into the alfalfa fields given to him by his own father. And then, reaching down, slow and wracked with pain throughout his body, Tío Eppy grabbed a fistful of dirt in both hands. His two fists trembled, shook with an unspoken and unnamed urgency, and he gripped the tierra between palms and fingers, nails and fingertips, his hands tense and tight on the very earth itself. Was he preparing to leave? Was he speaking back to the land in an unnamed desperation? Was he afraid, and thus clinging to that which he knew most intimately, the earth itself? Or was it much more? And am I allowed to even mention a moment so intimate? Am I allowed to question or ask? Tío Eppy knew he was dying—we all knew he was dying—yet all he wanted to do was grip dirt. His hands held the tierra, and the four men stood there in silence for a long time, the shade of the alamo[8] cradling both the living and soon-to-be dead.

Resiliencia en este valle is more than just strength, is more than just endurance.

* * *

Even before the sun rises up and over the Manzano Mountains, las golondrinas are awake and away from the nest. They position themselves on the adobe wall adjacent to the house, keeping a close eye as I walk out to water the flowers and trees. They watch me and then fly away.

* * *

Brother borrows my four-wheeler so he can finish irrigating his fields this afternoon and into tonight. "Mine is broken," he admits when he calls to see if he can borrow it. And as he drives away, the afternoon light resting easy

7 "Over on that other side of the road": a term of endearment our family had for a specific property/location across from my grandfather's original house and store where he raised his family.

8 Cottonwood, a riparian tree species native and important to central New Mexico.

on his dark, dark skin, I think about the cigarettes I never see him smoke. Instead, I only smell the smoke on him, subtle but often, and I wonder at this hidden addiction he keeps for himself. When he irrigates in summer, it throws off his entire routine—eating and sleeping patterns—and he can spiral into a depressive chasm that is both calmed and caused by his life as a farmer and rancher. Do I dare say that he struggles to stay afloat in his own mind during these times? Such are the things we do not mention, do not let others see. Others in the community, the neighbors and primos, all they see is his figure in the distance, trailing along the borders of his field, a strong body, an image often lost in the haze of smoke and distance.

* * *

Swallows are common throughout the continent of North America, with seven different types, including the barn swallow, bank swallow, cliff swallow, and tree swallow. The barn swallow is the most widespread species of swallow in the world, a distinctive passerine bird with blue upperparts and a long, deeply forked tail. It is found in Europe, Asia, Africa, and the Americas.

The preferred habitat of the barn swallow is open country with low vegetation: pasture, meadows, and farmland, preferably with nearby water. The presence of accessible open structures like barns, stables, or culverts to provide nesting sites and exposed locations such as wires, roof ridges, or bare branches for perching are also important in the bird's selection of its breeding range. Both sexes defend the nest, but the male is particularly aggressive and territorial. Once established, pairs stay together to breed for life.

* * *

Mama makes radish enchiladas on Tuesday afternoon. Walking into the kitchen, the familiar smell of freshly made tortillas greets me, along with red chile in a slow simmer. The television hums in the background, Mama watching her usual daily episode of *Judge Judy*.

"What's the case about today?" I ask. "Eee, there's a lady that's after her landlord por que he tried kicking her out of the apartment!" replies Mama, her apron spattered with specks of white flour and smelling of fresh-cut onion. "Can you grate some queso? That's the only thing I don't have cut up to put the enchiladas together," Mama instructs, and I move through her kitchen, knowing since childhood where every kitchen tool and plate belongs.

"Why did Abuelita make radish enchiladas?" I ask Mama, expecting her to explain it as some kind of Indigenous or cultural tradition.

"Sabes qué? I think she did it only because they were so poor . . . they didn't have money for carnitas, so Abuelita had to use the food she could grow in her own backyard . . ."

At Mama's answer, I realize that I too often overlook the pobreza experienced by my ancestors. On my Mama's side, they were just plain poor; no other way to explain it.

"I always remember my abuelita having the biggest and most beautiful garden . . ." explains Mama, and I lean into this thought as Mama begins arranging a tortilla with chopped cebolla, radishes, and cheese, her working hands remembering with fondness the good times with her abuelita, a woman I never met.

The reality of their poverty lingers in the kitchen, between Mama and I, and we are quiet as we work, because silence too has a basis in our resistencia, this pobreza, and the struggle to not only endure but strive for more. Both my mother and father were the first and only of their siblings to earn bachelor's and master's degrees. Yet Mama still makes radish enchiladas, out of sentiment, remembrance, and brilliant taste.

* * *

The Spanish word for barn swallow in this region is golondrina. Of all the birds of the vallé, golondrinas tend to be my favorite. But why? Is it the bold tapering of their tails that moves me? Their small and wild stature among the larger birds like paisanos, gavilanes, and grullas?[9] Is it their simplicity? Their abundance of numbers in spring?

For the first time in my life, I own my own house, have my own front porch, and I watch them come, watch them build between my front door and walkway that leads out to the postal box.

* * *

There is a hum of loneliness that often accompanies the end of a summer day; I walk the acequia trail adjacent to the house, the terrenos, and think

9 Great roadrunners, hawks, and sandhill cranes.

about the life my son will live. My first son. My only son. Named after Saint James, the patron saint of fishermen. I used to work on the rivers of the West, seeking innovative ways to ensure the continued existence of native southwestern fish and their habitats. I floated on the bellies of rivers known by their Spanish titles—the San Juan, Río Lucero, el Río Grande. In my work, I searched for meaning outside of my father's farm and ranch, seeking until life gave me a son.

* * *

Between miscarriages one and two, I stood beneath a magnolia tree in downtown Fort Worth, so far from home, in a landscape of both land and soul that was unfamiliar to me. The baby was gone. A gathering of birds hid within the thick green of the magnolia, and I looked up, trying to find the source of their wild song. It was difficult to see them. Easier to hear. And I, a daughter of the American Southwest, removed and living and working in a strange city, heard the sound of dozens of birds, repeating in song both the resiliencia and querencia I thought had left me.

Years later, my son's talisman also became his nickname. And today, when calling out to him with fondness or for attention, I say, "Oye,[10] Bird, let's go . . ."

* * *

San Isidro's feast day is the 15th of May, and while the old-school sembradores[11] of New Mexico bless their fields with formal ceremony and celebration, Papa whispers his prayer to himself, skipping the ceremony as he hurries to get all the chores done, roaring across the dirt road on his carrito, a Honda Ranger UTV, equipped with a hardtop but no windshield or sidewalls. The open air is his rezo, the prayer to his saints, San Isidro and San Antonio. He prays on their behalf, this hard-headed farmer who eats too many Hershey's bars despite having diabetes.

But it was Papa who taught me Papa Teo's prayer, and now this prayer has become my favorite of all. It begins like this: "Santisimo sacramento, Hijo del Eterno Padre, alúmbrame mis entendimentos . . ." Illuminate my own understanding, begs the prayer. I think of all the rezos I've said

10 "Hey," or "hey you."

11 Those who plant or farm.

my whole life, both memorized and desperate, both recited and participatory. During Lent, during the Christmas posadas, all those rezos, all those prayers—what do they add up to? And what of the weight of our own devoción? And I sit in the back row at Romero Funeral Home, intending to stay for the length of Mr. T.'s funeral rosary. Friends and community members move in and out, hugs and "lo siento mucho," giving their pésame to the familia. And I think, what if for this rosary I do not kneel? Would this be just in poor taste, or would it be pure and utter disrespect? Or, more so, what would this inaction of mine—choosing not to kneel during the velorio[12]—say about my own devotion? Would Dios Himself love me less?

* * *

One myth goes like this: Swallows stole fire from the sun, delivering light to the earth below. Then in anger and vengeance, God threw a lightning bolt of fire to punish the birds, burning their chests the color of light, scorching their tails.

Another myth goes like this: Golondrinas stole the fear from a girl's heart. They flew up and away, leaving her empty from the darkness that once held her.

* * *

Just before Holy Week this year, Tía Emilia taught me how to make torta. Mama didn't know how to make it, and Nana died before I could learn from her how to make it. So I asked Tía Emilia. "Of course!" she agreed, instructing me not to bring anything; she already had everything we would need. As we worked in the kitchen—the kitchen once belonging to my great-Nana, Ramoncita—Tía Emilia (with her hardness of hearing and shuffling across the kitchen) explained to me each of the small details—from using cold water to making sure the eggs are "room temperature" to making sure the puela[13] we used for the chile was small but strong and the cast iron we used to fry the huevo was heavy and thick. A simple, traditional food, made for and eaten primarily during la cuaresma,[14] Tía Emilia's torta is more than a recipe; it is a tradition now

12 Wake or rosary said as a funerary rite.

13 Regional term for small cast-iron pot.

14 Lent.

shared. And outside the kitchen window, in the budding pear trees planted by the Baca lineage of familia before us, spring birds chirped their closing songs of the day, afternoon slipping into early evening, the bosque full of cottonwoods visible in the distance.

* * *

Hirundo rustica, the most widespread species of swallow in the world.

* * *

La resiliencia de mi familia originates in the land, la tierra. También, also, la resiliencia en este vallé is more than just strength, is more than just endurance. It is as well those things unspoken, unseen, so subtle that we may deny they even exist. Our doubts, our struggles, our unwillingness to lean into the weaknesses as much as la tradición itself.

"Si Dios quiere,"[15] I often remember Nana replying to many of the questions she was asked during conversations with her sister, her children, her vecinos and friends. These dichos and refranes[16] that I grew up with were not only about language but about intention, attitude, tone. There is much lost in translation, and I think more about my Nana's heartfelt intention when she recited them than just the words and language themselves.

Fueled by the light, we are the lonely landscapes and diverse people of New Mexico. Whether Pueblo, Hispanic, or Anglo, our belonging here has been set forth by a complex and bloody history.

* * *

At the first appearance of new life in the nest, I call both my husband and son over to the front porch to see the birds. Mama bird feeds the three hungry mouths gaping out from the top of the mud nest. She nourishes her babies. We watch from below, and the male bird watches *us* from his post above on the adjacent adobe wall.

So begins the new, and there is a littering of mud and debris on the floor of my porch. Las golondrinas are now five instead of two. And perhaps it is not one thing—not food, nor family, nor place—that grounds me, but rather the sum of the whole that grounds us all.

15 If the Lord wills/wants.

16 Regional sayings of advice or small bits of regional wisdom.

I am grounded by comida, cultura, y tierra—these are the things that center me. Nana's quelites[17] served during Lent, Tía Bell's chile con papitas and a fresh tortilla con mantequilla, Abuelita's radish enchiladas born from pobreza and love. "Alúmbrame mis entendimentos," beg the words of my Papa Teo's favorite prayer—"illuminate my own understanding." And the golondrinas, their forked tails and rust-butter chests—they remind me of what it is to be human, of what it is to be loved, of what it is to belong.

17 A spinach, beans, and onion dish traditionally made during the Lenten season.

Deed

I own a home here // wood floors, new or poorly refinished // walls half a foot thick // someone else's screws sifted in dirt // We have given the shed to the mice, the scraps // to the chickens, the casita // long ago abandoned // is full of fur and the dogs // can smell it

I think a lot about owning // property // and its context and its becoming // and how my great-great-grandmother might look at me and say the word // "own" // with a tongue that was born // "owned" and a lip // that birthed her with each word, each word // like a church bell down some distant road // knelling her name her name // her names

Margaret and Martha and Mary and Rhoda, my foremothers // all with // good // Christian // names // and I own this house // and they were all // "good" // Christians who owned my grandmothers // and I have dreams of owning more, some land // to build something // and they, the mothers, never got // what // they, the owners, had dreams // of building something more, on flat land // and I know my desire is different // but sometimes I'm not sure how

First // the bodies // and then, the land // the // land // "the" // a determiner // impersonal // used to make a generalized reference to something // rather than identifying a particular // instance // but the land that I bought has a particular // instance // this land was a relationship, it required no deed // and this land // is still // unceded // Tiwa land // and the Spanish gave the land the houses the people // "good Christian names" // and then took // what they wanted and what // they wanted // was land // and granted it to themselves // and what can I own now // or ever // or ever

// again

Burritos Josefina

"This is a burrito town," I said out loud as I looked up at the menu at Burritos Josefina, the new place by my parents' house.

I could recite you the basic burrito menu at any respectable local restaurant: chile colorado, chile verde, chicharrón, frijol con queso, fajitas, rajas con queso, mole, huevos a la mexicana, huevos con chorizo, machaca, lengua, huevos con weenie (spelled "winnie"), papas con chorizo, papas a la mexicana, papas con huevo, barbacoa, bistec, deshebrada, desebrada a la mexicana. Everything with or without beans.

I know this building. For a long time, before it was a burrito shop, it was Estela's Look, a hair salon, and before that, Pepitas, a snack shop. When I was a little girl, Pepitas was the farthest point I was allowed to ride my bike away from our house. My mind quickly jumped to Christmas 1990 and my father walking into our living room smiling, wheeling a white bike with turquoise streamers coming out of its handlebars.

Suddenly next in line, I order dos de chile verde and take a seat on one of a row of metal folding chairs.

Scanning the place, it's mostly men on their lunch breaks, working men who have spent the morning roofing or laying cement. "Someone's husband, someone's brother, someone's dad, someone's son," I whisper, singsongy. *Someone's abuser, too*, I think to myself, always knowing too much. They look weary, their eyes red-rimmed and tired, faces and hands covered in powdery white dust or clay. I look around the small perimeter and decide that everyone here looks like they could use some softness in their lives.

Including me.

I'm just glad my mom is hungry today. She asked for burritos and I rushed to get them because she is dying.

I'm taking it all in; a telephone is ringing aimlessly in the background. It feels like the person calling keeps hanging up and then trying again. The señora who was behind the counter is now a young woman with thick eyeliner; the señora is busing tables and wiping them up with a bleach cloth. It's hot in here, everyone is sweating. I watch the old woman wipe up the last empty table with vigor and then set the food tray down to wipe her brow. The cell phone in her back jean pocket rings, and she reaches for it. "Bueno?" She listens intently for a moment and then says, "Ahorita no, gracias."

There are more people in line, and I watch while a little boy sticks his fingers into the spout that dispenses a handful of Skittles for a quarter from some dingy stand-alone dispensers while his grandmother orders. "Como están las rajas? ¿Muy picosas?"[1] she asks, and the muchacha shakes her head no. "Bueno pues, deme una. Y una de frijol para el niño."[2]

I smile at the little boy. He stares back blankly.

It's loud in here. The workers are laughing, saying cochinadas[3] and cracking open icy Coke cans. There's two viejitos, old men having lunch next to me, their canes up against their chairs.

I feel an urgency to remember this moment, everything about it. Staring intently at the front counter, I pull out my phone and begin to type out a list:

> (1) A toothpick holder (2) A glass case with blue and white string rosaries (3) a box of Mazapánes (4) Little plastic bags with pineapple-filled empanadas (5) Biscochos (6) Tamarindo candies and jamoncillo hearts[4] (7) A small gray radio with paint splatters

I take in every smell, every sound, every crack snaking down the wall. I tell myself this moment is a poem I'm one day going to write, but I know that really, what I *really* feel, is the gravity of holding on to a world quickly fading.

My mother's world.

1 How are the chili strips? Very spicy?

2 OK, I'll take one. And a bean burrito for the boy.

3 Dirty words.

4 Biscochos, tamarind candies, and jamoncillo hearts are traditional New Mexican candies.

Gliding my eyes above the counter, they rest on the image of La Virgen de Guadalupe featured on a Mexican grocery store wall calendar. From this distance, the dingy edges of the cardstock meld into the color of the surrounding wall.

I shut my eyes tightly and, in a flash, remember years ago going to Mexico City for my fourth and final year of Moondance, a Mexican Curanderismo[5] ceremony. Afterward, a good friend and I had visited the Basilica and, at the very top of the hill, had watched an elderly woman crawl on bloodied knees toward the gold-framed manta of the Virgen de Guadalupe. She was struggling, every inch a mile. After each movement, she would brace herself by placing her palms on the concrete, and every time she did, the glass rosary in her hand would clack against the ground. She had done it so much and with so much intensity that the beads had begun to break off and scatter around her.

* * *

In ceremony, we are taught that if a sacred object breaks, it is protecting you by taking something that was coming your way.

"Está cumpliendo una petición," my friend had whispered. "¿Crees en los milagros?"[6]

"Si," I responded quickly.

But that quickness has never faded, and a decade later, I still think about it. Did I? Did I believe in miracles? Do I even now?

I wondered how, among so many petitions, so much suffering, a single prayer could be heard.

The sharp sound of metal clanking in the kitchen brought me back to Burritos Josefina and the image that floated above us all.

"Madre," I pleaded, "No te la lleves."[7]

5 Curanderismo refers to the practice of traditional folk healing associated with Indigenous curative practices.

6 "She is completing a request" and "Do you believe in miracles?"

7 Mother, do not take her.

Pat Mora

Writing Year by Year

You like to write?

Through the years, I've been asked that question as if some people were asking, You like to eat sand?

Since elementary school, I've enjoyed writing. This doesn't mean it isn't a challenge, as writing this brief essay is. Yes, I've now had years of practice. Wonderful teachers and a mom who liked to read, write, and edit were gifts. I'm sure I groused at some writing assignments (maybe at all), but I feel at home writing, as some feel at home swimming or ice skating. Being a reader and the daughter of a reader helped.

I've had the pleasure and privilege (and I mean both words) of writing and publishing for various age groups—children, teens, and adults. Each group poses challenges and offers rewards. Being a grandmother of a preteen helps me remember the excitement and frustrations of being a young writer.

When I write for children, I'm hoping they'll find pleasure and even delight in words. Picture books enhance the pleasure visually, and I'm grateful to the illustrators.

Adults and teens who like to read can creatively connect children to stories and songs in books—at school, at after-school activities, and with art projects.

I'll admit: I love text.

For students to succeed at school, they need to feel almost as relaxed with words as they do with crayons or clay. This is a particular challenge, of course, if English is not a student's first language.

Bravo! to teachers and librarians who can meet students where they are linguistically and welcome them and their families to our complex language: English. I have always been bilingual, but I am English dominant. I feel fortunate to speak two languages and enjoy being able to meet and visit with children in English or Spanish. Here are some opening lines from "Jazzy Duet / Dueto de jazz":

Play
juega

with sounds
con sonidos.

Improvise!
¡Improvisa!

Slide into a river of music,
Resbala a un río d música.

Writing with our students of any age and sharing our writing deepens our understanding of the process and helps our students see that we are equals in a process that brings challenges and rewards. Writing together, we can tempt our students to explore playing with words. (This process may not feel like playing to many of our students, especially if they are not readers.) Some preteens and teens are quick to try; some find the page intimidating. Many adults find a blank page intimidating too.

How do we help students relax with words? How do we help them overcome past negative experiences? Graded experiences?

Big question: Do you like to write? Do you enjoy experimenting with words on the page? Creatively, it's hard to encourage a student to draw if we don't experience some pleasure in the process ourselves.

Teen writers may be particularly vulnerable. We should remember those years with compassion. Again, sharing the process with our students helps them take risks. Having poetry notebooks can provide space for experimentation with different kinds of poems.

I hope that my two poetry collections for teens, *My Own True Name* and *Dizzy in Your Eyes: Poems about Love*, prove helpful.

Back Then

I'd jump on my bike
some afternoons and pedal
by Cecilia's house,
pedaling faster, faster into the wind,
seeing the ordinary house,

sneaking a look as I sailed by
and feeling excited
that she was inside,

not really hoping she'd look out,
just pedaling by, privately
happy that I was near her,
knowing tomorrow at school, she'd smile
at me, and I'd feel like I swallowed
a slice of sun.

Dizzy in Your Eyes: Poems about Love

Honoring our students and their diverse lives can lure our students to risk writing, revealing and honoring themselves with words.

I remember how I felt in 1984, when, at the office of the vice president for academic affairs at the University of Texas at El Paso, I received my first copy of my first adult poetry book, *Chants*, published by Arte Público Press. I was assistant to the vice president for academic affairs. I had three children, my university work, family, and friends, and when I could, I wrote—primarily poetry, poetry for adults. Not bestsellers, but I began reading more poetry to improve writing mine; I still do, most mornings.

Many writers enjoy writing articles, essays, or books of nonfiction for adults. I did. Writing often begins with a desire: to express an opinion, to explore a topic, to convince a reading audience. Although each book is challenging, I enjoyed the challenge of writing books of essays and the family memoir. Writing is hard work. Are you willing to spend time alone writing? Are you willing to revise, to read your draft as if it's not yours? Can you handle rejection? And can you work hard for not much money? Are you hopeful? Creative?

Encantado: Desert Monologues, published by the University of Arizona Press, is my seventh poetry collection for adults. I've also written three books of nonfiction. In *Encantado*, which means "enchanted," I decided to create a small city in the Southwest near a river. We read/hear a variety of voices.

Señor Ortega

I live in languages, Spanish, English—
and shoes, yes, old *zapatos*, their leather tongues.
Seventy years of rhythm, my hammer's
tap-tap-tap,
the sewing machine *whirr*,

quiet *thud*, the screen door—
customers, nodding and shaking my hand,
the old *cortesías*—except for that man
years ago, who suggested I change my name
to improve my business. Crazy, some people.

Now, I reluctantly speak the language
of sadness—my wife whose last sigh
got lost inside her worn, weary body
and disappeared into her bones. Alone,
all I hear at home—TV, refrigerator.

Gnarled as tree roots, these hands mend
flamenco taps. My name still on my sign.
I speak words of faith—practice, practice.
I pick up the next shoe or boot—like us,
it needs patient attention and repair.

I'm working on new manuscripts. What have I learned and what am I learning? Be a reader. Not all readers are writers, but writers are readers. I read daily for pleasure and to keep learning.

Put your ego on a shelf you can't reach.

Luci Tapahonso

We Must Remember

We
Must remember the worlds
Our ancestors
Traveled.
Always wear the songs they gave us.
Remember we are made of prayers.
Now we leave wrapped in old blankets of love and wisdom

"We Must Remember" by Luci Tapahonso first appeared in *A Radiant Curve: Poems and Stories*, University of Arizona Press, 2008.

About the Contributors

Shelley Armitage, professor emerita and naturalist, is the author of eight award-winning books, including *Walking the Llano: A Texas Memoir of Place*. Honors include three NEH grants, an NEA grant, and a Rockefeller grant as well as serving as executive director of the New Mexico Humanities Council and as a board member on the Swann Foundation at the Library of Congress. She is a member of the Texas Institute of Letters and held the Roderick Professorship at the University of Texas at El Paso. She manages the family grasslands near Vega, Texas—a lasting foundation and inspiration for her new poetry collection, *A Habit of Landscape*.

Cordelia E. Barrera is professor in the Department of English at Texas Tech University, where she is cochair of the Literature of Social Justice and the Environment (LSJE) initiative. She specializes in Latinx literature, the American Southwest, and multiethnic speculative literatures. She has published essays in *The Quarterly Review of Film and Video*, *Western American Literature*, *Chicana/Latina Studies*, and *Utopian Studies*. Her 2022 book, *The Haunted Southwest: Towards an Ethics of Place in Borderlands Literature*, explores space, place, and the politics of haunting in the American Southwest.

Kimberly Blaeser is professor emerita at the University of Wisconsin-Milwaukee and an MFA faculty member in the low residency program in creative writing at the Institute of American Indian Arts in Santa Fe. The Wisconsin poet laureate for 2015–16, Blaeser is an Indigenous activist and environmentalist who grew up on White Earth Reservation. An enrolled member of the Minnesota Chippewa Tribe, she is the author of five poetry collections, including *Absentee Indians and Other Poems* and the 2024 collection *Ancient Light: Poems*. In 2021, she received the Lifetime Achievement Award from the Native Writers Circle of the Americas.

Norma E. Cantú is Norine R. and T. Frank Murchison Distinguished Professor of the Humanities at Trinity University. Her research areas include the US-Mexico borderlands, Chicanx literature, folklore studies, and literary theory. She founded the Society for the Study of Gloria Anzaldúa; cofounded CantoMundo, a national poetry workshop dedicated to supporting Latinx poets and poetry; and is a member of the board of directors of the American Folklore Society. Among her many publications are *Canícula: Snapshots of a Girlhood en la Frontera* and *Fiestas in Laredo: Matachines, Quinceañeras, and George Washington's Birthday*.

Sandra Cisneros, widely anthologized and pioneering Chicana, has published short-story and poetry collections and is the author of *The House on Mango Street*, *Caramelo*, and most recently, *Woman without Shame: Poems*. A recipient of a MacArthur Foundation Fellowship and two National Endowment for the Arts Fellowships, Cisneros founded the Macondo Foundation and the Alfredo Cisneros Del Moral Foundation, named in honor of her father and dedicated to promoting the work of Texas writing and writers. In 2022, Cisneros was awarded the Poetry Foundation's Ruth Lilly Poetry Prize in honor of a lifetime of extraordinary writing.

Anel I. Flores is a trans-queer artist and coach whose writing captures the essence of LGBTQIA+ experiences across professional and community spaces. They hold an MFA in creative writing and penned the chapbook *La Fea* as well as *Empanada: A Lesbiana Story en Probaditas*, forthcoming in a Spanish/English bilingual edition; also forthcoming is a novel, *Cortinas de Lluvia*. Anel's literary contributions can be found in *Switchgrass Review*, *Camino Real*, *The Fifth Wednesday Journal*, *RiverSEdge*, *Entre Guadalupe y Malinche*, *Rooted: Queer Women of Color Anthology*, and *La Voz*. Anel founded LezRideSA, Queer Voices Speak Out, and La Otra Taller Nepantla Residency.

Christine Granados began her writing career as a reporter for the *El Paso Times* and the *Austin-American Statesman* and has written two books of fiction, *Fight like a Man and Other Stories We Tell Our Children* and *Brides and Sinners in El Chuco*. *Fight like a Man* is the winner of the 2018 NACCS Tejas Foco Fiction Book Award and winner of the 2017 Writers'

League of Texas Fiction Discovery Prize. Both *Fight like a Man* and *Brides and Sinners* are set in El Paso. Christine is a reporter at the Fredericksburg Standard-Radio Post.

Stephanie Elizondo Griest is a globetrotting author from Corpus Christi and professor of creative nonfiction at the University of North Carolina Chapel Hill. Her books include *Around the Bloc: My Life in Moscow*, *Mexican Enough: My Life between the Borderlines*, *All the Agents and Saints: Dispatches from the U.S. Borderlands*, and the forthcoming *Art above Everything: Global Women with a Singular Vision*. Her work has won a Margolis Award for Social Justice Reporting, an International Latino Book Award, a PEN Southwest Book Award, and a Lowell Thomas Travel Journalism Gold Prize. A cancer survivor, Stephanie has been in remission since 2017.

Kali Fajardo-Anstine is the nationally bestselling author of the novel *Woman of Light* and the widely acclaimed short-story collection *Sabrina & Corina: Stories*, a finalist for the National Book Award and winner of an American Book Award. She is a 2023 Guggenheim Fellow and the 2021 recipient of the Addison M. Metcalf Award from the American Academy of Arts and Letters. Fajardo-Anstine is the 2022–24 Endowed Chair in Creative Writing at Texas State University. She is from Denver, Colorado.

María (Meg) Eugenia Guerra was editor and publisher of the independent monthly newspaper *LareDOS* from 1994 through 2014, which covered issues central to the Texas/Mexico borderlands. In 2011, *LareDOS* received the First Amendment Community Watchdog Award from the Society of Professional Journalists (Fort Worth chapter) for a series of articles concerning living conditions in the *colonias* (barrios) near Laredo, Texas, and damage done to the National Historic Landmark Fort Treviño in San Ygnacio, Texas. Meg's interest in the long-term vitality and sustainability of the borderlands is found in her deep tejana roots, which date back to 1750 and her stake in her family's ranch near Zapata, Texas.

Lisa Lee Herrick is the daughter of Hmong refugees and an award-winning Hmong-American writer, artist, and media producer based in California. Her creative nonfiction has appeared in *Best American Essays*,

Best American Food Writing, *The Rumpus*, *Orion Magazine*, *LitHub*, *Emergence Magazine*, and *Food52*. She is a PEN America Emerging Voices Fellow and a finalist for the Restless Books Prize for New Immigrant Writing. Lisa is cofounder of Fresno's LitHop literary arts festival and editor at large for *Hyphen* magazine. She is at work on a memoir and a novel.

ire'ne lara silva, the 2023 Texas State poet laureate, is the author of four poetry collections: *furia*; *Blood Sugar Canto*; *CUICACALLI / House of Song*; and *FirstPoems*; two chapbooks, *Enduring Azucares* and *Hibiscus Tacos*; and a short-story collection, *flesh to bone*. In 2021, ire'ne was awarded the Texas Institute of Letters Shrake Award for Best Short Nonfiction and a Tasajillo Writers Grant. Other awards include a NALAC Fund for the Arts Grant and the final Alfredo Cisneros del Moral Award. ire'ne is writer at large for *Texas Highways Magazine* and is working on a second collection of short stories titled *the light of your body*. Her latest poetry collection is *the eaters of flowers*.

Diana López is the author of *Sofia's Saints* and the middle-grade books *Confetti Girl*, *Ask My Mood Ring How I Feel*, *Nothing Up My Sleeve*, *Lucky Luna*, and the *Los Monstruos* series. Her novel *Choke* was adapted as *The Choking Game* for the Lifetime Movie Network. She also wrote *Coco, a Story about Music, Shoes, and Family*, a novel adaptation of the award-winning Disney/Pixar film, and a picture-book biography called *Sing with Me: The Story of Selena Quintanilla*. Her short fiction and essays have been featured in numerous journals and anthologies. She has served as the managing editor of *Huizache: The Magazine of Latino Literature* and as the president for the Texas Institute of Letters.

Pat Mora, born in El Paso, Texas, is an award-winning poet and author of books for adults, teens, and children. Her awards include a Poetry Fellowship from the National Endowment for the Arts, a Golden Kite Award, and a Lifetime Achievement Award from the Texas Institute of Letters. Her poetry collections include *Encantado: Desert Monologues*, *Adobe Odes*, *Aunt Carmen's Book of Practical Saints*, *Agua Santa / Holy Water*, *Borders*, and *Chants*. She is the founder of the family literacy initiative Children's Day, Book Day, El día de los niños / El día de los libros, a year-long commitment to "bookjoy," which culminates in celebrations across the country in April. Pat lives in Santa Fe, New Mexico.

Gris Muñoz is a poet and storyteller and the author of the bilingual poetry and short-story collection *Coatlicue Girl*. Her poetry and essays have been published by *The Rumpus*, *Huizache*, *Tasteful Rude*, and *The Smithsonian Latino Center*, among others, and have been featured by the Texas Book Festival, NEA's Big Read, and the Latino Collection & Resource Center at San Antonio Public Library in collaboration with Texas Public Radio. She was recently named vice president of the border women's writing initiative *Mujer Migrante*, founded by acclaimed poet Dolores Dorates. Gris is currently commissioned to write the biography of acclaimed LA artist Fabian Debora.

Michelle Otero is the author of *Vessels: A Memoir of Borders*, *Bosque: Poems*, and the essay collection *Malinche's Daughter*. She served as Albuquerque poet laureate from 2018–20 and coedited the *New Mexico Poetry Anthology 2023* and *22 Poems and a Prayer for El Paso*, a tribute to victims of the 2019 El Paso shooting and winner of a New Mexico–Arizona Book Award. A coach, community-based artist, and racial healing practitioner, she founded ArteSana Creative Consulting, dedicated to storytelling as the basis for organizational development and positive social change. Originally from Deming, New Mexico, Otero holds a BA in history from Harvard College, an MFA in creative writing from Vermont College, and is a member of the Macondo Writers Workshop.

Emmy Pérez is a Chicanx poet and writer originally from Santa Ana, California. A recipient of a National Endowment for the Arts Poetry Fellowship in 2017, she is professor and chair in the Department of Creative Writing at the University of Texas Río Grande Valley and has also taught at various detention facilities and as part of social justice projects. Her latest collective is Poets Against the Border Wall. Emmy was a fellow (2010–12) and organizing committee member of CantoMundo (2018–19) and is a longtime member of Macondo Writers Workshop. In 2019, she was named the 2020 poet laureate for Texas.

Petra Salazar is an educator and poet from Española, New Mexico, who refers to themself as a white (tres)passing "coyote" with an indohispano/anglo racial identity. Salazar's work has been published in *Indiana Review*, *Sonora Review*, *The Southampton Review*, and *Latin American Literature*

Today. They facilitate "philopoetics" courses and community groups as a means to bridge the divide between philosophy as an academic discipline and poetry. They consider education and poetry as healing, liberatory practices that occur both inside and outside traditional learning and literary spaces.

Sara Spurgeon is professor of American Literature at Texas Tech University, where she codirects the Literature of Social Justice and Environment (LSJE) initiative. She works and writes in literatures of the American West and Southwest and is also involved in nature/environmental writing, gender studies, and critical Indigenous and decolonial theory. She is the author of *Exploding the Western: Myths of Empire on the Postmodern Frontier*, coauthor of *Writing the Southwest*, editor of a critical anthology on Cormac McCarthy, and coeditor of *Weird Westerns: Race, Gender, Genre* and the forthcoming *Hellbent for Leather: Sex and Sexuality in the Weird Western*.

Carmen Tafolla served as the poet laureate of San Antonio from 2012 to 2014 and was named the poet laureate of Texas for 2015–16. She is the author of eight poetry collections, including *Sonnets and Salsa*, *Rebozos*, and *This River Here: Poems of San Antonio*. A Professor Emerita of Bicultural & Bilingual Studies at UT San Antonio, Tafolla has written over forty books, including numerous children's books. Well known as a storyteller and performance artist, Tafolla is a native of San Antonio's west side barrio.

Margo Tamez is a poet, herstorian, and Indigenous rights defender who grew up in unceded Lipan Apache territory in South Texas. Her research areas include the legacies of colonial violence and environmental injustice, family resilience, and narratives of resistance on the Mexico-US border. She is associate professor of Indigenous studies at the University of British Columbia. An enrolled citizen of the Lipan Apache band of Texas, Tamez is the author of the groundbreaking collection *Raven Eye, Father / Genocide* and *Naked Wanting*.

Luci Tapahonso is professor emerita of English literature at the University of New Mexico. She served as the inaugural poet laureate of the Navajo Nation between 2013 and 2015 and is a recipient of a 2018 Native Arts and

Culture Foundation Artist Fellowship. She is the author of three children's books and six books of poetry, including *A Radiant Curve: Poems and Stories* and *Blue Horses Rush In*. She recently completed a script for an exhibition titled *Creating Tradition: Innovation and Change in American Indian Art* for the American Heritage Gallery at Walt Disney World's Epcot. She lives in Santa Fe and is at work on her next book.

Laura Tohe is Diné, Sleepy-Rock People clan and born for the Bitter Water People clan. She is the current Navajo Nation poet laureate. Her books include *No Parole Today*, *Making Friends with Water*, *Sister Nations*, *Tséyi / Deep in the Rock*, and *Code Talker Stories*. Her commissioned librettos are *Enemy Slayer: A Navajo Oratorio* and *Nahasdzáán in the Glittering World*, which made its world premiere in France. Among her awards are the 2020 Academy of American Poetry Fellowship, a 2019 American Indian Festival of Writers Award, and the Arizona Book Association's Glyph Award. Twice nominated for the Pushcart Award, Tohe is professor emerita with distinction from Arizona State University.

Naima Yael Tokunow is a communications professional, educator, writer, artist, and editor. Her work (and life) explores Black femme identity, kinship, and futurity. She is the author of three chapbooks: *Make Witness*, published in 2016 by Zoo Cake Press; *Planetary Bodies*, out from *Black Warrior Review* in 2019; and *Shadow Black*, selected by Pulitzer Prize winner Jericho Brown for the *Frontier* Digital Chapbook Prize in 2020. She is a four-time Pushcart Prize nominee, a TENT Residency Fellow, and has attended the Home School workshop in Miami. Currently, she is the 2022–24 Nightboat Editorial Fellow, where she edits for *Tupelo Quarterly* and reads for *Nat. Brut.*

Krystal Monique Toney is a PhD candidate in environmental science at the University of North Texas. Her work focuses on the disparities in access to conservation education and nature among Black students and students of low socioeconomic status in Texas. As an undergrad, she used camera traps to build a photographic archive of animals living within the Trinity River Audubon Center and led hikes about conservation education, Blackness in nature, and community ecology. She created Black in Nature as an attempt to share her knowledge, creativity, and love for nature while encouraging other Black people to love and embrace our beautiful and natural world.

Leeanna T. Torres is a native daughter of the American Southwest, a Nuevomexicana who has worked as an environmental professional throughout the West since 2001. While often disguised as an environmental professional, she remains a student of both water and land—agua y tierra. In her writing, she speaks with and from that sacred sense of place that is inherent in the great Southwest, that intrinsic relationship between people and place—*el sagrado*, the sacred. Her essays have appeared in *Blue Mesa Review*, *High Country News*, and *High Desert Journal*. Her work can also be found in several anthologies, including Torrey House Press's 2022 *First & Wildest: The Gila Wilderness at 100*. Her creative-nonfiction work is often centered on landscape, culture, and *querencia*.

Diane Wilson is a fourth-generation shrimper and author of *An Unreasonable Woman: A True Story of Shrimpers, Politicos, Polluters, and the Fight for Seadrift, Texas*; *Holy Roller: Growing Up in the Church of Knock Down, Drag Out; or How I Quit Loving a Blue-Eyed Jesus*; and *Diary of an Eco Outlaw*. She is a cofounder of Code Pink; cofounder of Texas Jail Project, which advocates for inmates' rights; and founder and executive director of San Antonio Bay Estuarine Waterkeeper. In 2019, Wilson and Waterkeeper won a $50 million settlement in a citizen suit against Formosa Plastics, the largest settlement in US history. For this, Wilson was awarded a Goldman Environmental Award. She has been jailed more than twenty times for civil disobedience.

Diane Hueter Warner recently retired from Texas Tech University as a librarian for the James Sowell Family Collection in Literature, Community, and the Natural World, where she organized an annual conference on literature and place, a student essay contest, and a program for visiting scholars. More recently, she collaborates with Texas Tech University Press and editors at Terrain.org on an emerging writers award. She now divides her time between Lubbock and the Olympic Peninsula. She is the author of *After the Tornado*, and her poetry, which has been nominated for the Pushcart Prize, has appeared in *The Carolina Quarterly*, *Nelle*, *SWWIM*, and most recently in a special library issue of *Inlandia: a Literary Journal*.